The Wrath of Almighty God

Sermons on God's Judgment Against Sinners

Joathan Edwards

Edited by Don Kistler

Soli Deo Gloria Publications
An imprint of Reformation Heritage Books
Grand Rapids, Michigan

The Wrath of Almighty God
© 1996 by Soli Deo Gloria

All rights reserved. No part of this book may be used or reproduced in any manner whatsoever without written permission except in the case of brief quotations embodied in critical articles and reviews. Direct your requests to the publisher at the following addresses:

Soli Deo Gloria Publications
An imprint of Reformation Heritage Books
3070 29th St. SE
Grand Rapids, MI 49512
616-977-0889
orders@heritagebooks.org
www.heritagebooks.org

Paperback edition published 2025

ISBN 979-8-88686-194-5

Printed in the United States of America
25 26 27 28 29 30/10 9 8 7 6 5 4 3 2 1

Contents

Publisher's Preface		iv
1.	Natural Men in a Dreadful Condition	1
2.	Sinners in the Hands of an Angry God	61
3.	The Justice of God in the Damnation of Sinners	83
4.	The Final Judgment	139
5.	The Portion of the Wicked	186
6.	Wicked Men Useful in Their Destruction Only	232
7.	The Future Punishment of the Wicked Unavoidable and Intolerable	254
8.	Wrath to the Uttermost	277
9.	Concerning the Endless Punishment of Those Who Die Impenitent	291
10.	The Eternity of Hell Torments	337
11.	The End of the Wicked Contemplated by the Righteous	364

Publisher's Preface

Scripture says that sinners need to be "saved from the wrath to come." Modern evangelism seems to believe that a lack of love is the sinner's problem. Jonathan Edwards was an evangelist; therefore he warned sinners about hell.

These are by no means *all* the sermons or treatises Jonathan Edwards preached or wrote on the subjects of hell and the judgment of God against impenitent sinners. Most of his sermons on these ominous topics remain unpublished, and are in manuscript form at the Beinecke Rare Book Room at Yale University, where few have access.

However, that fact notwithstanding, these sermons and treatises contain the essential Edwards message on those subjects and are collected from the two volume edition known popularly as "The Hickman Edition," which is now in print by the Banner of Truth Trust. The late Edwardsian scholar Dr. John H. Gerstner called that set the best value in Christian literature available today, no matter what the cost! Those volumes, though, are large, double-columned, with very tiny print.

We have retypeset this material dealing specifically with the doctrine of hell and final judgment, making only the most minimal of corrections—most of those dealing with over-punctuation of the nineteenth century edition and with the addition of clarifying words.

Edwards believed the message of hell was essential to evangelism. We agree; hence it is that this collection is now in print. May God use it to glorify Himself in the salvation of sinners.

Natural Men in a Dreadful Condition

"Then he called for a light, and sprang in, and came trembling, and fell down before Paul and and Silas, and brought them out, and said, Sirs, what must I do to be saved?" Acts 16:29–30

We have here and in the context an account of the conversion of the jailer, which is one of the most remarkable instances of the kind in the Scripture. The jailer before seems not only to have been wholly insensible to the things of religion, but to have been a persecutor, and to have persecuted these very men, Paul and Silas; though he now comes to them in so earnest a manner, asking them what he must do to be saved. We are told in the context that all the magistrates and multitude of the city rose up jointly in a tumult against them, and took them and cast them into prison, charging the jailer to keep them safely. Whereupon he thrust them into the inner prison and made their feet fast in the stocks. And it is probable that he did not act in this merely as the servant or instrument of the magistrates, but that he joined with the rest of the people in their rage against them, and that he did what he did urged on by his own will as well as the magistrates' commands, which made him execute their commands with such rigor.

But when Paul and Silas prayed and sang praises at midnight, and there was suddenly a great earthquake, and

God had in so wonderful a manner set open the prison doors, and every man's bands were loosed, he was greatly terrified. In a kind of desperation, he was about to kill himself; but Paul and Silas cried out to him, "Do thyself no harm, for we are all here." Then he called for a light, and sprang in, as we have the account in the text. We may observe:

1. The objects of his concern. He is anxious about his salvation. He is terrified by his guilt, especially by his guilt in his ill treatment of these ministers of Christ. He is concerned to escape from that guilty state, the miserable state he was in by reason of sin.

2. The sense which he has of the dreadfulness of his present state. This he manifests in several ways.

By his great haste to escape from that state, and by his haste to inquire what he must do. He seems to be urged by the most pressing concern, sensible of his present necessity of deliverance, without any delay. Before, he was quiet and secure in his natural state; but now his eyes are opened and he is in the utmost haste. If the house had been on fire over his head, he could not have asked more earnestly or have been in greater haste. He could soon have come to Paul and Silas to ask them what he must do if he had only walked. But he was in too great haste to walk only or to run, for he *sprang* in; he leaped into the place where they were. He fled from wrath. He fled from the fire of divine justice, and so hastened as one who fled for his life.

By his behavior and gesture before Paul and Silas. He fell down. That he fell down before those whom he had persecuted and thrust into the inner prison, and made their feet fast in the stocks, shows what was the state of his mind. It shows some great distress that makes such an alteration in him, that brings him to this. He was broken down, as it were, by the distress of his mind, in a sense of the dreadfulness of his condition.

His earnest manner of inquiring of them what he shall do to escape from this miserable condition: "Sirs, what must I do to be saved?" So distressed is he that he is brought to be willing to do anything, to have salvation on any terms and by any means, however difficult; he is brought, as it were, to write a blank check and give it to God that God may prescribe his own terms.

DOCTRINE. They who are in a natural condition are in a dreadful condition.

This I shall endeavor to make appear by a particular consideration of the state and condition of unregenerate persons:

I. As to their actual condition in this world.
II. As to their relations to the future world.

I. The condition of those who are in a natural state is dreadful in the present world.

First, on account of the depraved state of their natures. As men come into the world, their natures are dreadfully depraved. Man in his primitive state was a noble piece of divine workmanship, but by the Fall it is dreadfully defaced. It is awful to think that so excellent a creature as man is should be so ruined. The dreadfulness of the condition which unconverted men are in in this respect appears in the following things:

1. The dreadfulness of their depravity appears in that they are so sottishly blind and ignorant. God gave man a faculty of reason and understanding, which is a noble faculty. Therein he differs from all other creatures here below. He is exalted in his nature above them, and is, in this respect, like the angels. Man is made capable to know God, and to know spiritual and eternal things. And God gave him understanding that he might know Him, and know heavenly things, and made him as capable to know these things as any others. But man has debased himself, and has lost his glory in this respect. He has become as ignorant of the excellency of God as the very beasts. His understanding is full of darkness; his mind is blind, is altogether blind to spiritual things. Men are ignorant of God and ignorant of Christ, ignorant of the way of salvation, ignorant of their own happiness, blind in the midst of the brightest and clearest light, ignorant under all manner of instructions. Romans 3:17: "The way of peace they have not known." Isaiah 27:11: "It is a people of no understanding." Jeremiah 4:22: "My people is foolish, they have not known Me; they are sottish* children, and have no understanding." Psalm 95:10–11: "It is a people that do err in their heart, and they have not known my ways; unto whom I swear in my wrath, that they should not enter into my rest." 1 Corinthians 15:34: "Some have not the knowledge of God; I speak this to your shame."

There is a spirit of atheism prevailing in the hearts of men, a strange disposition to doubt the very being of God, of another world, and of everything which cannot be seen with the bodily eyes. Psalm 14:1: "The fool hath said in his heart, There is no God." They do not realize that God sees them when they commit sin, and will call them to an account for it. And therefore, if they can hide sin from the eyes of men, they are not concerned, but are bold to commit it. Psalm 94:7–9: "Yet they say, the Lord shall not see, neither shall the God of Jacob regard it. Understand, ye brutish among the people; and, ye fools, when will ye be

---

* sottish = dull, insensitive, stupid

wise? He that planted the ear, shall he not hear? He that formed the eye, shall he not see?" Psalm 73:11: "They say, How doth God know? and is there knowledge in the Most High?" So sottishly unbelieving are they of future things, of heaven and hell, and will commonly run the venture of damnation sooner than be convinced. They are stupidly senseless to the importance of eternal things. How hard to make them believe, and to give them a real conviction that to be happy to all eternity is better than all other good, and that to be miserable forever under the wrath of God is worse than all other evil. Men show themselves senseless enough in temporal things, but in spiritual things far more so. Luke 12:56: "Ye hypocrites, ye can discern the face of the sky, and of the earth; but how is it that ye do not discern this time?" They are very subtle in evil designs, but sottish in those things which most concern them. Jeremiah 4:22: "They are wise to do evil, but to do good they have no knowledge." Wicked men show themselves more foolish and senseless of what is best for them than the very brutes. Isaiah 1:3: "The ox knoweth his owner, and the ass his master's crib; but Israel doth not know, My people doth not consider." Jeremiah 8:7: "Yea, the stork in the heaven knoweth her appointed times; and the turtle, and the crane, and the swallow observe the time of their coming; but My people know not the judgment of the Lord."

2. *They have no goodness in them*. Romans 7:18: "In me, that is, in my flesh, dwelleth no good thing." They have no principle that disposes them to anything that is good. Natural men have no higher principle in their hearts than self-love. And herein they do not excel the devils. The devils love themselves and love their own happiness and are afraid of their own misery. And they go no further. The devils would be as religious as the best of natural men if

they were in the same circumstances. They would be as moral and would pray as earnestly to God and take as much pains for salvation if there were the like opportunity. And as there is no good principle in the hearts of natural men, so there are never any good exercises of heart—never one good thought or motion of heart in them.

Particularly, there is no love to God in them. They never had the least degree of love to the infinitely glorious Being. They never had the least true respect to the Being who made them, in whose hand their breath is, and from whom are all their mercies. However they may seem to do things at times out of respect to God, and wear a face as though they honored Him and highly esteemed Him, it is all in mere hypocrisy. Though there may be a fair outside, they are like painted sepulchers: within, there is nothing but putrefaction and rottenness.

They have no love to Christ, the glorious Son of God, who is so worthy of their love and has shown such wonderful grace to sinners in dying for them. They never did anything out of any real respect to the Redeemer of the world since they were born. They never brought forth any fruit to that God who made them, and in whom they live and move and have their being. They never have in any way answered the end for which they were made. They have hitherto lived altogether in vain and to no purpose. They never so much as sincerely obeyed one command of God; never so much as moved one finger out of a true spirit of obedience to Him who made them to serve Him. And when they have seemed outwardly to comply with God's commands, their hearts were not in it. They did not do it out of any spirit of subjection to God, or any disposition to obey Him, but were merely driven to it by fear, or in some way influenced by their worldly interest.

They never gave God the honor of one of His attributes. They never gave Him the honor of His authority by obeying Him. They never gave Him the honor of His sovereignty by submitting to Him. They never gave Him the honor of His holiness and mercy by loving Him. They never gave Him the honor of His sufficiency and faithfulness by trusting in Him, but have looked upon God as one not fit to be believed or trusted, and have treated Him as if He were a liar. 1 John 5:10: "He that believeth not God hath made Him a liar." They never so much as heartily thanked God for one mercy they have received in their whole lives, though God has always maintained them, and they have always lived upon His bounty. They never so much as once heartily thanked Christ for coming into the world and dying to give them an opportunity to be saved. They never would show Him so much gratitude as to receive Him when He has knocked at their door, but have always shut the door against Him, though He has come to knock at their door upon no other ground but only to offer Himself to be their Savior.

They never so much as had any true desires after God or Christ in their whole lives. When God has offered Himself to them to be their portion and Christ to be the friend of their souls, they did not desire it. They never desired to have God and Christ for their portion. They would rather be without them than with them, if they could avoid going to hell without them.

They never had so much as an honorable thought of God. They always have esteemed earthly things before Him. And notwithstanding all they have heard in the commands of God and Christ, they have always preferred a little worldly profit or sinful pleasure before them.

3. Unconverted men are in a dreadful condition by reason of the dreadful wickedness which there is in them.

Sin is a thing of a dreadful nature, and that because it is against an infinitely great and infinitely holy God. There is in the nature of man enmity against God, contempt of God, rebellion against God. Sin rises up as an enemy against the Most High. It is a dreadful thing for a creature to be an enemy to the Creator, or to have any such thing in his heart as enmity against Him. This will be very clear if we consider the difference between God and the creature, and how all creatures, compared with Him, are as the small dust of the balance, are as nothing, less than nothing, and vanity. There is an infinite evil in sin. If we saw the hundredth part of the evil there is in sin, it would make us sensible that those who have any sin, let it be ever so small, are in a dreadful condition.

The hearts of natural men are exceedingly full of sin. If they had but one sin in their hearts, it would be sufficient to render their condition very dreadful. But they have not only one sin, but all manner of sin. There is every kind of lust. The heart is a mere sink of sin, a fountain of corruption whence issue all manner of filthy streams. Mark 7:21–22: "From within, out of the heart of men, proceed evil thoughts, adulteries, fornications, murders, thefts, covetousness, wickedness, deceit, lasciviousness, an evil eye, blasphemy, pride, foolishness." There is no one lust in the heart of the devil that is not in the heart of man. Natural men are in the image of the devil. The image of God is razed out and the image of the devil is stamped upon them. God is graciously pleased to restrain the wickedness of men, principally by fear and respect to their credit and reputation, and by education. And if it were not for such restraints as these, there is no kind of wickedness that men would not commit, whenever it came in their way. The commission of those things, at the mention of which men are now ready to start, and seem to be shocked when they hear them read, would be common and general; and earth would be a kind of hell. What would not natural men do if they were not afraid? Matthew 10:17: "But beware of men."

Men have not only every kind of lust, and wicked and perverse dispositions in their hearts, but they have them to a dreadful degree. There is not only pride, but an amazing degree of it—pride whereby a man is disposed to set himself even above the throne of God itself. The hearts of natural men are mere sinks of sensuality. Man has become like a beast in placing his happiness in sensual enjoyments. The heart is full of the most loathsome lusts. The souls of natural men are more vile and abominable than any reptile. If God should open a window in the heart so that we might look into it, it would be the most loathsome spectacle that ever was set before our eyes. There is not only malice in the hearts of natural men, but a fountain of it. Men naturally therefore deserve the language applied to them by John the Baptist in Matthew 3:7 ("O generation of vipers") and by Christ in Matthew 23:33: "Ye serpents, ye generation of vipers."

Men, if it were not for fear and other such restraints, would not only commit all manner of sin, but to what degree, to what length would they not proceed! What has a natural man to keep him from openly blaspheming God as much as any of the devils, yea, from dethroning Him, if that were possible, if fear and other such restraints were out of the way? Yea, would it not be thus with many of those who now appear with a fair face, and will speak most of God, and make many pretenses of worshipping and serving Him? The exceeding wickedness of natural men appears abundantly in the sins they commit, notwithstanding all these restraints. Every natural man, if he reflects, may see enough to show him how exceedingly sinful he is.

Sin flows from the heart as constantly as water flows from a fountain. Jeremiah 6:7: "As a fountain casteth out her waters, so she casteth out her wickedness." And this wickedness that so abounds in their hearts has dominion over them. They are slaves to it. Romans 7:14: "Sold under sin." They are so under the power of sin that they are driven on by their lusts in a course against their own conscience and against their own interest. They are hurried on to their own ruin, and that at the same time their reason tells them it will probably be their ruin. 2 Peter 2:14: they "cannot cease from sin." On account of wicked men's being so under the power of sin, the heart of man is said to be desperately wicked (Jeremiah 17:9). Ephesians 2:1: "Dead in trespasses and sins."

The hearts of natural men are dreadfully hard and incorrigible. There is nothing but the mighty power of God that will move them. They will cleave to sin, and go on in sin, let what will be done with them. Proverbs 27:22: "Though thou shouldest bray a fool in a mortar among wheat with a pestle, yet will not his foolishness depart from him." There is nothing that will awe our hearts; and there is nothing that will draw them to obedience—let there be mercies or afflictions, threatenings or gracious calls and invitations, frowning, or patience and long-suffering, or fatherly counsels and exhortations. Isaiah 26:10: "Let favor be shown to the wicked, yet will he not learn righteousness; in the land of uprightness will he deal unjustly, and will not behold the majesty of the Lord."

Secondly, the relative state of those who are in an unconverted condition is dreadful. This will appear if we consider:

1. Their relative state with respect to God; and that because:
(1) They are without God in the world. They have no interest or part in God. He is not their God. He has declared He will not be their God (Hosea 1:9). God and believers have a mutual covenant relation and right to each other. They are His people and He is their God. But He is not the covenant God of those who are in an unconverted state. There is a great alienation and estrangement between God and the wicked. He is not their Father and portion; they have nothing to challenge of God; they have no right to any one of His attributes. The believer can challenge a right in the power of God, in His wisdom and holiness, His grace and love. All are made over to Him, to be for His benefit. But the unconverted can claim no right in any of God's perfections. They have no God to protect and defend them in this evil world, to defend them from sin or from Satan or any evil. They have no God to guide and direct them in any doubts or difficulties, to comfort and support their minds under afflictions. They are without God in all their affairs, in all the business they undertake, in their family affairs, in their personal affairs, in their outward concerns, and in the concerns of their souls.

How can a creature be more miserable than to be separated from the Creator, and to have no God whom he can call his own God? He is wretched, indeed, who goes up and down in the world without a God to take care of him, to be his guide and protector, and to bless him in his affairs. The very light of nature teaches that a man's God is his all. Judges 18:24: "Ye have taken away my gods, and what have I more?" There is but one God, and in Him they have no right. They are without that God whose will must determine their whole well-being, both here and forever.

That unconverted men are without God shows that they

are liable to all manner of evil. They are liable to the power of the devil, to the power of all manner of temptation, for they are without God to protect them. They are liable to be deceived and seduced into erroneous opinions, and to embrace damnable doctrines. It is not possible to deceive the saints in this way. But the unconverted may be deceived. They may become papists, heathens, or atheists. They have nothing to secure them from it. They are liable to be given up of God to judicial hardness of heart. They deserve it; and since God is not their God they have no certainty that God will not inflict this awful judgment upon them.

As they are without God in the world, they are liable to commit all manner of sin, and even the unpardonable sin itself. They cannot be sure they shall not commit that sin. They are liable to build up a false hope of heaven, and so to go hoping to hell. They are liable to die in such a case as Saul and Judas did, fearless of hell. They have no security from it. They are liable to all manner of mischief since they are without God. They cannot tell what shall befall them, nor when they are secure from anything. They are not safe one moment. Ten thousand fatal mischiefs may befall them that may make them miserable forever.

They who have God for their God are safe from all such evils. It is not possible that they should befall them. God is their covenant God, and they have His faithful promise to be their refuge. But what mischief is there which may not befall natural men? Whatever hopes they may have may be disappointed. Whatever fair prospect there may seem to be of their conversion and salvation, it may vanish away. They may make great progress towards the kingdom of God, and yet come short at last. They may seem to be in a very hopeful way to be converted and yet never *be* converted. A natural man is sure of nothing. He is sure of no good, nor is he sure of escaping any evil. It is therefore a dreadful condition that a natural man is in. They who are in a natural state are lost. They have wandered from God, and they are like lost sheep that have wandered from their shepherd. They are poor helpless creatures in a howling wilderness, and have no shepherd to protect or to guide them. They are desolate, and exposed to innumerable fatal mischiefs.

(2) They are not only without God, but the wrath of God abides upon them. John 3:36: "He that believeth not the Son shall not see life, but the wrath of God abideth on him." There is no peace between God and them, but God is angry with them every day. He is not only angry with them, but that to a dreadful degree. There is a fire kindled in God's anger; it burns like fire. Wrath abides upon them, which, if it should be executed, would plunge them into the lowest hell and make them miserable there to all eternity. They have provoked the Holy One of Israel to anger. God has been angry with them ever since they began to sin. He has been provoked by them every day ever since they exercised any reason; and He is provoked by them more and more every hour. The flame of His wrath is continually burning. There are many now in hell who never provoked God more than they, nor so much as many of them. Wherever they go, they go about with the dreadful wrath of God abiding on them. They eat, drink, and sleep under wrath. How dreadful a condition, therefore, are they in!

It is the most awful thing for the creature to have the wrath of his Creator abiding on him. The wrath of God is a thing infinitely dreadful. The wrath of a king is as the roaring of a lion, but what is the wrath of a king, who is but a worm of the dust to the wrath of the infinitely great and dreadful God? How dreadful is it to be under the wrath of the First Being, the Being of beings, the great Creator and mighty possessor of heaven and earth! How dreadful is it for a person to go about under the wrath of God, who gave him being, and in whom he lives and moves; who is everywhere present, and without whom he cannot move a step nor draw a breath!

Natural men, inasmuch as they are under wrath, are under a curse. God's wrath and curse are continually upon them. They can have no reasonable comfort, therefore, in any of their enjoyments; for they do not know but that they are given them in wrath, and shall be curses to them and not blessings. As it is said in Job 18:15: "Brimstone shall be scattered upon his habitation." How can they take any comfort in their food or in their possession when they do not know but all are given them to fit them for the slaughter?

2. Their relative state will appear dreadful if we consider how they stand related to the devil.

(1) They who are in a natural state are the children of the devil. As the saints are the children of God, so the ungodly are the children of the devil. 1 John 3:10: "In this the children of God are manifest, and the children of the devil." Matthew 13:38-39: "The field is the world; the good seed are the children of the kingdom: but the tares are the children of the wicked one. The enemy that sowed them is the devil." John 8:44: "Ye are of your father, the devil, and the lusts of your father ye will do." They are, as it were, begotten of the devil; they proceed from him. 1 John 3:8: "He that committeth sin is of the devil." As Adam begat a son in his own likeness, so are wicked men in the likeness and image of the devil. They acknowledge this relation and own themselves as children of the devil by consenting that he should be their father. They subject themselves to him

[and] hearken to his counsels as children hearken to the counsels of a father. They learn of him to imitate him, and do as he does, as children learn to imitate their parents. John 8:38: "I speak that which I have seen with My Father, and ye do that which ye have seen with your father." How awful a state is this! How dreadful is it to be a child of the devil, the spirit of darkness, the prince of hell, that wicked, malignant, and cruel spirit! To have anything to do with him is very dreadful. It would be accounted a dreadful, frightful thing only to meet the devil, to have him appear to a person in a visible shape. How dreadful, then, must it be to be his child! How dreadful for any person to have the devil for his father!

(2) They are the devil's captives and servants. Man, before his fall, was in a state of liberty; but now he has fallen into Satan's hands. The devil has gotten the victory and carried him captive. Natural men are in Satan's possession and they are under his dominion. They are brought by him into subjection to his will, to go at his bidding and do what he commands. 2 Timothy 2:26: "Taken captive by him at his will." The devil rules over ungodly men. They are all his slaves and do his drudging. This argues their state to be dreadful. Men account it an unhappy state of life to be slaves, and especially to be slaves to a bad master, to one who is very hard, unreasonable, and cruel. How miserable do we look upon those persons who are taken captive by the Turks, or other such barbarous nations, and put by them to the meanest and most cruel slavery, and treated no better than they treat their cattle! But what is this to being taken captive by the devil, the prince of hell, and made a slave to him? Would not a man better be a slave to anyone on earth than to the devil?

The devil is, of all masters, the most cruel, and treats

his servants the worst. He puts them to the vilest service, to that which is the most dishonorable of any in the world. No work is so dishonorable as the practice of sin. The devil puts his servants to such work as debases them below the dignity of human nature. They must make themselves like beasts to do that work to serve their filthy lusts. And, besides the meanness of the work, it is a very hard service. The devil causes them to serve him at the expense of the peace of their own conscience, and, oftentimes, at the expense of their reputation, at the expense of their estates and the shortening of their days. The devil is a cruel master, for the service upon which he puts his slaves is to undo themselves. He keeps them hard at work day and night to work their own ruin. He never intends to give them any reward for their pains, but their pains are to work out their own everlasting destruction. It is to gather fuel and kindle the fire for themselves to be tormented into all eternity.

(3) The soul of a natural man is the habitation of the devil. The devil is not only their father, and rules over them, but he dwells in them. It is a dreadful thing for a man to have the devil near him, often coming to him. But it is a more dreadful thing to have him dwell with a man, to take up his constant abode with him, and [it is] more dreadful yet to have him dwell in him, to take up his abode in his heart. But thus it is with every natural man. The devil takes up his abode in a man's heart. As the soul of a godly man is the habitation of the Spirit of God, so the soul of a wicked man is the habitation of unclean spirits. As the soul of a godly man is the temple of God, so the soul of a wicked man is the synagogue of Satan. A wicked man's soul is in Scripture called Satan's house and Satan's palace. Matthew 12:29: "How can one enter into a strong man's

house?" meaning the devil. And Luke 11:21: "When a strong man armed keepeth his palace, his goods are in peace." Satan not only lives, but reigns, in the heart of a wicked man. He has not only taken up his abode there, but he has set up his throne there. The heart of a wicked man is the place of the devil's rendezvous. The doors of a wicked man's heart are open to devils. They have free access there, though the doors are shut against God and Jesus Christ. There are many devils, no doubt, that have to do with one wicked man, and his heart is the place where they meet. The soul of a wicked man is, as it was said of Babylon, the habitation of devils, and the hold of every foul spirit, a cage of every unclean and hateful bird. This dreadful state is the condition of a natural man by reason of the relation in which he stands to the devil.

II. The state of unconverted men is very dreadful if we consider its relation to the future world. Our state here is not lasting, but transitory. We are pilgrims and strangers here, and are principally designed for a future world. We continue in this present state but a short time; but we are to be in that future state to all eternity. And therefore men are to be denominated either happy or miserable chiefly with regard to that future state. It matters but little comparatively what our state is here, because it will continue but a short time; it is nothing to eternity. But that man is a happy man who is entitled to happiness, and he is miserable who is in danger of misery, in his eternal state. Prosperity or adversity in the present state alters them but very little, because this state is of so short continuance.

1. Those who are in a natural condition have no title to any inheritance in another world. There are glorious things in another world. There are unsearchable riches, an unspeakable and inconceivable abundance, but they have nothing to do with it. Heaven is a world of glory and blessedness, but they have no right to the least portion of those blessings. If they should die and go out of the world as they are, they would go destitute, having no inheritance, no friends, no enjoyments to go to. They will have no God to whom they may go, no Redeemer to receive their departing souls, no angel to be a ministering spirit to them, to take care of them, to guard or defend them; no interest in that Redeemer who has purchased those blessings. What is said of the Ephesians 2:12 is true of those who are in a natural condition. "At that time ye were without Christ, being aliens from the commonwealth of Israel, and strangers from the covenant of promise, having no hope, and without God in the world." What a dreadful case they are in who live in the world having no hope, without any title to any benefits hereafter, and without any ground to hope for any good in their future and eternal state!

2. Natural men are in a dreadful condition because of the misery to which they are exposed in the future world. This will be obvious, if we consider (1) how great the misery is of which they are in danger; and (2) how great is their danger of this misery.

(1) How great the misery is of which they are in danger. It is great in two respects: the torment and misery are great in themselves, and they are of endless duration.

First, the torment and misery of which natural men are in danger are exceedingly great in themselves. They are great beyond any of our words or thoughts. When we speak of them, our words are swallowed up. We say they are great, and exceedingly great and very dreadful. But when we have used all the words we can to express them, how faint is the idea that is raised in our minds in comparison with the reality! This misery will appear very dreadful if we consider what calamities meet together in it.

In it the wicked are deprived of all good, separated from God and all fruits of His mercy. In this world they enjoy many of the streams of God's goodness, but in the future world they will have no more smiles of God, no more manifestations of His mercy by benefits, by warnings, by calls and invitations. He will nevermore manifest His mercy by the exercise of patience and long-suffering by waiting to be gracious; no more use any forbearance with them for their good; no more exercising His mercy by strivings of His Spirit, by sending messengers and using means. They will have no more testimonies of the fruits of God's goodness in enjoying food and raiment, and comfortable dwellings and convenient accommodations, nor any of the comforts of this life; no more manifestations of His mercy by suffering them to draw near to Him with their prayers, to pray for what they need. God will exercise no pity towards them, no regard for their welfare. Cut off from all the comforts of this life, shut out of heaven, they will see Abraham, Isaac, and Jacob in the kingdom of heaven, but they shall be turned away from God and from all good into the blackness of darkness, into the pit of hell, into that great receptacle which God has provided on purpose to cast into it the filthy, polluted, and abominable of the universe. They will be in a most dreadful condition; they will have no friends. God will be their enemy; angels and the spirits of the just will be their enemies; devils and damned spirits will be their enemies. They will be hated with perfect hatred, [and] will have none to pity them, none to bemoan their case or be any comfort to them.

It appears that the state of the damned will be exceedingly dreadful in that they will suffer the wrath of God executed to the full upon them, poured out without mixture.

They shall bear the wrath of the Almighty. They shall know how dreadful the wrath of an Almighty God is. Now none knows, none can conceive. Psalm 90:11: "Who knoweth the power of thine anger?" Then they shall feel the weight of God's wrath. In this world they have the wrath of God abiding on them, but then it will be executed upon them; now they are the objects of it, but then they will be the subjects of it. Now it hangs over them, but then it shall fall upon them in its full weight without any alleviation or any moderation or restraint. Their souls and their bodies shall then be filled full with the wrath of God. Wicked men shall be as full of wrath as anything that glows in the midst of a furnace is of fire.

The wrath of God is infinitely more dreadful than fire. Fire, yea, the fiercest fire, is but an image and shadow of it. The vessels of wrath shall be filled up with wrath to the brim. Yea, they shall be plunged into a sea of wrath. And therefore hell is compared to a lake of fire and brimstone because there wicked men are overwhelmed and swallowed up in wrath, as men who are cast into a lake or sea are swallowed up in water. Oh, who can conceive of the dreadfulness of the wrath of an Almighty God! Everything in God is answerable to His infinite greatness. When God shows mercy, He shows mercy like a God. His love is infinitely desirable because it is the love of God. And so when He executes wrath is it like a God. This God will pour out without mixture. Revelation 14:10: "The same shall drink of the wine of the wrath of God, which is poured out without mixture into the cup of His indignation; and he shall be tormented with fire and brimstone in the presence of the holy angels, and in the presence of the Lamb." No mixture of mercy or pity; nothing thrown into the cup of wrath to assuage or moderate it. "God shall cast upon him and not spare," Job 27:22. They shall be cast into the winepress of the wrath of God where they shall be pressed down with wrath as grapes are pressed in a winepress. Revelation 14:19: they are "cast into the great winepress of the wrath of God." God will then make appear in their misery how terrible His wrath is so that men and angels may know how much more dreadful the wrath of God is than the wrath of kings or any creatures. They shall know what God can do towards His enemies, and how fearful a thing it is to provoke Him to anger.

If a few drops of wrath sometimes so distress the minds of men in this world so as to be more dreadful than fire or any bodily torment, how dreadful will be a deluge of wrath; how dreadful will it be when all God's mighty waves and billows of wrath pass over them! Every faculty of the soul shall be filled with wrath and every part of the body shall be filled with fire. After the resurrection, the body shall be cast into that great furnace which shall be so great as to burn up the whole world. These lower heavens, this air and this earth, shall all become one great furnace, a furnace that shall burn the earth even to its very center. In this furnace shall the bodies of the wicked lie to all eternity, and yet live and have their sense of pain and torment not at all diminished. Oh, how full will the heart, the vitals, the brain, the eyes, the tongue, the hands, and the feet be of fire, of this fire of such an inconceivable fierceness! How full will every member, and every bone, and every vein, and every sinew be of this fire! Surely it is a fearful thing to fall into the hands of the living God! Who can bear such wrath? A little of it is enough to destroy us. Psalm 2:12: "Kiss the Son, lest He be angry, and ye perish from the way, when His wrath is kindled but a little." But how will men be overwhelmed, how will they sink, when God's wrath is executed in so dreadful a degree! The misery which the damned will endure will be their perfect destruction. Psalm 50:22: "Now consider this, ye that forget God, lest I tear you in pieces, and there be none to deliver."

In several places the wicked are compared to the stubble, to briars and thorns before devouring flames, and to the fat of lambs which consumes into smoke. Psalm 37:20: "But the wicked shall perish, and the enemies of the Lord shall be as the fat of lambs; they shall consume; into smoke shall they consume away." They shall be, as it were, ground to powder under the weight of God's wrath (Matthew 21:44). Their misery shall be perfect misery; and because damnation is the perfect destruction of a creature, therefore it is called death. It is eternal death, of which temporal death, with all its awful circumstances, is but a faint shadow. The struggles and groans and gasps of the body when dying, its pale awful visage when dead, its state in the dark grave when it is eaten with worms, are but a faint shadow of the state of the soul under the second death.

How dreadful the state of the damned is we may argue from the desert of sin. One sin deserves eternal death and damnation, which, in the least degree of it, is the total destruction of the creature. How dreadful, then, is the misery of which natural persons are in danger, who have lived some time in the world, have committed thousands and thousands of sins, have filled up many years with a course of sinning, and have committed many great sins, with high aggravations, who have sinned against the glorious gospel of Christ and against great light, whose guilt is far more dreadful than that of the people of Sodom and Gomorrah! How dreadful is the punishment to which they are exposed in which all their sins shall be punished according to their desert, and the uttermost farthing shall be exacted of them! The punishment of one idle word or sinful thought would be more than they could bear. How then will they bear all the wrath that shall be heaped upon them for all their multiplied and aggravated transgression?

If one sin deserves eternal death and damnation, how many deaths and damnations will they have accumulated upon them at once! Such an aggravated, multiplied death must they die every moment, and always continue dying such a death and yet never be dead. Such misery as this may well be called "the blackness of darkness." Hell may well be called "the bottomless pit," if the misery is so unfathomably great. Men sometimes have suffered extreme torment in this world. Dreadful have been the sufferings of some of the martyrs; but how little those are in comparison of the sufferings of the damned we may learn from 1 Peter 4:16–18: "Yet if any man suffer as a Christian, let him not be ashamed, but let him glorify God on this behalf. For the time is come that judgment must begin at the house of God; and if it first begin at us, what shall the end be of those that obey not the gospel of God? And if the righteous scarcely be saved, where shall the ungodly and sinner appear?"

The apostle is here speaking of the sufferings of Christians; and from thence he argues that, seeing their sufferings are so great, how unspeakably great will be the sufferings of the wicked! And if judgment begins with them, what shall be the end of those who obey not the gospel! As much as to say that the sufferings of the righteous are nothing to what those who obey not the gospel are. How dreadful, therefore, does this argue their misery to be! Well may the sinners in Zion be afraid, fearful, and surprised. Well may the kings of the earth, the great men, the rich men, the chief captains, every bondman and every free man, hide themselves in the dens and in the rocks of the mountains at Christ's second coming and cry and say to the mountains and rocks, "Fall on us, and hide us from the face of Him that sitteth on the throne, and from the wrath of the Lamb; for the great day of His wrath is come, and who shall be able to stand?" Well may there be weeping and gnashing of teeth in hell, where there is such misery. Thus the misery of those who are in a natural condition, is, in itself, exceedingly great.

Second, this misery is of endless duration. The misery is not only amazingly great and extreme, but of long continuance, yea, of infinitely long continuance. It never will have any end. There will be no deliverance, no rest, no hope; but they will last throughout all eternity. Eternity is a thing in the thought of which our minds are swallowed up. As it is infinite in itself, so it is infinitely beyond the comprehension of our minds. The more we think of it, the more amazing will it seem to us. Eternity is a duration to which a long period of time bears no greater proportion than a short period. A thousand years or a thousand ages bear no greater proportion to eternity than a minute; or, which is the same thing, a thousand ages are as much less than eternity as a minute. A minute comes as near an equality to it; or you may take as many thousand ages out of eternity as you can minutes.

If a man, by the utmost skill in arithmetic, should denote or enumerate a great number of ages, and should rise by multiplication to ever so prodigious numbers, should make as great figures as he could, and rise in multiplying as fast as he could, and should spend his life in multiplying, the product of all would be no nearer equal to the duration which the wicked must spend in the misery of hell than one minute. Eternity is that which cannot be made less by subtraction. If we take from eternity a thousand years or ages, the remainder is not the less for it. Eternity is that which will forever be but beginning, and that because all the time which is past, let it be ever so long, is but a point to what remains. The wicked, after they have suffered millions of ages, will be, as it were, but in the first point, only setting out in their sufferings. It will be no comfort to them that so much is gone, for they will have none the less to bear. There will never a time come when, if what is past is compared to what is to come, it will not be as a point and as nothing. The continuance of their torment cannot be measured out by revolutions of the sun, or moon, or stars, by centuries or ages. They shall continue suffering after these heavens and this earth shall wax old as a garment, till the whole visible universe is dissolved. Yea, they shall remain in their misery through millions of such ages as are equal to the age of the sun, moon, and stars, and still it will be all one as to what remains, still no nearer the end of their misery. Matthew 25:41: "Depart from me, ye cursed, into everlasting fire, prepared for the devil and his angels." Mark 9:44: "Where their worm dieth not, and the fire is not quenched." Revelation 20:10: "They shall be tormented day and night for ever and ever." And 14:11: "The smoke of their torment ascendeth up for ever and ever."

The damned in hell, in their misery, will be in absolute despair. They shall know that their misery will have no end, and therefore they will have no hopes of it. Oh, who can conceive the dreadfulness of such despair as this in the midst of such torment! Who can express or think anything of how dreadful the thought of eternity is to them who are under so great torment! To what unfathomable depths of woe will it sink them! With what a gloom and blackness of darkness will it fill them! What a boundless gulf of sorrow and woe is the thought of eternity to the damned, who shall be in absolute and utter despair of any deliverance!

How dreadful, then, is the condition of those who are in a natural state, who are in danger of such misery.

(2) The dreadfulness of their condition will appear by considering how great their danger is of this misery. This will be obvious from the following things:

First, their danger is such that, continuing in their present state, they will unavoidably sink into this misery.

The state in which natural persons now are naturally tends to it. And this because they are separated from God, and destitute of any spiritual good. The soul that is in a state of separation from its Creator must be miserable because he is separated from the fountain of all good. He who is separate from God is in great danger of ruin because he is without any defense. He who is separated from God must perish, if he continues so, because it is from God only that he can have those supplies which can make him happy.

It is with the soul as it is with the body. The body, without supplies of sustenance, will miserably famish and die. So the souls of natural men are in a famishing condition. They are separate from God, and therefore are destitute of any spiritual good which can nourish the soul or keep it alive. They are like one who is remote in a wilderness where he has nothing to eat or drink, and therefore, if he continues so, will unavoidably die. So the state of natural men naturally tends to that dreadful misery of the damned in hell because they are separated from God.

They are under the power of a mortal disease, which, if it be not healed, will surely bring them to this death. They are under the power and dominion of sin, and sin is a mortal disease of the soul. If it is not cured, it will certainly bring them to death, that is, to that second death of which we have heard. The infection of the disease has powerfully seized their vital parts. The whole head is sick, the whole heart faint. The disease is inveterate. The infection is spread throughout the whole frame; the very nature is corrupted and ruined, and the whole must come to ruin if God, by His mighty power, does not heal the disease. The soul is under a mortal wound, a wound deep and dreadfully confirmed. Its roots reach the most vital parts, yea, they are principally seated there. There is a plague upon the heart which corrupts and destroys the source of life, ruins the whole frame of nature, and hastens an inevitable death. There is a most deadly poison which has been infused into and spread over the man. He has been bitten by a fiery serpent whose bite issues in a most tormenting death. Sin is that which as naturally tends to the misery and ruin of the soul as the most mortal poison tends to the death of the body.

We look upon persons far gone in a consumption, or with an incurable cancer or some such malady, as in doleful circumstances. But that mortal disease under whose power natural men are makes their case a thousand times more doleful. That mortal disease of natural men does, as it were, ripen them for damnation. We read of the clusters of the vine of the earth being for the winepress of the wrath of God (Revelation 14:18), where by the clusters of the vine are meant wicked men. The wickedness of natural men tends to sink them down to hell as the weight of a stone causes it to tend towards the center of the earth. Natural men have, as it were, the seeds of hell within their own hearts. Those principles of sin and corruption, which are in them if they remain unmortified, will at length breed the torment of hell in them, and that necessarily, and of their own tendency. The soul that remains under the power of sin will at length take fire of itself. Hell will kindle in them.

If they continue in their present state this misery appears to be unavoidable, if we consider the justice and truth of God.

If they continue in their present condition, so surely as God is just they shall suffer the eternal misery of which we have heard. The honor of God's justice requires it, and God will not disparage His own justice. He will not deny His own honor and glory, but will glorify Himself on the wicked as well as the godly. He will not lose His honor of any one of His creatures which He has made.

It is impossible that God should be frustrated or disappointed. And so surely as God will not be frustrated, so surely shall they who continue in a natural condition suffer that eternal misery of which we have heard. The avenging justice of God is one of the perfections of His nature, and He will glorify all His perfections. God is unalterable in this as well as His other perfections. His justice shall and must be satisfied. He has declared that He will by no means clear the guilty (Exodus 34:7), that He will not justify the wicked (Exodus 23:7), and that He will not at all acquit the wicked (Nahum 1:3).

God is a strictly just Judge. When men come to stand before Him, He will surely judge them according to their works. Those who have guilt lying upon them, He will surely judge according to their guilt. The debt they owe to justice must be paid to the uttermost farthing. It is impossible that anyone who dies in his sins should escape everlasting condemnation and punishment before such a Judge. He will render to every man according to his deeds. Romans 2:8–9: "Unto them that are contentious, and do not obey the truth, but obey unrighteousness, indignation and wrath, tribulation and anguish, upon every soul of man that doeth evil." It is impossible to influence God to be otherwise than just in judging ungodly men. There is no bribing Him. He accepts not the person of princes, nor regards the rich more than the poor. Deuteronomy 10:17: "He regardeth not persons, nor taketh reward." It is impossible to influence Him to be otherwise than strictly just by any supplications, tears, or cries. God is inexorably just. The cries and the moans of the malefactor will have no influence upon this Judge to pass a more favorable judgment on them, so as in any way to acquit or release them. The eternal cries, groans, and lamentations of the wicked will have no influence upon Him. Though they are ever so long continued, they will not prevail upon God.

So surely as God is true, if they die in the state they are now in, they shall suffer that eternal misery. God has threatened it in a positive and absolute manner. The threatenings of the law are absolute; and they who are in a natural state are under the condemnation of the law. The threatening of the law takes hold upon them; and if they continue under guilt God is obliged by His Word to punish them according to that threatening. And He has often, in the most positive and absolute manner, declared that the wicked shall be cast into hell; that they who believe not shall be damned; that they shall have their portion in the lake that burns with fire and brimstone; and that their misery shall never have an end. And therefore, if there is any truth in God, it shall surely be so. It is as impossible that he who dies in a natural condition should escape suffering that eternal misery as that God should lie. The Word of God is stronger and firmer than mountains of brass and shall not fail. We shall sooner see heaven and earth pass away than one jot or tittle of all that God has said in His Word not be fulfilled. So much for the first thing that evinces the greatness of the danger that natural men are in of hell, that is, that they will unavoidably sink into hell if they continue in such a condition.

Second, their danger will appear very dreadful if we consider how uncertain it is whether they will ever get out of this condition. It is very uncertain whether they will ever be converted. If they should die in their present condition, their misery is certain and inevitable. But it is very doubtful whether they will not die in such a condition. There is great danger that they will, great danger of their never being converted. And this will appear if we consider two things:

They have nothing on which to depend for conversion. They have nothing in the world by which to persuade themselves that they shall ever be converted. Left to themselves, they never will repent and turn to God. If they are ever converted, therefore, it is God who must do it. But they have no promise of God that they ever shall be converted. They do not know how soon they may die. God has not promised them long life; and He has not promised them that they shall be ready for death before they die. It is but a "peradventure" whether God will ever give them repentance to the acknowledging of the truth (2 Timothy 2:25). Their resolutions are not to be depended on. If they have convictions, they are not to be depended on; they may lose those convictions. Their conversion depends on innumerable uncertainties. It is very uncertain, then, whether they will be converted before they die.

Another thing which shows the danger that they shall never be converted is that there are but few, comparatively, who are ever converted. But few of those who have been natural persons in time past have been converted. Most of them have died unconverted. So it has been in all ages, and hence we have reason to think that but few of them who are unconverted now will ever be converted; most of them will die unconverted and will go to hell. Natural persons are ready to flatter themselves that they shall be converted. They think there are signs of it. But a man would not run the venture of so much as a sixpence in such an uncertainty as they are in about their ever being converted or not going to hell. This shows the doleful condition of natural men, as it is uncertain whether they shall ever be converted.

They who are in a natural condition are in danger of going to hell every day. Those now present who are in a natural condition are in danger of dropping into hell before tomorrow morning. They have nothing to depend on to keep them out of hell one day or one night. We know not what a day may bring forth. God has not promised to spare them one day; and He is every day angry with them. The black clouds that are full of the thunder of God's wrath hang over their heads every day, and they know not how soon the thunder will break forth upon their heads. Natural men are, in Scripture, compared to those who walk in slippery places. They know not when their feet will slip. They are continually in danger. Psalm 73:18–19: "Surely thou didst set them in slippery places; thou castedst them down into destruction. How are they brought into desolation as in a moment!" Natural men hang over the pit of hell, as it were, by a thread that has a moth continually gnawing it. They know not when it will snap in twain and let them drop. They are in the utmost uncertainty; they are not secure one moment. A natural man never goes to sleep but he is in danger of waking in hell. Experience abundantly teaches the matter to be so. It shows by millions of instances that man is not certain of life one day. And how common a thing is it for death to come suddenly and unexpectedly! And thousands, beyond all reasonable question, are going to hell every day, and death comes upon them unexpectedly. "When they shall say, 'peace and safety,' then sudden destruction cometh upon them, as travail upon a woman with child; and they shall not escape." It is a dreadful condition that natural persons are in upon this account; and no wise person would be in their condition for a quarter of an hour in exhange for the whole world, because such is the danger that they will drop into hell before that quarter of an hour is expired.

Thus I have shown how dreadful the condition of natural men is, relatively considered. I shall mention two or three things more, which yet further make it appear how doleful their condition is.

1. The longer it continues, the worse it grows. This is an awful circumstance in the condition of a natural man. Any disease is looked upon as the more dreadful for its growing and increasing nature. Thus cancer and gangrene are regarded as dreadful calamities because they continually grow and spread; and the faster they grow, the more dreadful are they accounted. It would be dreadful to be in a natural condition if a person could continue as he is and his condition grow no worse; if he could live in a natural condition and never have it any more dreadful than when he first begins to sin. But it is yet much more dreadful when we consider that every day it becomes worse and worse.

The condition of natural men is worse today than it was yesterday, and that on several accounts. The heart grows more and more polluted and hardened. The longer sin continues unmortified, the more is it strengthened and rooted. Their guilt also grows greater, and hell every day grows hotter; for they are every day adding sin to sin, and so their iniquity is increasing over their heads more and more. Every new sin adds to the guilt. Every sin deserves eternal death for its punishment. And therefore, in every sin that a man commits, there is so much added to the punishment to which he lies exposed. There is, as it were, another eternal death added to augment his damnation. And how much is added to the account in God's book every day; how many new sins are set down, that all may be answered for; each one of which sins must be punished, that by itself would be an eternal death! How fast do wicked men heap up guilt, treasure up wrath, so long as they continue in a natural condition! How is God more and more provoked, His wrath more and more incensed; and how does hellfire continually grow hotter and hotter! If a man has lived twenty years in a natural condition, the fire has been increased every day since he has lived. It has been, as it were, blown up to a greater and greater degree of fierceness. Yea, how dreadfully does one day's continuance in sin add to the heat of hellfire!

2. All blessings are turned into curses to those who live and die in such a condition. Those things which are most pleasant and comfortable, and which men esteem the blessings of life, are but curses unto such—as their meat, their drink, and their raiment. There is a curse that goes with every mouthful of meat and every drop of drink to such a person. There is a curse with his raiment which he puts on; it all contributes to his misery. Though it may please him, yet it does him no good, but he is the more miserable for it. If he has any enjoyment which is sweet and pleasant to him, the pleasure is a curse to him; he is

really the more miserable for it. It is an occasion of death to him. His possessions, which he values himself upon and sets his heart upon, are turned into a curse to him. His house has the curse of God upon it, and his table is a snare and a trap to him (Psalm 69:22). His bed has God's curse upon it. When he lies down to sleep, a curse attends his rest; and when he goes forth to labor he is followed with a curse on that.

The curse of God is upon his fields, on his corn, and herds, and all he has. If he has friends and relations who are pleasant and dear to him, they are no blessings to him. He receives no comfort by them, but they prove a curse to him. I say it is thus with those who live and die in a natural condition. Deuteronomy 28:16–20: "Cursed shalt thou be in the city, and cursed shalt thou be in the field. Cursed shall be thy basket and thy store. Cursed shall be the fruit of thy body, and the fruit of thy land, and the increase of thy cows, and the flocks of thy sheep. Cursed shalt thou be when thou comest in, and cursed shalt thou be when thou goest out. The Lord shall send upon thee cursing, vexation, and rebuke, in all that thou settest thine hand unto for to do, until thou be destroyed, and until thou perish quickly, because of the wickedness of thy doings, whereby thou hast forsaken Me."

Man's faculties of reason and understanding, and all his natural powers, are turned into a curse. Yea, spiritual mercies and privileges shall also be turned into a curse to those who live and die in a natural condition. A curse goes with the worship of God, with sabbaths and sacraments, with instruction, counsels, warnings, and with the most precious advantages. They are all turned into a curse. They are a savor of death unto death. They do but harden the heart, aggravate the guilt and misery, and inflame the divine wrath. Isaiah 6:9–10: "Go, make the heart of this people fat." 2 Corinthians 2:16: "To the one we are the savor of death unto death." It will only be an occasion of their misery that God ever sent Christ into the world to save sinners. That which is in itself so glorious a manifestation of God's mercy, so unspeakable a gift, that which is an infinite blessing to others who receive Christ, will be a curse unto them. It will be, says 1 Peter 2:8, "a stone of stumbling, and a rock of offense." The blood of Christ, which is the price of eternal life and glory to some, is an occasion of sinking them vastly the lower into eternal burnings.

And that is the case of such persons: the more precious any mercies are in themselves, the more of a curse are they to them. The better the things are in themselves, the more will they contribute to their misery. And spiritual privileges, which are in themselves greater mercies than any outward enjoyments, will above all things prove a curse to them. Nothing will enhance their condemnation so much as these. On account of these, it will be more tolerable for Sodom and Gomorrah in the day of judgment than for them. Yea, so doleful is the condition of natural men that, if they live and die in that condition, not only the enjoyments of life, but life itself, will be a curse to them. The longer they live, the more miserable will they be; the sooner they die, the better. If they live long in such a condition and die in it at last, it would have been better for them if they had died before. It would have been far better for them to have spent the time in hell than on earth, yea, better for them to have spent ten thousand years in hell instead of one on earth. When they look back and consider what enjoyments they have had, they will wish they had never had them. Though when on earth they set their hearts on their earthly enjoyments, they will hereafter wish they had been without them; for they will see they have only fitted them for the slaughter. They will wish they never had had their houses and lands, their garments, their earthly friends, their earthly possessions.

And so they will wish that they had never enjoyed the light of the gospel, that they had been born among the heathen in some of the most dark and barbarous places of the earth. They will wish that Christ had never come into the world to die for sinners so as to give men any opportunity to be saved. They will wish that God had cast off fallen man as He did the fallen angels, and had never made him the offer of a Savior. They will wish that they had died sooner, and had not had so much opportunity to increase their guilt and their misery. They will wish they had died in their childhood and been sent to hell then. They will curse the day that ever they were born, and wish they had been made vipers and scorpions or anything rather than rational creatures.

3. They have no security from the most dismal horrors of mind in this life. They have no security but their stupidity. A natural man can have no comfort or peace in a natural condition but that of which blindness and senselessness are the foundation. And from what has been said, that is the very evil. A natural man can have no comfort in anything in this world any further than thought and consideration of mind are deep down in him, just as you can make a condemned malefactor senseless of his misery by putting him to sleep with opium, or make him merry just before his execution by giving him something to deprive him of the use of reason so that he shall not be sensible of his own circumstances. Otherwise, there is no peace or comfort which a natural man can have in a natural condition. Isaiah 48:22: "There is no peace, saith the Lord, to

Natural Men in a Dreadful Condition

the wicked." Job 15:20-21: "The wicked man travaileth with pain all his days; a dreadful sound is in his ears."

The doleful state of a natural man appears especially from the horror and amazement to which he is liable on a deathbed. To have the heavy hand of God upon one in some dangerous sickness, which is wasting and consuming the body and likely to destroy it, and to have a prospect of approaching death and of soon going into eternity, there to be in such a condition as this—to what amazing apprehensions must the sinner be liable! How dismal must his state be when the disease prevails, so that there is no hope that he shall recover, when the physician begins to give him over, and friends to despair of his life; when death seems to hasten on, and he is at the same time perfectly blind to any spiritual object, altogether ignorant of God, of Christ, and of the way of salvation, having never exercised one act of love to God in his life, or done one thing for His glory; having then every lust and corruption in its full strength; having then such enmity in the heart against God, as to be ready to dethrone Him, if that were possible; having no right in God or interest in Christ; having the terrible wrath of God abiding on him; being yet the child of the devil, entirely in his possession and under his power; with no hope to maintain him, and with the full view of never-ending misery just at the door—what a dismal case must a natural man be in under such circumstances! How will his heart die within him at the news of his approaching death, when he finds that he must go, that he cannot deliver himself, that death stands with his grim countenance looking him in the face, and is just about to seize him, and carry him out of the world, and that he at the same time has nothing to depend on!

How often are there instances of dismal distress of unconverted persons on a deathbed! No one knows the fears, the exercise, and torment in their hearts but they who feel them. They are such that all the pleasures of sin which they have had in their whole lives will not pay them for. As you may sometimes see godly men go triumphing out of the world full of joy, with the foretastes of heaven, so sometimes wicked men, when dying, anticipate something of hell before they arrive there. The flames of hell do, as it were, come up and reach them in some measure before they are dead. God then withdraws and ceases to protect them; the tormentor begins his work while they are alive. Thus it was with Saul and Judas; and there have been many other similar instances since, and none who are in a natural condition have any security from it. The state of a natural man is doleful on this account, though this is but a prelude and foretaste of the everlasting misery which follows.

Thus I have in some measure shown in what a doleful condition those are who are in a natural condition. Still I have said but little. It is beyond what we can speak or think. They who say most of the dreadfulness of a natural condition say but little. And they who are most sensible are sensible of but a small part of the misery of a natural state.

Application

We may derive from this doctrine much useful and practical instruction.

1. Hence we may learn the stupidity and sottishness of many natural persons. If we consider those things which we have now heard concerning their dreadful condition, and then see how the greater part of natural men behave

themselves, we may well be astonished that there should be such stupidity in the heart of man. If we rightly considered it, we should be ready to cry out with astonishment. Their sottishness appears in the following things:

Though they are in such a dreadful condition, they can go about easy and quiet, and in little or no concern respecting it. What might rationally be expected of such persons? If it were a new thing to us, and we had heard there was a person in a particular town or country of such a name who was in this awful condition, who had no interest in his Creator, who had the wrath of Almighty God abiding on him—that wrath which is great and terrible enough to make him miserable with devils in hell to all eternity; that he was a captive in the hands of the devil, was made his slave, and was under his power and dominion; that his soul was a habitation of devils; that he was condemned to be cast into the lake that burns with fire and brimstone, to drink of the wine of the wrath of God which is poured out without mixture into the cup of His indignation, and to suffer in an inexpressible, inconceivable extremity in both body and soul forever and ever without hope or end; to be liable to sink in this misery every day, and the longer he continued out of it, the worse his condition, the more dreadful the wrath, and the hotter the flames of hell; I say, supposing we had just now for the first time heard there was a person in this awful condition, how should we expect to see him behave himself? If he was in the exercise of his reason, should we not expect to see him trembling and quaking on account of his misery, with all the manifestations of continual terror and amazement, regardless of all things else, spending his days and nights in tears and groans, and lamentations, crying for pity and help, crying with an exceedingly loud and bitter cry, crying to everyone to pity him and pray for him? Yea, how many are there in this dreadful condition who are easy and quiet, and appear to have nothing to trouble them! They go about the world without anxiety or alarm, as if they had no more reason to be disquieted than if they had already secured their salvation. Though they are told how dreadful their condition is hundreds of times, their tranquility is wholly undisturbed. They can sit and hear of its certainty and its nearness, of its dreadful nature and its inconceivable degree, and then can go away with as quiet and easy hearts as they had before. There is no moving them by telling them of such things. They can sleep as quietly, and go about their business with as perfect unconcern. They can eat and drink and enjoy the pleasures of social life with no apparent load on their minds, and without being sensible of anything in their circumstances which should hinder them from such enjoyment.

And not only so, but they can go about with a merry heart. There are many of them, who not only seem to be quiet in their minds, but they are very cheerful, as if all were well with them and everything smiled upon them; as if they were in happy circumstances, and had everything as they desired; and are even disposed to be merry and sportive about their own condition and the dreadful realities of the future world. For their part they choose to take their ease and pleasure, and not disturb or molest themselves with such dark and melancholy thoughts, like the persons mentioned in Isaiah 56:12: "Come ye, say they, I will fetch wine, and we will fill ourselves with strong drink; and tomorrow shall be as this day, and much more abundant."

They are so senseless that they do not think it worth their while to make any considerable effort to escape from this dreadful condition. They will not take half so much pains for it as for a little worldly gain, and they do not think it worth the while even to ask God to deliver them from it. They think it too much labor to withdraw once or twice each day to ask God to be merciful to them, that they might not continue in their natural state. And they foolishly neglect the precious opportunities which they enjoy to get into a better state. God gives them great advantages for it, and they are called upon, warned, and exhorted to improve them. They are told what good opportunities they have and the danger of letting them slip, but all is to no purpose. These persons will let slip the time of youth, which is a precious season to escape from their natural condition. So they will let slip a time of the moving of God's Spirit in the place where they live. They act as if they had a wish to continue in the same state. They will put themselves so little out of the way to escape from it; they are so backward to deny themselves a little, or to make only a little effort; they seem to begrudge it, and think it needless. If they have a great advantage put into their hands, it is to no purpose. They would be as good without it as with it, for they have no heart to improve it. Proverbs 17:16: "Wherefore is there a price in the hand of a fool to get wisdom, seeing he hath no heart to it?"

Instead of using means to get into a better state, they are willfully doing those things which make it worse and worse. Instead of striving for deliverance, they are striving against it. They are provoking God more, increasing their guilt, hardening their hearts, and setting themselves farther and farther from conversion; and this, too, when they are told that the things which they practice have this tendency. They act as if they wished to be sure never to be converted. Thus it is with innumerable multitudes. So exceedingly senseless and stupid are many natural persons.

2. Hence we need not wonder that we are directed in Scripture to strive and to be very earnest to be delivered

from our natural condition. This is the direction which God gives us from time to time. Luke 13:24: "Strive to enter in at the strait gate." Matthew 11:12: "The kingdom of heaven suffereth violence." Ecclesiasties 9:10: "Whatsoever thy hand findeth to do, do it with thy might." 2 Peter 1:10: "Give diligence to make your calling and election sure." Hebrews 6:18: we "have fled for refuge to lay hold upon the hope set before us." The direction which was given to Lot, relating to his flight out of Sodom, was designed for the direction of all who are in a natural condition. Genesis 19:17: "Escape for thy life; look not behind thee, neither stay thou in all the plain; escape to the mountain, lest thou be consumed."

This doctrine shows us the reason why persons should be directed in such a way as this to seek their salvation. That it is such a dreadful condition is reason enough why persons should thus vehemently strive and be violent to get into a better state, and why they should hasten for their lives and flee from the wrath to come. If the case of natural men is as we have heard, no wonder that they should have such advice given them, and that God expects that the pains which they take, and the endeavors they use for it, should be in some measure answerable to its importance. No wonder that the jailer, when made sensible of his condition, should conduct himself as we have the account in the text. No wonder that he should be in such haste as not only to run in, but to spring or leap into the place where Paul and Silas were, and fall down before them and ask in such an earnest manner, "What must I do to be saved?" If he had not been indeed in a dreadful state, he would have acted like one distracted. But considering that he was in a natural condition, which is so dreadful, it was not the least wonder.

Natural Men in a Dreadful Condition

3. Hence we may learn how dismal are the effects which the fall of man has brought upon the world. It has brought all mankind into this dreadful condition of which we have heard. The far greater part of those who live in this world are in this state, and the greater part of those who die in the world die in this state. What a miserable world, therefore, is the world in which we live! This world lies under a curse. God has pronounced woe against it; and what an immeasurable amount of woe is brought upon it! What woeful devastation has sin made in the world!

What has been said of the dreadfulness of their condition may well awaken and terrify the impenitent. How many things are there in your circumstances which are awful and terrible to think of. There is not one of those things which have been mentioned but that the thought of it may well be frightful to you. It may well be a dreadful thought that you have no goodness in you, nor have ever done anything which has the least goodness in it; that you never exercised one act of love or true thankfulness or obedience to God in your life, nor ever did the least thing out of true respect to God. The consideration of the dreadful depravity and wickedness of your heart may well be frightful to you; to think what a sink of corruption it is, how full of all manner of wickedness, how full of enmity against God; that there are the same corruptions in your heart as in the heart of the devil, and that there are the seeds of the same enmity against God, and that you are in the very image of the devil.

If you look into your own heart and strictly examine what it would entice you to do, if all restraints of fear and self-interest were taken off, it might well affright you. How awful may the thought well be to you when you consider that you are a creature separated from your Creator; that there is an alienation between you and that great Being in whom you live and move and have your being; that you are a poor desolate creature who has no God to protect you, guide you, and provide for you in the world; and that you are secure from no manner of mischief into which human nature is capable of falling either in soul or body! How terrifying should it be to you to think how good, how mighty and terrible that God is under whose wrath you lie down and rise up, and eat and drink, and engage in the daily business of life! How frightful should it be to you when you consider in what relation you stand to the devil; that you are his child, and that he owns you; that you are his servant, his possession, and that your heart is his dwelling-place; that you are without Christ, and so without hope, and have no good thing in another world in which you have any inheritance! And how amazing may it well be to you when you consider how great that future misery is to which you are exposed and condemned, wherein God shows His wrath and makes His power known in the destruction of the ungodly, in which they are vessels of wrath filled to the brim; and that you are in danger of being plunged in a bottomless gulf or deluge of wrath, where mighty waves and billows of wrath shall pass over you; and when you consider the torment of your body in that great furnace of fire, where every part, every organ, every vein, and every limb shall be filled full of fire, and yet full of quick sense, and that this torment shall remain to an endless duration, a duration which shall always be beginning, but never ending!

And how well may it frighten you, and strike a terror upon you, when you consider that if you die in your present condition it is as impossible that you should escape this misery as it is that God should cease to be just and true;

and that the greater part of those who are in your condition will suffer this misery, and that you have no security that you shall be kept from it one day or one hour! How terrifying may it well be to you when you consider how much more dreadful your case continually grows! How frightful may it be to you every night when you sit down and consider how much greater your guilt is, and how much deeper your condemnation is than it was in the morning! How awful and doleful may it be to you to consider that if you live and die in your present state, everything is cursed to you: even your greatest mercies and best enjoyments, your food, your raiment, your nearest friends, and your earthly possessions; and not only so, but the light of the gospel, and the means of grace, and life itself will be cursed to you! All will be but an occasion of your greater misery. Such persons shall wish they had been born and brought up among the heathen. They shall wish that Christ had never come into the world; they shall wish they had never been born. How awful may it be to you when you think that death will most certainly come upon you, and you know not how soon; and what dismal circumstance you would be in if you were in your present condition on a deathbed! How many things are there in your case which are of a terrifying, awful nature! How can you live in such circumstances without living in continual terror? Here consider further the following things:

1. There is nothing which you see but what may justly minister torment to you while you remain in a natural condition. If you lift up your eyes and behold the sun, moon, and stars, and cast your eyes abroad on the face of the earth, and see the mountains, fields, and trees, it may justly put you in mind of the dolefulness of your condition: that the great God who made all these things, who

stretched forth the heavens as a curtain, who ordained the sun, moon, and stars, and laid the foundations of the earth, and causes the grass and trees to grow, is a God in whom you have no interest, but who is continually angry with you, and that His wrath abides on you.

So when you look on your own body, and consider how it is formed and contrived, it may be a frightful thing to you to consider that He who made you is not at peace with you, and that you are the object of His displeasure. If you have pleasures and enjoyments and are in flourishing circumstances, if you see the faces of your near friends and dear relations, and look upon your children and other dear friends, and behold your costly possessions, these things may justly minister torment to you while you are in a natural state. For consider that you do not know but that all these things are given you in wrath. When you sit down to eat and drink you may do it in torment, because you know not but this may be in wrath. When you lie down upon your beds it may justly be in torment, for you do not know but you shall awake in hell. And when you awake in the morning, it may justly be with torment in your heart to think you are still in that doleful condition. When you go forth to your daily labor, you have reason to go with a terrified heart; for you know not but you are followed with God's curse in all that to which you put your hands.

Whatever dispensations of Providence you may have, all may justly put you in mind of the dolefulness of your condition. If you meet with afflictions, these may remind you that you have no God to pity you, and that a God who is angry with you every day sends these afflictions upon you. If you meet with prosperity, you may justly receive it with a sorrowful sense of the dolefulness of your state; for you know not but it is to fit you for the slaughter. If you hear of the death of others, it may justly terrify you and put you in mind of your own mortality, and of your danger of dying as you now are. If you hear of others' conversion, it may justly renew in you a sense of the dolefulness of your own state, that you still remain unconverted. If you see the Bible, an awful thought may justly go with the sight that you have never yet received any good by that book, and that all the curses written in it stand against you. Every time you enter the house of God, it may justly renew awful thoughts of your circumstances, that you have entered there so often and obtained no good; entered so often, and gone away worse than you came.

And what danger there is that you shall be one of those spoken of in Ecclesiastes 8:10: "I saw the wicked buried, who had come and gone from the place of the holy, and they were forgotten in the city where they had so done." And wheresoever you turn yourself, whatever you meet with, and whatever you behold or hear may justly renew a sense of the dolefulness of your state. The thought of your condition may justly cast a darkness upon everything.

2. Consider that the time will soon come when you will be sensible that the dolefulness of your condition is as great as I have represented it; that I have not enlarged or magnified the matter, but that the case is as I have declared it. You will then see that it is so. Whether you are sensible of it now or not, yet in a little time you will surely be sensible, and will need no argument to convince you of it. Yea, you will be sensible that it is *more* doleful than I have represented. After all that has been told you now, and at other times, the time will come when you will say that the one half was not told you.

Your condition is thus doleful, notwithstanding everything with which you may flatter yourself. You may be ready to flatter yourself that, though the condition of some natural persons is thus doleful, yet yours is not; that you are in better circumstances than other natural men commonly are. Or, particularly, you may flatter yourself that you are not so bad as others; you do not find such dreadful corruptions in your heart as you hear are in others. Herein you deceive yourself. It is because you are ignorant of your own heart. What has been said of the depraved state of natural men, of their blindness, their hardness, their deadness, all belongs to you. You may possibly flatter yourself that your condition is not so doleful because you have always walked orderly; you have been moral and religious. Here also you deceive yourself. For, notwithstanding your moral and religious behavior and all your sobriety, you never did the least thing from a gracious respect to God.

You have a heart in the likeness of the heart of the devil. You are without God in the world. God is angry with you every day. His wrath is not at all appeased. You may flatter yourself that you are the children of godly parents, that you have many godly friends who may put up many prayers for you, that your case is not so doleful on that account, and that your danger is not extremely great. But in this you miserably deceive yourself. You are children of the devil, notwithstanding all this. If you die in your present condition, it is impossible that you shall escape eternal misery. And there is great danger that you will die in it. You have no security that you shall not be in hell before tomorrow morning. Do not flatter yourself from such things as these that you are not in a doleful condition. Some of those who flatter themselves most, and think their condition the least doleful, are indeed in the most doleful condition. It is more dreadful than their neighbors'; more so than that of many whom they esteem ten times worse than themselves.

And this is one thing which adds to the dolefulness of their condition, that they so flatter themselves and think their state so good. So it was of old with the scribes and Pharisees. Matthew 21:31: "Verily I say unto you, the publicans and harlots go into the kingdom of God before you."

This subject may well excite joy and thankfulness in the hearts of the truly penitent, that God has found out a way to deliver them from such a condition; that God has been pleased to send His Son into the world to die for them; that He has given them the gospel and the means of grace; and that He has delivered them from this dreadful condition. You were in the same circumstances. 1 Corinthians 6:11: "Such were some of you; but ye are washed, but ye are sanctified, but ye are justified in the name of the Lord Jesus, and by the Spirit of our God." It is mere grace which has made the difference. There is no cause of boasting. God might have taken others and left you. You deserved no more than they. You had no more righteousness of your own. Probably you have done worse than many who have eternally perished. Take heed that you entertain no boasting thought, and that your joy in this is a humble joy, accompanied with continual praise to God who has done such great things for you, and from all eternity set His love upon you.

This subject should lead those who are in a natural condition earnestly to seek for deliverance. Will you rest in such a condition when there is a way of salvation provided and an opportunity for an escape? Will you of choice continue still in this state? Though your case is very dangerous, yet there is a possibility of rescue if you have but a heart to improve your opportunity.

But besides what has been said, I would desire you further to consider how happy will be your state should you obtain deliverance. A converted state is not less happy than a natural condition is miserable and dreadful. You will be brought out of darkness into marvelous light. It will be like the dawning of the morning after a long night of darkness. It will be a joyful morning to you. The daystar will arise in your heart. Then will be given you the morning star. You will then have a discovery of the glory of God and the beauty and excellency of Jesus Christ made to your soul; and then will be opened to your view the glorious fountain of divine grace. You will then look back and see how you have dwelt in darkness throughout your lives, and in the region and shadow of death. Matthew 4:16: "The people which sat in darkness saw great light, and to them which sat in the region and shadow of death light is sprung up." You will then be brought out of a dreadful bondage into glorious liberty. You will come forth as from a dark dungeon to see the glorious light of the Sun of righteousness. Your eyes will then be opened and you will be brought out of the prison house. Isaiah 61:1: "The Spirit of the Lord God is upon me, because the Lord hath anointed me to preach good tidings unto the meek; He hath sent me to bind up the broken-hearted, to proclaim liberty to the captives, and the opening of the prison to them that are bound." Then you who were dead will be made alive; and you who have been lost will be found. What you will then obtain will richly repay you for all the labor which you have undergone. If you have spent ever so many years in wrestling with corruption and temptation in striving to enter in at the strait gate, you will not regret it. But more particularly consider:

 1, How glorious will be the alteration made in your nature. Old things will be done away with and all things will become new. Sin will be mortified in you and the glorious image of God conferred upon you. You will have holy and spiritual principles imparted to you, a spirit of divine love and heavenly-mindedness, a relish for spiritual enjoyments, a delight in the Lord Jesus Christ, a truly meek, humble, charitable, and benevolent spirit. You will be changed from being more filthy and hateful than a reptile into the likeness of the glorious Son of God. You will be taken out of the mire of brutal lusts and spiritual abominations, will be washed from all your filthiness, and will be adorned with the most glorious ornaments—those ornaments of mind which in the sight of God are of great price, ornaments which will render you a thousand times more beautiful and lovely than the robes of princes. You will obtain those graces of the Spirit of God which are the ornaments of angels.

2. Consider the safety of the condition in which you will then be. The terrible wrath of the great God which abides on wicked men will then be removed from you. Christ will be to you as a hiding place from the storm, and as a shadow from the heat of God's wrath. You will then be safe from hell, and will be forever delivered from that dreadful misery which is endured by the damned, and to which you are now condemned. Revelation 20:6: "On such the second death hath no power."

You will be safe from the power of Satan. Christ will be your protector; you shall be out of Satan's reach so that he will not be able to destroy you. You shall dwell on high. Your place of defense shall be the munition of rocks, where you may laugh at the power of the enemy. And though you are in a world full of enemies and sinners, yet God will be your Rock, and the most high God your Redeemer. God will carry you as on eagles' wings through the world, aloft out of the reach of your enemies. They may see you and wish your ruin and gnash their teeth, but shall not be able to accomplish it. Satan will desire to have you, but Christ will have prayed for you, and that will be your security. You will be safe from death; it will not be able to hurt you. Natural men are in continual danger from death. They know not when nor how death may come. But if it comes while they are in that condition, it sinks them into hell. But you need not be afraid to meet death, either by day or night. Whenever it comes, and in whatever form, you are safe. While others walk in slippery places, your feet will be established on a rock. In a time of sickness and mortality, while others tremble, you need not fear. If you are sick, you need not dread the issue. For though your flesh and your heart should fail you, yet God will be the strength of your heart, your present help, and your portion forever. Though the earth should be removed, you will be safe. Psalm 46:1-3: "God is our refuge and strength, a very present help in trouble. Therefore will not we fear though the earth be removed, and though the mountains be carried into the midst of the sea; though the waters thereof roar and be troubled, though the mountains shake with the swelling thereof." If you are once in Christ Jesus, none shall ever pluck you out of his hands. John 10:28: "They shall never perish, neither shall any pluck them out of My hand."

You will be freed from condemnation, for who is he who shall condemn you? It is Christ who died, yea rather, who is risen again. Who shall separate you from the love of Christ? "Neither life, nor death, nor angels, nor principalities, nor powers, nor things present, nor things to come, nor height, nor depth, nor any other creature." What a glorious foundation will there be for your peace and quietness! Isaiah 32:17: "And the work of righteousness shall be peace; and the effect of righteousness, quietness and assurance for ever." Let this consideration, therefore, prompt you earnestly to seek that you may obtain that happy condition. Can you consider how happy the change would be to you, how desirable such safety is, and not be willing earnestly to seek and do everything which lies in your power, that you may obtain it?

3. Consider how exceedingly it will be for the comfort and pleasure of your life if you are converted. You are not only under the greatest necessity to become converted, because a natural condition is so dreadful a condition, but you will gain by it in every way. You will not only gain eternal life by it, but you will gain unspeakably by it while in this world. Your pains will be richly rewarded while here, though that is but little to your future reward. You cannot take a more direct course to make your life pleasant. You will obtain by it the most excellent delight and pleasure in comparison with which the pleasures which are to be had in worldly things are low and vile. Hereby you may obtain the most substantial, soul-satisfying, soul-refreshing pleasures. You may then live a life of divine love and communion with that glorious Being who is the object of your love. Then you will be blessed with the best company and with heavenly society. Far better is a little with the fear of the Lord than great treasures with that trouble which wicked men have with their enjoyments. Then you may enjoy what God in his providence bestows upon you with peace of conscience, and may rejoice in it as the fruit of the love of God. Then you may have the comfort of considering that you have God's blessing on what you possess.

Your enjoyments will then be sweet to you, for you will

enjoy God in the fruits of His bounty. Your life will be abundantly more pleasant in all the circumstances and concerns of it. It will make God's house a more delightful resort; your own house a more pleasant residence, for then the blessing of heaven will rest upon it; and your closet a sweeter retirement. It will make your labor sweeter to you, and it will sweeten your rest. You may then say with the psalmist (Psalm 4:8), "I will both lay me down and sleep, for thou, Lord, only makest me dwell in safety." It will tend to make your life pleasant, and to make your deathbed comfortable to you. When all other comforts fail, this will stand you instead. It will remain as a living spring, which will never fail. John 4:14: "The water that I shall give him shall be in him a well of water springing up into everlasting life." This will make time comfortable, and will make the thought of eternity comfortable to you when you shall have those pleasures which are at God's right hand forever in more immediate prospect; and you shall have that faithful promise of God that hereafter you shall see God, and shall dwell in His presence, and shall from the hands of Christ receive a crown of life.

DIRECTION. In general be directed to act as if you were in a dreadful condition; as one who looks upon his case to be dreadful, not merely as one looks upon his case as undesirable and worse than that of another; but as one who is sensible that his state is inexpressibly dismal and terrible. Consider how men act when they apprehend their circumstances to be very dreadful, though only in temporal respects. For instance, if they are in danger of being consumed by fire, or only having their substance consumed; or if in danger of being seized by an enemy, or otherwise in danger of some dreadful evil, how do the thoughts of danger awaken their powers! What earnestness appears in them! In what haste are they! Be directed to seek for deliverance from a natural condition in like manner if you would be delivered. The jailer acted as one who was sensible that his condition was dreadful. So be you directed to act, if you would have the like success. Particularly:

1. *Be in haste.* The jailer, when he was made sensible of his dreadful condition, sprang into the presence of Paul and Silas and cried out, "What must I do to be saved?" So you cannot be in too much haste. When ministers direct those who are seeking salvation to wait until God's time comes, if they understand the Scriptures they cannot mean that they should not be in haste to obtain a better condition, or that they should be at rest, or continue in such a condition one hour or one moment. They can only mean these two things: that they should wait or persevere in opposition to giving up in discouragement; and that they should wait in opposition to quarreling with God for not delivering them, and not in opposition to being uneasy in a natural condition. For persons ought to be uneasy, and it argues awful stupidity to be otherwise but in opposition to a quarreling spirit because God does not show mercy sooner. We should persevere in our efforts to obtain salvation as being sensible that God is not obliged to bestow it in our time or at all; that He may, if He wills, refuse to show mercy, and, if He does show mercy, that He may do it in His own time. Remember that the command of Christ to you is, "Repent and believe the Gospel." You cannot lawfully continue in your present state one day or hour. Those who defer and put off repentance till another time are not in a likely way to obtain deliverance. The way is to improve the present time; to do now what must be done ever. We should make securing our salvation our present and im-

mediate business.

Therefore, inquire whether you do not put it off. If you do not put off the whole of the work, yet do you not put off part of it? Do you think you now strive as much for salvation as it will ever be needful that you should? If not, delay no longer. Let it not be said of you tomorrow that there is anything delayed today, which you yourself thought needful to be done, or in your power to do, in order to secure your salvation. If you are sensible that you are in this dreadful condition, you certainly will make haste; you will need no other motive to it.

2. *Let nothing which you do in seeking salvation be done with slackness.* The direction is, "Whatsoever thy hand findeth to do, do it with thy might." Therefore, let nothing be done with a slack hand. Do everything which you do in this great work earnestly. There are many things which you have to do, many duties to be performed, many means to be employed—let all be done with your strength. Be earnest in prayer, earnest in hearing the Word preached, diligent and faithful in watching over your own heart, diligent in searching your heart, diligent in reflecting on your past life, diligent and laborious in meditation, laborious and earnest in striving against temptation.

And do not perform merely the duties of religion towards God earnestly, but also its duties towards your neighbor. Be earnest that you may do every duty required of you towards all men. Be earnest and diligent to do justly and honestly, and to render every man his due. Be earnest to watch against an envious, malicious, and vengeful spirit. Be earnest to do all the duties of charity: labor with your might that you may behave charitably towards men, and neglect no duty of charity required of you. Be earnest in performing every relative duty: in rendering suitable honor

Natural Men in a Dreadful Condition

to your parents; in manifesting kindness and confidence to your husband or your wife; in instructing and governing your children, bringing them up in religion, and seeking their salvation in the very way pointed out in the Scriptures. Do this earnestly and with all your strength. You should not merely do *some* things earnestly, but all.

3. Take heed lest your earnestness is not transient, but that you continue in it to the end. It is the misery of many persons that they seem to be very warmly engaged for a little time, but it does not last. It is a very rare thing that any who are thoroughly and perseveringly in earnest for salvation fail of it, unless they have put off the work until they are near death before they began. How unstable is the heart of man, and how many are there who go to hell through backsliding! It is often the case, when persons begin with much seeming earnestness, that they do it upon a secret dependence that they shall not need to make these efforts very long. They flatter themselves that in a little time they shall obtain what they seek and then they may take their ease; therefore, when they have gone on awhile and fail of that expectation, they soon slacken their exertions. They never consented to seek in this diligent persevering manner always; but they appointed a time of their own, and sought it on terms of their own fixing. But a man is then in a hopeful way to be converted when he has so great a sense of his misery and his necessity of conversion that he is disposed to do his utmost to be violent for the kingdom of heaven, and to devote his life to it.

If you are seeking salvation, inquire how it is with you as to this matter. Do you feel a disposition in yourself to be at the pains and difficulty of a most laborious seeking God's grace in the denial of every lust, and in a painful performance of every duty as long as you live? Or does this seem to you to be too much, more than you can find a heart to comply with? You may be ready to say that you could be willing to do all this if you knew you should obtain at last. But that is not sufficient. You should be willing to run the venture of that, and seek upon what encouragement is given you, and to wait for God's sovereign will and pleasure in that way. And if you cannot become willing for this, be sensible there is a defect in your manner of seeking which it behoves you to mend. And do not think that you seek it in the right way until you come to it. If you have a right sense of the dolefulness of your condition, it will bring you to it. Consider the great encouragement there is for this way of seeking. Hosea 6:3: "Then shall we know, if we follow on to know the Lord."

4. *Seek that you may be brought to lie at God's feet in a sense of your own exceeding sinfulness.* Seek earnestly that you may have such a sight yourself: what an exceedingly sinful creature you are, what a wicked heart you have, and how dreadfully you have provoked God to anger; that you may see that God would be most just if He should never have any mercy upon you. Labor that all quarreling with God's dispensations towards sinners may be wholly subdued; that your heart may be abased and brought down to the dust before God; that you may see yourself in the hands of God; and that you can challenge nothing of God but that God and His throne are blameless in the eternal damnation of sinners, and would be in your damnation.

Seek that you may be brought off from all high opinion of your own worth, all trust in your own righteousness, and to see that all you do in religion is so polluted and defiled that it is utterly unworthy of God's acceptance, and that you commit sin enough in your best duties to condemn you forever.

Seek that you may come to see that God is sovereign, that He is the potter and you the clay, and that His grace is His own, and that He may bestow it on whom He will, and that He might justly refuse to show you mercy. Seek that you may be sensible that God is sovereign as to the objects of His grace, and also as to the time and manner of bestowing it, and seek God and wait upon Him as a sovereign God. Seek that you may be sensible that God's anger is infinitely dreadful, yet, at the same time, be sensible that it is just. Labor that when you have a sense of the awfulness of the wrath of God in your mind, you may fall down before an angry God and lie in the dust.

Seek that you may see that you are utterly undone, and that you cannot help yourself, and yet that you do not deserve that God should help you, and that He would be perfectly just if He should refuse ever to help you.

If you have come to this, then you will be prepared for comfort. When persons are this humble, it is God's manner soon to comfort them. When you are thus brought low, doubtless God will soon lift you up. God will not bestow such a great and infinite mercy as eternal life upon persons who will not acknowledge His sovereignty in that matter. When once there has been that conviction upon the heart which casts down imaginations and every high thing that exalts itself against God, then God is wont speedily to reveal His grace and love, and to pour the oil of comfort into the soul.

5. *Abound in earnest prayer to God that He would open your eyes that you may behold the glorious and rich provision made for sinners in Jesus Christ.* The souls of natural men are so blinded that they see no beauty or excellency in Christ. They do not see His sufficiency. They see no beauty in the work of salvation by Him; and as long as they remain thus blind it is

impossible that they should close with Christ. The heart will never be drawn to an unknown Savior. It is impossible that a man should love that, and freely choose that, and rejoice in that in which he sees no excellency. But if your eyes were opened to see the excellency of Christ, the work would be done. You would immediately believe on Him, and you would find your heart going after Him. It would be impossible to keep it back.

But take heed that you do not entertain a wrong notion of what it is spiritually to see Christ. If you do, you may seek that which God never bestows. Do not think that spiritually to see Christ is to have a vision of Him as the prophets had, to see Him in some bodily shape, to see the features of His countenance. Do not pray or seek for any such thing as this. But what you are to seek is that you may have a sight of the glorious excellency of Christ, and of the way of salvation through Him in your heart. This is a spiritual sight of Christ. This is that for which you must cry to God day and night. God is the fountain of spiritual light. He opens the eyes of the blind. He commands the light to shine out of darkness. It is easy with God to enlighten the soul, and fill it with these glorious discoveries, though it is beyond the power of men and angels.

Sinners in the Hands of an Angry God

"Their foot shall slide in due time."
Deuteronomy 32:35

In this verse is threatened the vengeance of God on the wicked unbelieving Israelites who were God's visible people and lived under means of grace, and that notwithstanding all God's wonderful works that He had wrought towards that people yet remained, as is expressed in verse 28, void of counsel, having no understanding in them, and that, under all the cultivations of heaven, brought forth bitter and poisonous fruit, as is shown in the two verses preceding the text.

The expression that I have chosen for my text ("their foot shall slide in due time") seems to imply the following things relating to the punishment and destruction that these wicked Israelites were exposed to:

1. They were always exposed to destruction, as one who stands or walks in slippery places is always exposed to fall. This is implied in the manner of their destruction's coming upon them being represented by their foot's sliding. The same is expressed in Psalm 73:18: "Surely thou didst set them in slippery places; thou castedst them down into destruction."

2. It implies that they were always exposed to sudden, unexpected destruction. As he who walks in slippery places is every moment liable to fall, he cannot foresee one mo-

ment whether he shall stand or fall the next; and when he does fall, he falls at once without warning, which is also expressed in Psalm 73:18–19: "Surely thou didst set them in slippery places; thou castedst them down into destruction. How are they brought into desolation, as in a moment."

3. Another thing implied is that they are liable to fall of themselves without being thrown down by the hand of another, as he who stands or walks on slippery ground needs nothing but his own weight to throw him down.

4. The reason why they are not fallen already, and do not fall now, is only that God's appointed time is not come. For it is said that when that due time or appointed time comes, "their feet shall slide." Then they shall be left to fall, as they are inclined by their own weight. God will not hold them up in these slippery places any longer, but will let them go; and then, at that very instant, they shall fall into destruction as he who stands in such slippery, declining ground on the edge of a pit so that he cannot stand alone, when he is let go he immediately falls and is lost.

The observation from the words that I would now insist upon is this: There is nothing that keeps wicked men at any one moment out of hell but the mere pleasure of God.

By the mere pleasure of God I mean His sovereign pleasure, His arbitrary will, restrained by no obligation, hindered in no manner of difficulty any more than if nothing else but God's mere will had in the least degree or in any respect whatsoever any hand in the preservation of wicked men one moment.

The truth of this observation may appear by the following considerations:

1. There is no lack of power in God to cast wicked men

into hell at any one moment. Men's hands cannot be strong when God rises up. The strongest have no power to resist Him, nor can any deliver out of His hands. He is not only able to cast wicked men into hell, but he can most easily do it. Sometimes an earthly prince meets with a great deal of difficulty to subdue a rebel who has found means to fortify himself, and has made himself strong by the number of his followers. But it is not so with God. There is no fortress that is any defense against the power of God. Though hand joins in hand, and vast multitudes of God's enemies combine and associate themselves, they are easily broken in pieces; they are as great heaps of light chaff before the whirlwind, or as large quantities of dry stubble before devouring flames. We find it easy to tread on and crush a worm that we see crawling on the earth; so it is easy for us to cut or singe a slender thread that anything hangs by. Thus easy is it for God, when He pleases, to cast His enemies down to hell. What are we that we should think to stand before Him at whose rebuke the earth trembles and before whom the rocks are thrown down!

2. They deserve to be cast into hell, so that divine justice never stands in the way; it makes no objection against God's using His power at any moment to destroy them. Yea, on the contrary, justice calls aloud for an infinite punishment of their sins. Divine justice says of the tree that brings forth such grapes of Sodom: "Cut it down, why cumbereth it the ground?" (Luke 13:7). The sword of divine justice is every moment brandished over their heads, and it is nothing but the hand of arbitrary mercy and God's mere will that holds it back.

3. They are already under a sentence of condemnation to hell. They not only justly deserve to be cast down there,

but the sentence of the law of God, that eternal and immutable rule of righteousness that God has fixed between Him and mankind, has gone out against them and stands against them, so that they are bound over already to hell. John 3:18: "He that believeth not is condemned already." So that every unconverted man properly belongs to hell; that is his place; from thence he is. John 8:23: "Ye are from beneath." And there he is bound. It is the place that justice, God's Word, and the sentence of His unchangeable law assign to him.

4. They are now the objects of that very same anger and wrath of God that is expressed in the torments of hell; and the reason why they do not go down to hell at each moment is not because God, in whose power they are, is not then very angry with them—as angry as He is with many of those miserable creatures as He is now tormenting in hell, and there feel and bear the fierceness of His wrath. Yea, God is a great deal more angry with great numbers who are now on earth—yea, doubtless, with many who are now in this congregation who, it may be, are at ease and quiet—than He is with many of those who are now in the flames of hell.

So it is not because God is unmindful of their wickedness and does not resent it that He does not let loose His hand and cut them off. God is not altogether such a one as ourselves, though they may imagine Him to be so. The wrath of God burns against them; their damnation does not slumber; the pit is prepared; the fire is made ready; the furnace is now hot and ready to receive them; the flames now rage and glow. The glittering sword is whetted and held over them, and the pit has opened her mouth under them.

5. The devil stands ready to fall upon them and seize

them as his own at what moment God shall permit him. They belong to him; he has their souls in his possession and under his dominion. The Scripture represents them as his goods, Luke 11:21. The devils watch them; they are ever by them at their right hand. They stand waiting for them like greedy, hungry lions that see their prey and expect to have it, but are, for the present, held back. If God should withdraw His hand by which they are restrained, they would in one moment fly upon their poor souls. The old serpent is gaping for them. Hell opens its mouth wide to receive them, and, if God would permit it, they would be hastily swallowed up and lost.

6. There are in the souls of wicked men those hellish principles reigning that would presently kindle and flame out into hellfire if it were not for God's restraints. There is laid in the very nature of carnal men a foundation for the torments of hell. There are those corrupt principles, in reigning power in them and in full possession of them, that are the beginnings of hellfire. These principles are active and powerful, exceedingly violent in their nature, and, if it were not for the restraining hand of God upon them, they would soon break out; they would flame out after the same manner as the same corruptions, the same enmity does in the hearts of damned souls, and would beget the same torments in them as they do in them. The souls of the wicked are in Scripture compared to the troubled sea (Isaiah 57:20). For the present, God restrains their wickedness by His mighty power as He does the raging waves of the troubled sea, saying, "Hitherto shalt thou come and no further." But if God should withdraw that restraining power it would soon carry all before it. Sin is the ruin and misery of the soul. It is destructive in its nature, and if God should leave it without restraint there would be

nothing else needed to make the soul perfectly miserable. The corruption of the heart of man is a thing that is immoderate and boundless in its fury, and, while wicked men live here, it is like fire pent up by God's restraints; whereas, if it were let loose, it would set on fire the course of nature. And as the heart is now a sink of sin, so if sin was not restrained it would immediately turn the soul into a fiery oven or a furnace of fire and brimstone.

7. It is no security to wicked men for one moment that there are no visible means of death at hand. It is no security to a natural man that he is now in health, and that he does not see which way he should now immediately go out of the world by any accident, and that there is no visible danger in any respect in his circumstances. The manifold and continual experience of the world in all ages shows that this is no evidence that a man is not on the very brink of eternity, and that the next step will not be in another world. The unseen, unthought-of ways and means of persons' going suddenly out of the world are innumerable and inconceivable. Unconverted men walk over the pit of hell on a rotten covering, and there are innumerable places in this covering so weak that they will not bear their weight; and these places are not seen. The arrows of death fly unseen at noonday; the sharpest sight cannot discern them. God has so many different, unsearchable ways of taking wicked men out of the world and sending them to hell that there is nothing to make it appear that God needs to be at the expense of a miracle, or go out of the ordinary course of His providence to destroy any wicked man at any moment. All the means that there are of sinners' going out of the world are so in God's hands, and so absolutely subject to His power and determination, that it does not depend at all less on the mere will of God whether sinners

shall at any moment go to hell than if means were never made use of or at all concerned in the case.

8. Natural men's prudence and care to preserve their own lives, or the care of others to preserve them, do not secure them a moment. To this, divine providence and universal experience also bear testimony. There is this clear evidence that men's own wisdom is no security to them from death; that if it were otherwise we would see some difference between the wise and judicious men of the world, and others, with regard to their liableness to early and unexpected death. But how is it in fact? Ecclesiastes 2:16: "How dieth the wise man? As the fool."

9. All the pains and contrivances wicked men use to escape hell, while they continue to reject Christ and so remain wicked men, do not secure them from hell one moment. Almost every natural man who hears of hell flatters himself that he shall escape it. He depends upon himself for his own security. He flatters himself in what he has done, in what he is now doing, or what he intends to do. Every one lays out matters in his own mind how he shall avoid damnation, and flatters himself that he contrives well for himself, and that his schemes will not fail. They hear indeed that there are but few saved, and that the bigger part of men who have died heretofore have gone to hell; but each one imagines that he lays out matters better for his own escape than others have done. He does not intend to come to that place of torment. He says within himself that he intends to take care that he shall be effectual, and to order matters so for himself as not to fail.

But the foolish children of men miserably delude themselves in their own schemes, and in their confidence in their own strength and wisdom; they trust nothing but a shadow. The bigger part of those who heretofore have lived under the same means of grace and are now dead are undoubtedly gone to hell. And it was not because they were not as wise as those who are now alive; it was not because they did not lay out matters as well for themselves to secure their own escape. If it were so that we could come to speak with them and could inquire of them, one by one, whether they expected, when alive, and when they used to hear about hell, ever to be subjects of that misery, we, doubtless, would hear one and another reply, "No, I never intended to come here. I had laid out matters otherwise in my mind. I though I would contrive well for myself. I thought my scheme was good. I intended to take effectual care, but it came upon me unexpectedly. I did not look for it at that time and in that manner. It came as a thief; death outwitted me. God's wrath was too quick for me. O my cursed foolishness! I was flattering myself, and pleasing myself with vain dreams of what I would do hereafter; and when I was saying 'peace and safety,' then sudden destruction came upon me."

10. God has laid Himself under no obligation, by any promise, to keep any natural man out of hell one moment. God certainly has made no promises either of eternal life or of any deliverance or preservation from eternal death but what are contained in the covenant of grace, the promises that are given in Christ in whom all the promises are "yea" and "amen." But surely they have no interest in the promises of the covenant of grace who are not the children of the covenant and who do not believe in any of the promises of the covenant and have no interest in the Mediator of the covenant.

So that whatever some have imagined and pretended about promises made to natural men's earnest seeking and knocking, it is plain and manifest that whatever pains a natural man takes in religion, whatever prayers he makes, till he believes in Christ God is under no manner of obligation to keep him a moment from eternal destruction. So that thus it is that natural men are held in the hand of God over the pit of hell. They have deserved the fiery pit and are already sentenced to it. And God is dreadfully provoked. His anger is as great towards them as to those who are actually suffering the executions of the fierceness of His wrath in hell. And they have done nothing in the least to appease or abate that anger; neither is God in the least bound by any promise to hold them up one moment. The devil is waiting for them; hell is gaping for them; the flames gather and flash about them, and would fain lay hold on them and swallow them up; the fire pent up in their own hearts is struggling to break out, and they have no interest in any Mediator. There are no means within reach that can be any security to them. In short, they have no refuge, nothing to take hold of. All that preserves them every moment is the mere arbitrary will and uncovenanted, unobliged forbearance of an incensed God.

Application

The use may be of awakening to unconverted persons in this congregation. This that you have heard is the case of every one of you who are out of Christ. That world of misery, that lake of burning brimstone, is extended abroad under you. There is the dreadful pit of the glowing flames of the wrath of God; there is hell's wide gaping mouth open, and you have nothing to stand upon, nor anything to take hold of. There is nothing between you and hell but the air; it is only the power and mere pleasure of God that holds you up.

You probably are not sensible of this. You find you are kept out of hell, but do not see the hand of God in it. But you look at other things as the good state of your bodily constitution: your care of your own life and the means you use for your own preservation. But indeed these things are nothing. If God should withdraw His hand they would avail no more to keep you from falling than the thin air would to hold up a person who is suspended in it.

Your wickedness makes you, as it were, heavy as lead, and to tend downwards with great weight and pressure towards hell. And if God should let you go, you would immediately sink and swiftly descend and plunge into the bottomless gulf, and your healthy constitution and your own care and prudence and best contrivance and all your righteousness would have no more influence to uphold you and keep you out of hell than a spider's web would have to stop a falling rock. Were it not that such is the sovereign pleasure of God, the earth would not bear you one moment for you are a burden to it. The creation groans with you. The creature is made subject to the bondage of your corruption, not willingly. The sun does not willingly shine upon you to give you light to serve sin and Satan. The earth does not willingly yield her increase to satisfy your lusts, nor it is willingly a stage for your wickedness to be acted upon. The air does not willingly serve you for breath to maintain the flame of life in your vitals while you spend your life in the service of God's enemies. God's creatures are good, and were made for men to serve God with, and do not willingly subserve to any other purpose; they groan when they are abused to purposes so contrary to their nature and end. And the world would spew you out were it not

Sinners in the Hands of an Angry God

for the sovereign hand of Him who has subjected it in hope. There are the black clouds of God's wrath now hanging directly over your heads, full of the dreadful storm and big with thunder; and were it not for the restraining hand of God it would immediately burst forth upon you. The sovereign pleasure of God for the present stays His rough wind; otherwise it would come with fury and your destruction would come like a whirlwind, and you would be like the chaff of the summer threshing floor.

The wrath of God is like great waters that are dammed for the present: they increase more and more and rise higher and higher till an outlet is given. And the longer the stream is stopped, the more rapid and mighty is its course when once it is let loose. It is true that judgment against your evil work has not been executed hitherto; the floods of God's vengeance have been withheld, but your guilt in the meantime is constantly increasing and you are every day treasuring up more wrath. The waters are continually rising and waxing more and more mighty, and there is nothing but the mere pleasure of God that holds the waters back that are unwilling to be stopped and press hard to go forward. If God should only withdraw His hand from the floodgate it would immediately fly open, and the fiery floods of the fierceness and wrath of God would rush forth with inconceivable fury and would come upon you with omnipotent power. And if your strength were ten thousand times greater than it is, yea, ten thousand times greater than the strength of the stoutest, sturdiest devil in hell, it would be nothing to withstand or endure it.

The bow of God's wrath is bent and the arrow made ready on the string, and justice bends the arrow at your heart and strains the bow; and it is nothing but the mere pleasure of God, and that of an angry God, without any promise or obligation at all, that keeps the arrow one moment from being made drunk with your blood.

Thus are all you who never passed under a great change of heart by the might power of the Spirit of God upon your souls. All who were never born again and made new creatures and raised from being dead in sin to a state of new—and before altogether unexperienced—light and life (however you may have reformed your life in many things, and may have had religious affections, and may keep up a form of religion in your families and closets, and in the houses of God, and may be strict in it), you are thus in the hands of an angry God. It is nothing but His mere pleasure that keeps you from being this moment swallowed up in everlasting destruction.

However unconvinced you may now be of the truth of what you hear, by and by you will be convinced of it. Those who are gone from being in the like circumstances with you see that it was so with them; for destruction came suddenly upon most of them. When they expected nothing of it, and while they were saying, "Peace and safety," now they see that those things that they depended on for peace and safety were nothing but thin air and empty shadows.

The God who holds you over the pit of hell, much as one holds a spider or some loathsome insect over the fire, abhors you and is dreadfully provoked. His wrath towards you burns like fire. He looks upon you as worthy of nothing else but to be cast into the fire. He is of purer eyes than to bear to have you in His sight. You are ten thousand times more abominable in His eyes than the most hateful and venomous serpent is in ours. You have offended Him infinitely more than ever a stubborn rebel did his prince; and yet it is nothing but His hand that holds you from falling into the fire every moment. It is ascribed to nothing else that you did not go to hell the last night, that you were suffered to awake again in this world after you closed your eyes to sleep; and there is no other reason to be given why you have not dropped into hell since you arose in the morning but that God's hand has held you up. There is no other reason to be given why you have not gone to hell since you have sat here in the house of God, provoking His pure eyes by your sinful wicked manner of attending His solemn worship; yea, there is nothing else that is to be given as a reason why you do not this very moment drop into hell.

O sinner! Consider the fearful danger you are in. It is a great furnace of wrath, a wide and bottomless pit, full of the fire of wrath, that you are held over in the hand of that God whose wrath is provoked and incensed as much against you as against many of the damned in hell. You hang by a slender thread with the flames of divine wrath flashing about it, and ready every moment to singe it and burn it asunder; and you have no interest in any Mediator, and nothing to lay hold of, nothing that you have ever done, nothing that you can do to induce God to spare you one moment.

And consider here more particularly several things concerning that wrath that you are in such danger of:

1. Whose wrath it is. It is the wrath of the infinite God. If it were only the wrath of man, though it was the most potent prince, it would be comparatively little to be regarded. The wrath of kings is very much dreaded, especially of absolute monarchs who have the possessions and lives of their subjects wholly in their power to be disposed of at their mere will. Proverbs 20:2: "The fear of a king is as the roaring of a lion; whoso provoketh him to anger sinneth against his own soul." That subject who very much enrages

an arbitrary prince is liable to suffer the most extreme torments that human art can invent or human power can inflict. But the greatest earthly potentates, in their greatest majesty and strength, and when clothed in their greatest terrors, are but feeble, despicable worms of the dust in comparison of the great and almighty Creator and King of heaven and earth. It is but little they can do when most enraged and when they have exerted the utmost of their fury. All the kings of the earth before God are as grasshoppers; they are nothing and less than nothing. Both their love and their hatred are to be despised. The wrath of the great King of kings is as much more terrible than theirs as His majesty is greater than theirs. Luke 12:4–5: "And I say unto you, my friends, Be not afraid of them that kill the body, and after that have no more that they can do. But I will forewarn you whom you shall fear: fear Him, which after He hath killed, hath power to cast into hell; yea, I say unto you, Fear Him."

2. It is the fierceness of His wrath that you are exposed to. We often read of the fury of God, such as in Isaiah 59:18: "According to their deeds, accordingly He will repay fury to His adversaries." Also Isaiah 66:15: "For behold, the Lord will come with fire, and with His chariots like a whirlwind, to render His anger with fury, and His rebuke with flames of fire." And so in many other places. So we read of God's fierceness in Revelation 19:15, where we read of "the winepress of the fierceness and wrath of Almighty God." The words are exceedingly terrible. If it had only said "the wrath of God," the words would have implied that which is infinitely dreadful; but it not only says so, but "the fierceness and wrath of God." The fury of God! The fierceness of Jehovah! Oh, how dreadful must that be! Who can utter or conceive what such expressions carry in them! But it not

Sinners in the Hands of an Angry God

only says this, but "the fierceness and wrath of Almighty God." As though there would be a very great manifestation of His almighty power in what the fierceness of His wrath should inflict, as though omnipotence should be, as it were, enraged and exerted, as men are wont to exert their strength in the fierceness of their wrath. Oh, then, what will be the consequence! What will become of the poor worm that shall suffer it! Whose hands can be strong! And whose heart can endure! To what a dreadful, inexpressible, inconceivable depth of misery must the poor creature be sunk who shall be the subject of this!

Consider this, you who are here present, who yet remain in an unregenerate state: That God will execute the fierceness of His anger implies that He will inflict wrath without any pity. When God beholds the ineffable extremity of your case, and sees your torment so vastly disproportioned to your strength, and sees how your poor soul is crushed and sinks down, as it were, into an infinite gloom, He will have no compassion on you. He will not forbear the executions of His wrath or in the least lighten His hand. There shall be no moderation or mercy, nor will God then at all stay His rough wind. He will have no regard to your welfare, nor be at all careful lest you should suffer too much in any other sense than only that you should not suffer beyond what strict justice requires. Nothing shall be withheld because it is so hard for you to bear. Ezekiel 8:18: "Therefore will I also deal in fury; Mine eye shall not spare, neither will I have pity; and though they cry in Mine ears with a loud voice, yet will I not hear them." Now God stands ready to pity you. This is the day of mercy. You may cry now with some encouragement of obtaining mercy, but when once the day of mercy is past, your most lamentable and dolorous cries and shrieks will be in vain. You will be wholly lost and thrown away of God as to any regard of your welfare. God will have no other use to put you to but only to suffer misery. You shall be continued in being to no other end; for you will be a vessel of wrath fitted to destruction, and there will be no other use of this vessel but only to be filled full of wrath. God will be so far from pitying you when you cry to Him that it is said He will only "laugh and mock" (Proverbs 1:25–26).

How awful are those words in Isaiah 63:3, which are the words of the great God: "I will tread them in Mine anger, and trample them in My fury, and their blood shall be sprinkled upon My garments, and I will stain all My raiment." It is perhaps impossible to conceive of words that carry in them greater manifestations of these three things: contempt, hatred, and fierceness of indignation. If you cry to God to pity you, He will be so far from pitying you in your doleful case, or showing you the least regard or favor, that instead of that He will only tread you under foot. And though He will know that you cannot bear the weight of omnipotence treading upon you, yet He will not regard that, but He will crush you under His feet without mercy. He will crush out your blood and make it fly, and it shall be sprinkled on His garments so as to stain all His raiment. He will not only hate you, but He will have you in the utmost contempt. No place shall be thought fit for you but under His feet, to be trodden down as the mire in the streets.

3. The misery you are exposed to is that which God will inflict to the end that He might show what that wrath of Jehovah is. God has had it on His heart to show to men and angels both how excellent His love is and also how terrible His wrath is. Sometimes earthly kings have a mind to show how terrible their wrath is by the extreme punish-

ments they would execute on those who provoke them. Nebuchadnezzar, that mighty and haughty monarch of the Chaldean empire, was willing to show his wrath when enraged with Shadrach, Meshech, and Abednego, and accordingly gave order that the burning fiery furnace should be heated seven times hotter than it was before. Doubtless it was raised to the utmost degree of fierceness that human art could raise it; but the great God is also willing to show His wrath and magnify His awful majesty and mighty power in the extreme sufferings of His enemies. Romans 9:22: "What if God, willing to show His wrath, and to make His power known, endured with much long-suffering the vessels of wrath fitted to destruction?" And seeing this is His design, and what He has determined to show how terrible the unmixed, unrestrained wrath, the fury and fierceness of Jehovah is, He will do it to effect. There will be something accomplished and brought to pass that will be dreadful with a witness. When the great and angry God has risen up and executed His awful vengeance on the poor sinner, and the wretch is actually suffering the infinite weight and power of His indignation, then God will call upon the whole universe to behold that awful majesty and power that is to be seen in it. Isaiah 33:12–14: "And the people shall be as the burnings of lime; as thorns cut up shall they be burnt in the fire. Hear, ye that are afar off, what I have done; and ye that are near, acknowledge My might. The sinners in Zion are afraid; fearfulness hath surprised the hypocrites."

Thus it will be with you who are in an unconverted state if you continue in it. The infinite might, majesty, and terribleness of the omnipotent God shall be magnified upon you in the ineffable strength of your torments. You shall be tormented in the presence of the holy angels and in the presence of the Lamb. And when you shall be in this state of suffering, the glorious inhabitants of heaven shall go forth and look on the awful spectacle that they may see what the wrath and fierceness of the Almighty is; and when they have seen it they will fall down and adore that great power and majesty. Isaiah 66:23–24: "And it shall come to pass that from one moon to another, and from one sabbath to another, shall all flesh come to worship before Me, saith the Lord. And they shall go forth and look upon the carcasses of the men that have transgressed against Me; for their worm shall not die, neither shall their fire be quenched, and they shall be an abhorring unto all flesh."

4. It is an everlasting wrath. It would be dreadful to suffer this fierceness and wrath of Almighty God one moment, but you must suffer it to all eternity. There will be no end to this exquisite, horrible misery. When you look forward, you shall see a long forever, a boundless duration before you which will swallow up your thoughts and amaze your soul; and you will absolutely despair of ever having any deliverance, any end, any mitigation, any rest at all. You will know certainly that you must wear out long ages, millions of millions of ages, in wrestling and conflicting with this Almighty's merciless vengeance. And then, when you have done so, when so many ages have actually been spent by you in this manner, you will know that all is but a point to what remains. So that your punishment will indeed be infinite. Oh, who can express what the state of a soul in such circumstances is! All that we can possibly say about it gives but a very feeble, faint representation of it. It is inexpressible and inconceivable, for "who knows the power of God's anger?" (Psalm 90:11)

How dreadful is the state of those who are daily and hourly in danger of this great wrath and infinite misery!

But this is the dismal case of every soul in this congregation who has not been born again, however moral and strict, sober and religious they may otherwise be. Oh, that you would consider it whether you are young or old! There is reason to think that there are many in this congregation now hearing this discourse who will actually be the subjects of this very misery to all eternity. We know not who they are or in what seats they sit, or what thoughts they now have. It may be they are now at ease, and hear all these things without much disturbance, and are now flattering themselves that they are not the persons, promising themselves that they shall escape. If we knew that there was one person, and but one, in the whole congregation who was to be the subject of this misery, what an awful thing it would be to think of! If we knew who it was, what an awful sight would it be to see such a person! How might all the rest of the congregation lift up a lamentable and bitter cry over him! But, alas! Instead of one, how many is it likely will remember this discourse in hell! And it would be a wonder if some who are now present should not be in hell in a very short time, before this year is out. And it would be no wonder if some persons who now sit here in some seats of this meeting house in health, and who are quiet and secure, should be there before tomorrow morning. Those of you who finally continue in a natural condition, who shall keep out of hell longest, will be there in a little time! Your damnation does not slumber; it will come swiftly and, in all probability, very suddenly upon many of you. You have reason to wonder that you are not already in hell. It is doubtless the case of some whom you have seen and known who never deserved hell more than you, and who heretofore appeared as likely to have been now alive as you. Their case is past all hope; they are crying in extreme misery and perfect despair, but here you are in the land of the living, in the house of God, and have an opportunity to obtain salvation. What would not those poor damned, hopeless souls give for one day's opportunity such as you now enjoy!

And now you have an extraordinary opportunity, a day wherein Christ has thrown the door of mercy wide open, and stands callling and crying with a loud voice to poor sinners; a day wherein many are flocking to Him and pressing into the kingdom of God. Many are daily coming from the east, west, north, and south; many who were very lately in the same miserable condition that you are now in are now in a happy state with their hearts filled with love to Him who has loved them and washed them from their sins in His own blood, and are rejoicing in hope of the glory of God. How awful it is to be left behind at such a day! To see so many others feasting while you are pining and perishing! To see so many rejoicing and singing for joy of heart while you have cause to mourn for sorrow of heart and howl for vexation of spirit! How can you rest one moment in such a condition? Are not your souls as precious as the souls of the people at Suffield, where they are flocking from day to day to Christ?

Are there not many here who have lived long in the world and are not to this day born again, and so are aliens from the commonwealth of Israel, and have done nothing ever since they lived but treasure up wrath against the day of wrath? Oh, sirs, your case in a special manner is extremely dangerous. Your guilt and hardness of heart are extremely great. Do you not see how generally persons of your years are passed over and left in the present remarkable and wonderful dispensation of God's mercy? You need to consider yourselves and awake thoroughly out

Sinners in the Hands of an Angry God

of sleep. You cannot bear the fierceness and wrath of the infinite God.

And you, young men and women, will you neglect this precious season which you now enjoy, when so many others of your age are renouncing all youthful vanities and flocking to Christ? You especially now have an extraordinary opportunity, but if you neglect it it will soon be with you as with those persons who spent all the precious days of youth in sin, and are now come to such a dreadful pass in blindness and hardness.

And you children who are unconverted, do you not know that you are going down to hell to bear the dreadful wrath of that God who is now angry with you every day and every night? Will you be content to be the children of the devil when so many other children in the land are converted, and have become the holy and happy children of the King of kings?

And let everyone who is yet out of Christ, and hanging over the pit of hell, whether they are old men and women or middle aged or young people or little children, now hearken to the loud calls of God's Word and providence. This acceptable year of the Lord, a day of such great favor to some, will doubtless be a day of as remarkable vengeance to others. Men's hearts harden and their guilt increases swiftly, at such a day as this, if they neglect their souls; and never was there so great danger of such persons being given up to hardness of heart and blindness of mind. God seems now to be hastily gathering in His elect in all parts of the land; and probably the greater part of adult persons who ever shall be saved will be brought in now in a little time, and it will be as it was at the great outpouring of the Spirit upon the Jews in the apostles' days: the elect will obtain and the rest will be blinded.

If this should be the case with you, you will eternally curse this day, and will curse the day that ever you were born to see such a season of the pouring out of God's Spirit, and will wish that you had died and gone to hell before you had seen it.

Now, undoubtedly, it is as it was in the days of John the Baptist: the axe is in an extraordinary manner laid at the root of the trees so that every tree which does not bring forth good fruit may be hewn down and cast into the fire.

Therefore, let everyone who is out of Christ now awake and fly from the wrath to come. The wrath of Almighty God is now undoubtedly hanging over a great part of this congregation. Let everyone fly out of Sodom: "Haste and escape for your lives, look not behind you, escape to the mountains lest you be consumed."

The Justice of God in the Damnation of Sinners

"That every mouth may be stopped." Romans 3:19

The main subject of the doctrinal part of this epistle is the free grace of God in the salvation of men by Jesus Christ, especially as it appears in the doctrine of justification by faith alone. And the more clearly to evidence this doctrine and show the reason of it, the apostle, in the first place, establishes the point that no flesh living can be justified by the deeds of the law. And to prove it, he is very large and particular in showing that all mankind—not only the Gentiles, but Jews—is under sin, and so under the condemnation of the law, which is what he insists upon from the beginning of the epistle to this place.

He first begins with the Gentiles, and in the first chapter shows that they are under sin by setting forth the exceeding corruptions and horrid wickedness that overspread the Gentile world. And then, through the second chapter and the former part of this third chapter to the text and following verse, he shows the same of the Jews, that they also are in the same circumstances with the Gentiles in this regard. They had a high thought of themselves because they were God's covenant people, because they were circumcised and were the children of Abraham. They despised the Gentiles as polluted, condemned, and accursed, but looked on themselves, on account of their external privileges and ceremonial and moral righteousness, as a pure and holy people and the children of God, as the apostle observes in the second chapter. It was therefore strange doctrine to them that they also were unclean and guilty in God's sight, and under the condemnation and curse of the law.

The apostle, therefore, on account of their strong prejudices against such doctrine, the more particularly insists upon it and shows that they are no better than the Gentiles. In the 9th verse of this chapter: "What then? are we better than they? No, in no wise; for we have before proved both Jews and Gentiles, that they are all under sin." And to convince them of it he produces certain passages out of their own law, the Old Testament (to whose authority they pretended a great regard), from the 9th verse to our text.

And it may be observed that the apostle, first, cites certain passages to prove that all mankind is corrupt (verses 10–12): "As it is written, There is none righteous, no, not one. There is none that understandeth, there is none that seeketh after God. They are all gone out of the way, they are together become unprofitable; there is none that doeth good, no, not one."

Second, the passages he cites next are to prove that not only are all corrupt, but each one is *wholly* corrupt, as it were, all over unclean from the crown of the head to the soles of his feet. And therefore several particular parts of the body are mentioned—the throat, the tongue, the lips, the mouth, the feet (verses 13–15): "Their throat is an open sepulchre; with their tongues they have used deceit; the poison of asps is under their lips; whose mouth is full of cursing and bitterness: their feet are swift to shed blood."

Third, he quotes other passages to show that each one is not only all over corrupt, but corrupt to a desperate degree (verses 16–18) by affirming the most pernicious tendency of their wickedness: "Destruction and misery are in their ways"; and then by denying all goodness or godliness in them: "And the way of peace have they not known; there is no fear of God before their eyes."

And then, lest the Jews should think these passages of their law do not concern them, and that only the Gentiles are intended in them, the apostle shows in the text not only that they are not exempt, but that they especially must be understood: "Now we know that whatsoever things the law saith, it saith to them who are under the law." By "those that are under the law" are meant the Jews, and the Gentiles by "those that are without law," as appears by the 12th verse of the preceding chapter. There is special reason to understand the law as speaking to and of them to whom it was immediately given. And therefore the Jews would be unreasonable in exempting themselves. And if we examine the places of the Old Testament from whence these passages are taken, we shall see plainly that special respect is had to the wickedness of the people of that nation in every one of them. So that the law shuts all up in universal and desperate wickedness that every mouth may be stopped, the mouths of the Jews as well as of the Gentiles, notwithstanding all those privileges by which they were distinguished from the Gentiles.

The things that the law says are sufficient to stop the mouths of all mankind in two respects:

1. To stop them from boasting of their righteousness, as the Jews were wont to do, as the apostle observes in the 23rd verse of the preceding chapter. That the apostle has respect to stopping their mouths in this respect appears by the 27th verse of the context: "Where is boasting then? It is excluded." The law stops our mouths from making any plea for life or the favor of God or any positive good from

our own righteousness.

2. To stop them from making any excuse for themselves, or objection against the execution of the sentence of the law, or the infliction of the punishment that it threatens. That this is intended appears by the words immediately following: "That all the world may become guilty before God." That is, that they may appear to be guilty and stand convicted before God, and justly liable to the condemnation of His law as guilty of death, according to the Jewish way of speaking.

And thus the apostle proves that no flesh can be justified in God's sight by the deeds of the law. He draws the conclusion in the following verse, and so prepares the way for establishing the great doctrine of justification by faith alone, which he proceeds to do in the following part of the chapter and of the epistle.

DOCTRINE. It is just with God eternally to cast off and destroy sinners, for this is the punishment which the law condemns to.

The truth of this doctrine may appear by the joint consideration of two things: man's sinfulness and God's sovereignty.

It appears from the consideration of man's sinfulness, and that whether we consider the infinitely evil nature of all sin or how much sin men are guilty of.

1. If we consider the infinite evil and heinousness of sin in general, it is not unjust in God to inflict what punishment is deserved, because the very notion of deserving any punishment is that it may be justly inflicted. A deserved punishment and a just punishment are the same thing. To say that one deserves such a punishment and yet to say that he does not justly deserve it is a contradiction; and if he

The Justice of God in the Damnation of Sinners

justly deserves it then it may be *justly* inflicted.

Every crime or fault deserves a greater or lesser punishment in proportion as the crime itself is greater or less. If any fault deserves punishment, then so much the greater the fault, so much the greater is the punishment deserved. The faulty nature of anything is the formal ground and reason of its desert of punishment; and therefore the more anything has of this nature, the more punishment it deserves. And therefore the terribleness of the degree of punishment, let it be never so terrible, is no argument against the justice of it, if the proportion does but hold between the heinousness of the crime and the dreadfulness of the punishment. So that if there is any such thing as a fault infinitely heinous, it will follow that it is just to inflict a punishment for it that is infinitely dreadful.

A crime is more or less heinous according as we are under greater or less obligations to the contrary. This is self-evident, because it is herein that the criminalness or faultiness of any thing consists: that it is contrary to what we are obliged or bound to or what ought to be in us. So the faultiness of one being hating another is in proportion to his obligation to love him. The crime of one being despising and casting contempt on another is proportionately more or less heinous as he was under greater or less obligations to honor him. The fault of disobeying another is greater or less as anyone is under greater or less obligations to obey him. And therefore, if there is any being that we are under infinite obligations to love, honor, and obey, the contrary towards him must be infinitely faulty.

Our obligation to love, honor, and obey any being is in proportion to his loveliness, honorableness, and authority; for that is the very meaning of the words. When we say anyone is very lovely, it is the same as to say that he is one very much to be loved. Or if we say such a one is more honorable than another, the meaning of the words is that he is one whom we are more obliged to honor. If we say anyone has great authority over us, it is the same as to say that he has great right to our subjection and obedience.

But God is a being infinitely lovely, because He has infinite excellency and beauty. To have infinite excellency and beauty is the same thing as to have infinite loveliness. He is a being of infinite greatness, majesty, and glory, and, therefore, He is infinitely honorable. He is infinitely exalted above the greatest potentates of the earth and highest angels in heaven, and, therefore, He is infinitely more honorable than they. His authority over us is infinite and the ground of His right to our obedience is infinitely strong; for He is infinitely worthy to be obeyed Himself, and we have an absolute, universal, and infinite dependence upon Him. So that sin against God, being a violation of infinite obligations, must be a crime infinitely heinous, and so deserving infinite punishment.

Nothing is more agreeable to the common sense of mankind than that sins committed against anyone must be proportionally heinous to the dignity of the being offended and abused. It is also agreeable to the Word of God in 1 Samuel 2:25: "If one man sin against another, the judge shall judge him [i.e., shall judge him, and inflict a finite punishment, such as finite judges can inflict], but if a man sins against the Lord, who shall entreat for him?" This was the aggravation of sin that made Joseph afraid of it. "How shall I commit this great wickedness, and sin against God?" (Genesis. 39:9). This was the aggravation of David's sin, in comparison of which he esteemed all others as nothing, because they were infinitely exceeded by it. Psalm 51:4: "Against Thee, Thee only have I sinned." The

The Justice of God in the Damnation of Sinners

eternity of the punishment of ungodly men renders it infinite; and it renders it no more than infinite, and, therefore, renders it no more than proportionate to the heinousness of what they are guilty of.

If there is any evil or faultiness in sin against God, there is certainly infinite evil; for if it is any fault at all, it has an infinite aggravation in that it is against an infinite object. If it is ever so small upon other accounts, yet if it is anything it has one infinite dimension, and so is an infinite evil. This may be illustrated by this: if we suppose a thing to have infinite length, but no breadth and thickness (a mere mathematical line), it is nothing; but if it has any breadth and thickness, though never so small, and infinite length, the quantity to it is infinite. It exceeds the quantity of any thing, however broad, thick, and long, wherein these dimensions are all finite.

So that the objections made against the infinite punishment of sin from the necessity, or rather previous certainty, of the future existence of sin, arising from the unavoidable original corruption of nature, if they argue anything, argue against any faultiness at all; for if this necessity or certainty leaves any evil at all in sin, that fault must be infinite by reason of the infinite object.

But every objector who would argue from this that there is no fault at all in sin confutes himself and shows his own insincerity in his objection. For at the same time that he objects that men's acts are necessary, and that this kind of necessity is inconsistent with faultiness in the act, his own practice shows that he does not believe what he objects to be true; otherwise why does he at all blame men? Or why are such persons at all displeased with men for abusive, injurious, and ungrateful acts towards them? Whatever they pretend, by this they show that indeed they believe that there is no necessity in men's acts that is inconsistent with blame. And if their objection is that this previous certainty is by God's own ordering, and that where God orders an antecedent certainty of acts He transfers all the fault from the actor onto Himself, their practice shows that at the same time they do not believe this, but fully believe the contrary; for when they are abused by men they are displeased with men, and not with God only.

The light of nature teaches all mankind that when an injury is voluntary it is faulty, without any consideration of what there might be previously to determine the future existence of that evil act of the will. And it really teaches this as much to those who object and cavil most as to others, as their universal practice shows. By this it appears that such objections are insincere and perverse. Men will mention others' corrupt nature when they are injured as a thing that aggravates their crime, and that wherein their faultiness partly consists. How common is it for persons, when they look on themselves greatly injured by another, to inveigh against him and aggravate his baseness by saying, "He is a man of most perverse spirit. He is naturally of a selfish, niggardly, or proud and haughty temper. He is one of a base and vile disposition." And yet men's natural and corrupt dispositions are mentioned as an excuse for them, with respect to their sins against God, as if they rendered them blameless.

2. That it is just with God eternally to cast off wicked men may more abundantly appear if we consider how much sin they are guilty of. From what has been already said, it appears that if men were guilty of sin but in one particular, that is sufficient ground of their eternal rejection and condemnation. If they are sinners, that is enough. Merely this might be sufficient to keep them from

ever lifting up their heads, and cause them to smite on their breasts with the publican who cried, "God be merciful to me a sinner." But sinful men are full of sin, full of principles and acts of sin. Their guilt is like great mountains heaped one upon another till the pile is grown up to heaven.

They are totally corrupt in every part, in all their faculties, in all the principles of their nature, their understandings and wills, and in all their dispositions and affections. Their heads and their hearts are totally depraved; all the members of their bodies are only instruments of sin, and all their senses (seeing, hearing, tasting) are only inlets and outlets of sin, channels of corruption. There is nothing but sin, no good at all. Romans 7:18: "In me, that is, in my flesh, dwells no good thing." There is all manner of wickedness. There are the seeds of the greatest and blackest crimes. There are principles of all sorts of wickedness against men, and there is all wickedness against God. There is pride; there is enmity; there is contempt; there is quarreling; there is atheism; there is blasphemy. There are these things in exceeding strength. The heart is under the power of them; it is sold under sin, and is a perfect slave to it. There is hard-heartedness, hardness greater than that of a rock or an adamant-stone. There is obstinacy and perverseness, incorrigibleness and inflexibleness in sin that will not be overcome by threatenings or promises, by awakenings or encouragements, by judgments or mercies, neither by that which is terrifying nor that which is winning. The very blood of God our Savior will not win the heart of a wicked man.

And there are actual wickednesses without number or measure. There are breaches of every command in thought, word, and deed; a life full of sin; days and nights filled up with sin; mercies abused and frowns despised; mercy and justice, and all the divine perfections trampled on; and the honor of each person in the Trinity is trod in the dirt. Now if one sinful word or thought has so much evil in it as to deserve eternal destruction, how do they deserve to be eternally cast off and destroyed who are guilty of so much sin!

If with man's sinfulness we consider God's sovereignty, it may serve further to clear God's justice, in the eternal rejection and condemnation of sinners, from men's cavils and objections. I shall not now pretend to determine precisely what things are and what things are not proper acts and exercises of God's holy sovereignty, but only that God's sovereignty extends to the following things:

1. Such is God's sovereign power and right that He is originally under no obligation to keep men from sinning, but may in His providence permit and leave them to sin. He was not obliged to keep either angels or men from falling. It is unreasonable to suppose that God should be obliged, if He makes a reasonable creature capable of knowing His will and receiving a law from Him, and being subject to His moral government, at the same time to make it impossible for him to sin or break His law. For if God is obliged to this, it destroys all use of any commands, laws, promises, or threatenings and the very notion of any moral government of God over those reasonable creatures. For to what purpose would it be for God to give such and such laws, and declare His holy will to a creature, and annex promises and threatenings to move him to his duty and make him careful to perform it, if the creature, at the same time, has this to think of: that God is obliged to make it impossible for him to break His laws? How can God's

The Justice of God in the Damnation of Sinners 93

threatenings move to care or watchfulness when, at the same time, God is obliged to render it impossible that he should be exposed to the threatenings? Or to what purpose is it for God to give a law at all? For according to this supposition it is God, and not the creature, who is under law. It is the Lawgiver's care, and not the subject's, to see that His law is obeyed; and this care is what the Lawgiver is absolutely obliged to! If God is obliged never to permit a creature to fall, there is an end of all divine laws or government or authority of God over the creature; there can be no manner of use of these things.

God may permit sin, though the being of sin will certainly ensue on that permission: and so, by permission, He may dispose and order the event. If there were any such thing as chance or mere contingence, and the very notion of it did not carry a gross absurdity (as might easily be shown that it does), it would have been very unfit that God should have left it to mere chance whether man should fall or not. For chance, if there should be any such thing, is undesigning and blind. And certainly it is more fit that an event of so great importance, and which is attended with such an infinite train of great consequences, should be disposed and ordered by infinite wisdom than that it should be left to blind chance.

If it is said that God need not have interposed to render it impossible for man to sin, and yet not leave it to mere contingence or blind chance either, but might have left it with man's free will to determine whether to sin or not, I answer that if God did leave it to man's free will, without any sort of disposal or ordering (or, rather, adequate cause) in the case, whence it should be previously certain how that free will should determine, then still that first determination of the will must be merely contingent or by chance. It could not have any antecedent act of the will to determine it; for I speak now of the very first act or motion of the will, respecting the affair that may be looked upon as the prime ground and highest source of the event. To suppose this to be determined by a foregoing act is a contradiction. God's disposing this determination of the will by His permission does not at all infringe on the liberty of the creature. It is in no respect any more inconsistent with liberty than mere chance or contingence; for if the determination of the will is from blind, undesigning chance, it is no more from the agent himself or from the will itself than if we suppose in the case a wise, divine disposal by permission.

2. It was fit that it should be at the ordering of the divine wisdom and good pleasure whether every particular man should stand for himself or whether the first father of mankind should be appointed as the moral and federal head and representative of the rest. If God has not liberty in this matter to determine either of these two as He pleases, it must be because determining that the first father of men should represent the rest, and not that everyone should stand for himself, is injurious to mankind. For if it is not injurious, how is it unjust? But it is not injurious to mankind; for there is nothing in the nature of the case itself that makes it better that each man should stand for himself than that all should be represented by their common father, as the least reflection or consideration will convince anyone. And if there is nothing in the nature of the thing that makes the former better for mankind than the latter, then it will follow that they are not hurt in God's choosing and appointing the latter rather than the former, or, which is the same thing, that it is not injurious to mankind.

The Justice of God in the Damnation of Sinners

3. When men are fallen and become sinful, God, by His sovereignty, has a right to determine about their redemption as He pleases. He has a right to determine whether He will redeem any or not. He might, if He had pleased, have left all to perish, or might have redeemed all. Or He may redeem some and leave others; and if He does so, He may take whom He pleases and leave whom He pleases. To suppose that all have forfeited His favor and deserved to perish, and to suppose that He may not leave any one individual of them to perish, implies a contradiction, because it supposes that such a one has a claim to God's favor and is not justly liable to perish, which is contrary to the supposition.

It is meet that God should order all these things according to His own pleasure. By reason of His greatness and glory, by which He is infinitely above all, He is worthy to be sovereign, and that His pleasure should in all things take place. He is worthy that He should make Himself His end, and that He should make nothing but His own wisdom His rule in pursuing that end, without asking leave or counsel of any and without giving account of any of His matters. It is fit that He who is absolutely perfect and infinitely wise, and the Fountain of all wisdom, should determine every thing (that He effects) by His own will, even things of the greatest importance. It is fitting that He should be this sovereign because He is the first Being, the eternal Being from whence all other beings are. He is the Creator of all things, and all are absolutely and universally dependent on Him; and therefore it is fitting that He should act as the sovereign possessor of heaven and earth.

Application

In the improvement of this doctrine, I would chiefly direct myself to sinners who are afraid of damnation in a use of conviction. This may be matter of conviction to you, that it would be just and righteous with God eternally to reject and destroy you. This is what you are in danger of. You who are a Christ-less sinner are a poor condemned creature: God's wrath still abides upon you and the sentence of condemnation lies upon you. You are in God's hands, and it is uncertain what He will do with you. You are afraid what will become of you. You are afraid that it will be your portion to suffer eternal burnings, and your fears are not without grounds. You have reason to tremble every moment. But be you never so much afraid of it, let eternal damnation be never so dreadful, yet it is just. God may nevertheless do it and be righteous, holy, and glorious. Though eternal damnation is what you cannot bear, and however much your heart shrinks at the thoughts of it, yet God's justice may be glorious in it. The dreadfulness of the thing on your part, and the greatness of your dread of it, do not render it the less righteous on God's part. If you think otherwise, it is a sign that you do not see yourself, that you are not sensible what sin is, nor how much of it you have been guilty of.

Therefore, for your conviction, be directed, first, to look over your past life. Inquire at the mouth of conscience, and hear what that has to testify concerning it. Consider what you are, what light you have had, and what means you have lived under, and yet how you have behaved yourself! What have those many days and nights you have lived been filled up with? How have those years that have rolled over your heads, one after another, been spent? What has the sun shone upon you for, from day to day, while you have improved his light to serve Satan by it? What has God kept your breath in your nostrils for, and given you meat and drink, that you have spent your life and strength, supported by them, in opposing God and rebellion against Him?

How many sorts of wickedness have you not been guilty of! How manifold have been the abominations of your life! What profaneness and contempt of God have been exercised by you! How little regard have you had to the Scriptures, to the Word preached, to sabbaths and sacraments! How profanely have you talked, many of you, about those things that are holy! After what manner have many of you kept God's holy day, not regarding the holiness of the time, nor caring what you thought of in it! Yea, you have not only spent the time in worldly, vain, and unprofitable thoughts, but immoral thoughts, pleasing yourself with the reflection on past acts of wickedness, and in contriving new acts. Have not you spent much holy time in gratifying your lusts in your imaginations; yea, not only holy time, but the very time of God's public worship when you have appeared in God's more immediate presence? How have you not only not attended to the worship, but have in the meantime been feasting your lusts, and wallowing yourself in abominable uncleanness! How many sabbaths have you spent, one after another, in a most wretched manner, some of you not only in worldly and wicked thoughts, but also a very wicked outward behavior! When you on sabbath days have gotten together with your wicked companions, how has holy time been treated among you! What kind of conversation has there been! Yea, how have some of you, by a very indecent carriage, openly dishonored and cast contempt on the sacred services of God's house and holy day! And what you have done, some of you alone, what wicked practices there have been in secret, even in holy time, God and your own consciences know.

And how have you behaved yourself in the time of family prayer! And what a trade have many of you made of absenting yourselves from the worship of the families you belong to for the sake of vain company! And how have you continued in the neglect of secret prayer, therein willfully living in a known sin, going abreast against as plain a command as any in the Bible! Have you not been one who has cast off fear and restrained prayer before God?

What wicked carriage have some of you been guilty of towards your parents! How far have you been from paying that honor to them which God has required! Have you not even harbored ill will and malice towards them? And when they have displeased you, have you wished evil to them? Yea, and have you shown your vile spirit in your behavior? And it is well if you have not mocked them behind their backs, and, like the accursed Ham and Canaan, as it were, derided your parents' nakedness instead of covering it and hiding your eyes from it. Have not some of you often disobeyed your parents, yea, and refused to be subject to them? Is it not a wonder of mercy and forbearance that the proverb has not before now been accomplished on you: "The eye that mocketh at his father, and refuseth to obey his mother, the ravens of the valley shall pick it out, and the young eagles shall eat it" (Proverbs 30:17)?

What revenge and malice have you been guilty of towards your neighbors! How have you indulged this spirit of the devil, hating others and wishing evil to them, rejoicing when evil befalls them, and grieving at others' prosperity, and lived in such a way for a long time! Have not some of you allowed a passionate, furious spirit, and behaved yourselves in your anger more like wild beasts than like Christians?

What covetousness has been in many of you! Such has been your inordinate love of the world, and care about the things of it, that it has taken up your heart; you have allowed no room for God and religion; you have minded the world more than your eternal salvation. For the vanities of the world you have neglected reading, praying, and meditation; for the things of the world you have broken the sabbath; for the world you have spent a great deal of your time in quarreling. For the world you have envied and hated your neighbor; for the world you have cast God, Christ, and heaven behind your back; for the world you have sold your own soul. You have, as it were, drowned your soul in worldly cares and desires; you have been a mere earthworm that is never in its element but when groveling and buried in the earth.

How much of a spirit of pride has appeared in you, which is in a peculiar manner the spirit and condemnation of the devil! How have some of you vaunted yourselves in your apparel, others in their riches, others in their knowledge and abilities! How has it galled you to see others above you! How much has it gone against the grain for you to give others their due honor! And how have you shown your pride by setting up your wills in opposing others, and stirring up and promoting division and a party spirit in public affairs!

How sensual have you been! Are there not some here who have debased themselves below the dignity of human nature by wallowing in sensual filthiness as swine in the mire, or as filthy vermin feeding with delight on rotten carrion? What intemperance have some of you been guilty of! How much of your precious time have you spent away at the tavern and in drinking companies, when you ought to have been at home seeking God and your salvation in your families and closets!

And what abominable lasciviousness have some of you been guilty of! How have you indulged yourself from day to day and night to night in all manner of unclean imaginations! Has not your soul been filled with them till it has become a hold of foul spirits and a cage of every unclean and hateful bird? What foul-mouthed persons have some of you been, often in lewd and lascivious talk and unclean songs, wherein were things not fit to be spoken! And such company, where such conversation has been carried on, has been your delight. And with what unclean acts and practices have you defiled yourself! God and your own consciences know what abominable lasciviousness you have practiced in things not fit to be named when you have been alone, when you ought to have been reading or meditating or on your knees before God in secret prayer. And how have you corrupted others as well as polluted yourselves! What vile uncleanness have you practiced in company! What abominations have you been guilty of in the dark! Such as the apostle doubtless had respect to in Ephesians 5:12: "For it is a shame even to speak of those things that are done of them in secret." Some of you have corrupted others, and done what in you lay to undo their souls (if you have not actually done it), and by your vile practices and example have made room for Satan, invited his presence, and established his interest in the town where you have lived.

What lying have some of you been guilty of, especially in your childhood! And have not your heart and lips often disagreed since you came to riper years? What fraud, deceit, and unfaithfulness have many of you practiced in your own dealings with your neighbors, of which your own heart is conscious, if you have not been noted by others.

And how have some of you behaved yourselves in your family relations! How have you neglected your children's souls! And not only so, but have corrupted their minds by your bad examples; and instead of training them up in the nurture and admonition of the Lord have rather brought them up in the devil's service!

How have some of you attended that sacred ordinance of the Lord's Supper without any manner of serious preparation, and in a careless, slighty frame of spirits, and chiefly to comply with custom! Have you not ventured to put the sacred symbols of the body and blood of Christ into your mouth, while at the same time you lived in ways of known sins, and intended no other than still to go on in the same wicked practices! And, it may be, you have sat at the Lord's table with rancor in your heart against some of your brethren that you have sat there with. You have come even to that holy feast of love among God's children with the leaven of malice and envy in your heart, and so have eaten and drunk judgment to yourself.

What stupidity and sottishness have attended your course of wickedness, which has appeared in your obstinacy under awakening dispensations of God's Word and providence. And how have some of you backslidden after you have set out in religion, and quenched God's Spirit after He had been striving with you! And what unsteadiness, slothfulness, and long misimprovement of God's strivings with you have you been chargeable with!

Now, can you think when you have thus behaved yourself, that God is obliged to show you mercy? Are you not after all this ashamed to talk of its being hard with God to cast you off? Does it become one who has lived such a life to open his mouth to excuse himself, to object against God's justice in his condemnation, or to complain of it as hard in God not to give him converting and pardoning grace, and make him His child, and bestow on him eternal life? Or to talk of his duties and great pains in religion, as if such performances were worthy to be accepted, and to draw God's heart to such a creature? If this has been your manner, does it not show how little you have considered yourself, and how little a sense you have had of your own sinfulness?

Second, be directed to consider that if God should eternally reject and destroy you, what an agreeableness and exact mutual answerableness there would be between God so dealing with you and your spirit and behavior. There would not only be an equality, but a similitude. God declares that His dealings with men shall be suitable to their disposition and practice. Psalm 18:25–26: "With the merciful man, Thou wilt show Thyself merciful; with an upright man, Thou wilt show Thyself upright; with the pure, Thou wilt show Thyself pure; and with the froward, Thou wilt show Thyself froward." However much you dread damnation, and are frightened and concerned at the thoughts of it, yet, if God should indeed eternally damn you, you would be met with but in your own way; you would be dealt with exactly according to your own dealing. Surely it is but fair that you should be made to buy in the same measure in which you sell.

Here I would particularly show (1) that if God should eternally destroy you, it would be agreeable to your treatment of God; (2) that it would be agreeable to your treatment of Jesus Christ; (3) that it would be agreeable to your behavior towards your neighbors; and (4) that it would be

according to your own foolish behavior towards yourself.
  1. If God should forever cast you off, it would be exactly agreeable to your treatment of Him. That you may be sensible of this, consider:
    (1) You never have exercised the least degree of love to God; and therefore it would be agreeable to your treatment of Him if He should never express any love to you. When God converts and saves a sinner, it is a wonderful and unspeakable manifestation of divine love. When a poor lost soul is brought home to Christ, and has all his sins forgiven him and is made a child of God, it will take up a whole eternity to express and declare the greatness of that love. And why should God be obliged to express such wonderful love to you who never exercised the least degree of love to Him in all your life? You never have loved God, who is infinitely glorious and lovely; and why then is God under obligation to love you, who are all over deformed and loathsome as a filthy worm, or rather a hateful viper? You have no benevolence in your heart towards God; you never rejoiced in God's happiness; if He had been miserable, and if that had been possible, you would have liked it as well as if He were happy; you would not have cared how miserable He was, nor mourned for it, any more than you now do for the devil's being miserable. And why then should God be looked upon as obliged to take so much care for your happiness as to do such great things for it as He does for those who are saved? Or why should God be called hard in case He should not be careful to save you from misery? You care not what becomes of God's glory; you are not distressed however much His honor seems to suffer in the world; and why should God care any more for your welfare? Has it not been so that if you could but promote your private interest and gratify your own lusts, you

cared not how much the glory of God suffered? And why may not God advance His own glory in the ruin of your welfare, not caring how much your interest suffers by it? You never so much as stirred one step, sincerely making the glory of God your end, or acting from real respect to Him; and why then is it hard if God does not do such great things for you as the changing of your nature, raising you from spiritual death to life, conquering the powers of darkness for you, translating you out of the kingdom of darkness into the kingdom of His dear Son, delivering you from eternal misery, and bestowing upon you eternal glory? You were not willing to deny yourself for God; you never cared to put yourself out of your way for Christ; whenever anything cross or difficult came in your way that the glory of God was concerned in, it has been your manner to shun it and excuse yourself from it. You did not care to hurt yourself for Christ, whom you did not see worthy of it; and why then must it be looked upon as a hard and cruel thing if Christ has not been pleased to spill His blood and be tormented to death for such a sinner?

(2) You have slighted God; and why then may not God justly slight you? When sinners are sensible in some measure of their misery, they are ready to think it hard that God will take no more notice of them; that He will see them in such a lamentable, distressed condition, beholding their burdens and tears, and seem to slight it and manifest no pity to them. Their souls, they think, are precious: it would be a dreadful thing if they should perish and burn in hell forever. They do not see through it that God should make so light of their salvation. But then, ought they not to consider that as their souls are precious, so is God's honor precious? The honor of the infinite God, the great King of heaven and earth, is a thing of as great importance

(and surely may justly be so esteemed by God) as the happiness of you, a poor, little worm. But yet you have slighted that honor of God and valued it no more than the dirt under your feet. You have been told that such and such things were contrary to the will of a holy God and against His honor; but you cared not for that. God called upon you, and exhorted you to be more tender of His honor; but you went on without regarding Him. Thus have you slighted God! And yet is it hard that God should slight you? Are you more honorable than God, that He must be obliged to make much of you, however light you make of Him and His glory?

And you have not only slighted God in time past, but you slight Him still. You indeed now make a pretense and show of honoring Him in your prayers, and attendance on other external duties, and by sober countenance and seeming devoutness in your words and behavior; but it is all mere dissembling. That downcast look and seeming reverence are not from any honor you have to God in your heart, though you would have God take it so. You who have not believed in Christ have not the least jot of honor of God; that show of it is merely forced, and what you are driven to by fear, like those mentioned in Psalm 66:3: "Through the greatness of Thy power shall Thine enemies submit themselves to Thee." In the original it is "shall lie unto Thee"; that is, "yield feigned submission, and dissemble respect and honor to Thee."

There is a rod held over you that makes you seem to pay such respect to God. This religion and devotion, even the very appearance of it, would soon be gone and all vanish away, if that were removed. Sometimes, it may be, you weep in your prayers and in your hearing sermons, and hope God will take notice of it and take it for some honor; but

He sees it to be all hypocrisy. You weep for yourself; you are afraid of hell; and do you think that that is worthy of God to take much notice of you, because you can cry when you are in danger of being damned, when at the same time you indeed care nothing for God's honor?

Seeing you thus disregard so great a God, is it a heinous thing for God to slight you, a little, wretched, despicable creature, a worm, a mere nothing, and less than nothing, a vile insect that has risen up in contempt against the Majesty of heaven and earth?

(3) Why should God be looked upon as obliged to bestow salvation upon you when you have been so ungrateful for the mercies He has bestowed upon you already? God has tried you with a great deal of kindness, and He never has sincerely been thanked by you for any of it. God has watched over you, preserved you, provided for you, and followed you with mercy all your days; and yet you have continued sinning against Him. He has given you food and raiment, but you have improved both in the service of sin. He has preserved you while you slept, but when you arose it was to return to the old trade of sinning. God, notwithstanding this ingratitude, has still continued His mercy; but His kindness has never won your heart or brought you to a more grateful behavior towards Him. It may be you have received many remarkable mercies, recoveries from sickness, or preservations of your life when exposed by accidents, when, if you had died, you would have gone directly to hell; but you never had any true thankfulness for any of these mercies. God has kept you out of hell, and continued your day of grace and the offers of salvation so long a time, while you did not regard your own salvation so much as in secret to ask God for it. And now God has greatly added to His mercy to you by giving you the striv-

ings of His Spirit whereby a most precious opportunity for your salvation is in your hands. But what thanks has God received for it? What kind of returns have you made for all this kindness? As God has multiplied mercies, so have you multiplied provocations.

And yet now are you ready to quarrel for mercy and to find fault with God, not only that He does not bestow more mercy, but to contend with Him because He does not bestow infinite mercy upon you, heaven with all it contains, and even Himself, for your eternal portion. What ideas have you of yourself that you think God is obliged to do so much for you, though you treat Him ever so ungratefully for His kindness wherewith you have been followed all the days of your life?

(4) You have voluntarily chosen to be with Satan in his enmity and opposition to God; how justly therefore might you be with him in his punishment! You did not choose to be on God's side, but rather chose to side with the devil, and have obstinately continued in it against God's often-repeated calls and counsels. You have chosen rather to hearken to Satan than to God, and would be with him in his work. You have given yourself up to him to be subject to his power and government in opposition to God; how justly therefore may God also give you up to him, and leave you in his power to accomplish your ruin! Seeing you have yielded yourself to his will, to do as he would have you, surely God may leave you in his hands to execute his will upon you. If men will be with God's enemy, and on his side, why is God obliged to redeem them out of his hands, when they have done his work? Doubtless you would be glad to serve the devil and be God's enemy while you live, and then to have God as your friend and deliver you from the devil when you come to die. But will God be unjust if

He deals otherwise by you? No, surely! It will be altogether and perfectly just that you should have your portion with him with whom you have chosen to work, and that you should be in his possession to whose dominion you have yielded yourself; and if you cry to God for deliverance, He may most justly give you that answer in Judges 10:14: "Go to the gods which you have chosen."

(5) Consider how often you have refused to hear God's calls to you, and how just it would therefore be if He should refuse to hear you when you call upon Him. You are ready, it may be, to complain that you have often prayed and earnestly begged God to show you mercy, and yet have no answer to prayer. One says, "I have been constant in prayer for so many years, and God has not heard me." Another says, "I have done what I can. I have prayed as earnestly as I am able. I do not see how I can do more, and it will seem hard if after all this I am denied." But do you consider how often God has called and you have denied Him? God has called earnestly for a long time. He has called and called again in His Word and in His providence, and you have refused. You were not uneasy for fear you should not show regard enough to His calls. You let Him call as loud and as long as He would; for your part, you had no leisure to attend to what He said. You had other business to mind; you had these and those lusts to gratify and please, and worldly concerns to attend. You could not afford to stand considering what God had to say to you. When the ministers of Christ have stood and pleaded with you in His name, sabbath after sabbath, and have even spent their strength in it, how little were you moved! It did not alter you, but you went on still as you used to do. When you went away, you returned again to your sins, to your lasciviousness, to your vain mirth, to your covetousness, to

your intemperance, and this has been the language of your heart and practice: "Who is the Lord, that I should obey His voice?" (Exodus 5:20). Was it no crime for you to refuse to hear when God called? And yet is it now very hard that God does not hear your earnest calls, and that though your calling on God is not from any respect to Him, but merely from self-love?

The devil would beg as earnestly as you if he had any hope to get salvation by it, and a thousand times as earnestly, and yet be as much of a devil as he is now. Are your calls more worthy to be heard than God's? Or is God more obliged to regard what you say to Him than you to regard His commands, counsels, and invitations to you? What can be more justice than this: "Because I have called, and ye refused, I have stretched out My hand, and no man regarded; but ye have set at naught all My counsel, and would none of My reproof. I will also laugh at your calamity, I will mock when your fear cometh; when your fear cometh as desolation, and your destruction cometh as a whirlwind; when distress and anguish cometh upon you. Then shall they call upon Me, but I will not answer; they shall seek me early, but they shall not find me" (Proverbs 1:24-28).

(6) Have you not taken encouragement to sin against God on the very presumption that God would show you mercy when you sought it? And may not God justly refuse you that mercy which you have so presumed upon? You have flattered yourself that though you did so yet God would show you mercy when you cried earnestly to Him for it. How righteous therefore would it be in God to disappoint such a wicked presumption! It was upon that very hope that you dared to affront the Majesty of heaven so dreadfully as you have done; and can you now be so sottish

as to think that God is obliged not to frustrate that hope?

When a sinner takes encouragement to neglect secret prayer which God has commanded, to gratify his lusts, to live a carnal vain life, to thwart God, to run upon Him and condemn Him to his face, thinking with himself, "If I do so, God would not damn me. He is a merciful God; and therefore, when I seek His mercy, He will bestow it upon me"—must God be accounted hard because He will not do according to such a sinner's presumption?

Cannot He be excused from showing such a sinner mercy when he is pleased to seek it without incurring the charge of being unjust? If this is the case, God has no liberty to vindicate His own honor and majesty, but must lay Himself open to all manner of affronts, and yield Himself up to the abuses of vile men, though they disobey, despise, and dishonor Him as much as they will. And when they have done, His mercy and pardoning grace must not be in His own power and at His own disposal, but He must be obliged to dispense it at their call. He must take these bold and vile condemners of His majesty, when it suits them to ask it, and must forgive all their sins; and not only so, but must adopt them into His family, make them His children, and bestow eternal glory upon them. What mean, low, and strange thoughts have such men of God who think thus of Him! Consider that you have injured God the more, and have been the worse enemy to Him, for His being a merciful God. So have you treated that attribute of God's mercy! How just is it therefore that you never should have any benefit of that attribute!

There is something peculiarly heinous in sinning against the mercy of God more than other attributes. There is such base and horrid ingratitude in being the worse to God because He is a being of infinite goodness and grace, that it above all things renders wickedness vile and detestable. This ought to win us and engage us to serve God better; but instead of that to sin against Him the more has something inexpressibly bad in it, and does, in a peculiar manner, enhance guilt, and incense wrath, as seems to be intimated in Romans 2:4–5: "Or despisest thou the riches of His goodness, and forbearance, and long-suffering, not knowing that the goodness of God leadeth thee to repentance? But after thy hardness and impenitent heart treasurest up unto thyself wrath against the day of wrath, and revelation of the righteous judgment of God."

The greater the mercy of God is, the more should you be engaged to love Him and live to His glory. But it has been contrariwise with you; the consideration of the mercies of God being so exceedingly great is the thing wherewith you have encouraged yourself in sin. You have heard that the mercy of God was without bounds, that it was sufficient to pardon the greatest sinner, and you have upon that very account ventured to be a very great sinner. Though it was very offensive to God, though you heard that God infinitely hated sin, and that such practices as you went on in were exceedingly contrary to His nature, will, and glory, yet that did not make you uneasy. You heard that He was a very merciful God, and had grace enough to pardon you, and so cared not how offensive your sins were to Him. How long have some of you gone on in sin, and what great sins have some of you been guilty of on that presumption! Your own conscience can give testimony that this has made you refuse God's calls, and has made you regardless of His repeated commands. Now, how righteous would it be if God should swear in His wrath that you should never be the better for His being infinitely merciful!

Your ingratitude has been the greater that you have not only abused the attribute of God's mercy, taking encouragement from it to continue in sin, but you have also presumed that God would exercise infinite mercy to you in particular, which consideration should have especially endeared God to you. You have taken encouragement to sin the more from the consideration that Christ came into the world and died to save sinners; such thanks has Christ had from you for enduring such a tormenting death for His enemies! Now, how justly might God refuse that you should ever be the better for His Son's laying down His life! It was because of these things that you put off seeking salvation. You would take the pleasures of sin still longer, hardening yourself because mercy was infinite, and it would not be too late if you sought it afterwards. Now, how justly may God disappoint you in this, and so order it that it shall be too late.

(7) How have some of you risen up against God, and in the frame of your minds opposed Him in His sovereign dispensations! And how justly upon that account might God oppose you, and set Himself against you! You never yet would submit to God, never willingly comply that God should have dominion over the world, and that He should govern it for His own glory, according to His own wisdom. You, a poor worm, a potsherd, a broken piece of an earthen vessel, have dared to find fault and quarrel with God. Isaiah 45:9: "Woe to him that strives with his Maker. Let the potsherd strive with the potsherds of the earth. Shall the clay say to him that fashioned it, What makest thou?" But yet you have ventured to do it. Romans 9:20: "Who art thou, O man, that repliest against God?" But yet you have thought you were big enough; you have taken upon yourself to call God to an account as to why He does thus and thus. You

The Justice of God in the Damnation of Sinners

have said to Jehovah, "What doest Thou?" If you have been restrained by fear from openly venting your opposition and enmity of heart against God's government, yet it has been in you. You have not been quiet in the frame of your mind; you have had the heart of a viper within, and have been ready to spit your venom at God. It is well if sometimes you have not actually done it by tolerating blasphemous thoughts and malignant risings of heart against Him; yea, and the frame of your heart in some measure appeared in impatient and fretful behavior.

Now, seeing you have thus opposed God, how just is it that God should oppose you! Or is it because you are so much better and so much greater than God that it is a crime for Him to make that opposition against you which you make against Him? Do you think that the liberty of making opposition is your exclusive prerogative, so that you may be an enemy to God but God must by no means be an enemy to you, but must be looked upon as under obligation nevertheless to help you and save you by His blood, and bestow His best blessings upon you?

Consider how in the frame of your mind you have thwarted God in those very exercises of mercy towards others that you are seeking for yourself. God exercising His infinite grace towards your neighbors has put you into an ill frame, and, it may be, set you in a tumult of mind. How justly therefore may God refuse ever to exercise that mercy towards you! Have you not thus opposed God showing mercy to others, even at the very time when you pretended to be earnest with God for pity and help for yourself, yea, and while you were endeavoring to get something wherewith to recommend yourself to God? And will you look to God still with a challenge of mercy, and contend with Him for it notwithstanding? Can you who have such a heart, and have thus behaved yourself, come to God for anything other than mere sovereign mercy?

2. *If you should forever be cast off by God, it would be agreeable to your treatment of Jesus Christ.* It would have been just with God if He had cast you off forever, without ever making you the offer of a Savior. But God has not done that. He has provided a Savior for sinners, and offered Him to you, even His own Son Jesus Christ, who is the only Savior of men. All who are not forever cast off are saved by Him. God offers men salvation through Him, and has promised us that if we come to Him we shall not be cast off. But if you have treated, and still treat, this Savior after such a manner, if you should be eternally cast off by God it would be most agreeable to your behavior towards Him, which appears by this: you reject Christ and will not have Him for your Savior.

If God offers you a Savior from deserved punishment, and you will not receive Him, then surely it is just that you should go without a Savior. Or is God obliged, because you do not like this Savior, to provide you another? He has given an infinitely honorable and glorious person, even His only begotten Son, to be a sacrifice for sin and so provide salvation; and this Savior is offered to you. Now if you refuse to accept Him, is God therefore unjust if He does not save you? Is He obliged to save you in a way of your own choosing because you do not like the way of His choosing? Or will you charge Christ with injustice because He does not become your Savior when, at the same time, you will not have Him when He offers Himself to you and beseeches you to accept Him as your Savior?

OBJECTION 1. I am sensible that by this time many persons are ready to object against this. If all should speak what they now think, we would hear murmuring all over the meeting house. And one and another would say, "I cannot see how this can be, that I am not willing that Christ should be my Savior, when I would give all the world that He was my Savior. How is it possible that I should not be willing to have Christ for my Savior when this is what I am seeking after, praying for, and striving for as for my life?"

Here therefore I would endeavor to convince you that you are under a gross mistake in this matter. First, I would endeavor to show the grounds of your mistake, and, second, to demonstrate to you that you *have* rejected and do *willfully* reject Jesus Christ.

First, that you may see the weak grounds of your mistake, consider:

(1) There is a great deal of difference between a willingness not to be damned and being willing to receive Christ for your Savior. You have the former; there is no doubt of that. Nobody supposes that you love misery so as to choose an eternity of it; and so doubtless you are willing to be saved from eternal misery. But that is a very different thing from being willing to come to Christ. Persons very commonly mistake the one for the other, but they are quite two things. You may love the deliverance, but hate the Deliverer. You tell of a willingness, but consider what is the object of that willingness. It does not respect Christ; the way of salvation by Him is not at all the object of it; but it is wholly terminated on your escape from misery. The inclination of your will goes no further than self; it never reaches Christ. You are willing not to be miserable; that is, you love yourself, and there your will and choice terminate. And it is but a vain pretense and delusion to say or think that you are willing to accept Christ.

(2) There is certainly a great deal of difference be-

tween a forced compliance and a free willingness. Force and freedom cannot consist together. Now that willingness, whereby you think you are willing to have Christ for a Savior, is merely a forced thing. Your heart does not go out after Christ of itself, but you are forced and driven to seek an interest in Him. Christ has no share at all in your heart; there is no manner of closing of the heart with Him. This forced compliance is not what Christ seeks of you. He seeks a free and willing acceptance. Psalm 110:3: "Thy people shall be willing in the day of Thy power." He seeks not that you should receive Him against your will, but with a free will. He seeks entertainment in your heart and choice. And if you refuse thus to receive Christ, how just is it that Christ should refuse to receive you! How reasonable are Christ's terms, who offers to save all those who willingly, or with a good will, accept Him for their Savior! Who can rationally expect that Christ should force Himself upon any man to be his Savior? Or what can be looked for as more reasonable than that all who would be saved by Christ should heartily and freely entertain Him? And surely it would be very dishonorable for Christ to offer Himself upon lower terms.

But I would now proceed, second, to show that you are not willing to have Christ for a Savior. To convince you of it, consider:

(1) How it is possible that you should be willing to accept Christ as a Savior from the desert of a punishment that you are not sensible you have deserved. If you are truly willing to accept Christ as a Savior, it must be as a sacrifice to make atonement for your guilt. Christ came into the world on this errand, to offer Himself as an atonement, to answer for our desert of punishment. But how can you be willing to have Christ for a Savior from a desert of hell if

you are not sensible that you have a desert of hell? If you have not really deserved everlasting burnings in hell, then the very offer of an atonement for such a desert is an imposition upon you. If you have no such guilt upon you, then the very offer of a satisfaction for that guilt is an injury, because it implies in it a charge of guilt that you are free from. Now therefore it is impossible that a man who is not convinced of his guilt can be willing to accept such an offer, because he cannot be willing to accept the charge which the offer implies. A man who is not convinced that he has deserved so dreadful a punishment cannot willingly submit to be charged with it. If he thinks he is willing, it is but a mere forced, feigned business, because in his heart he looks upon himself as greatly injured and therefore cannot freely accept Christ under that notion of a Savior from the desert of such a punishment; for such an acceptance is an implicit owning that he does deserve such a punishment.

I do not say but that men may be willing to be saved from an undeserved punishment; they may rather not suffer it than suffer it. But a man cannot be willing to accept salvation at God's hands under the notion of a Savior from punishment deserved from him which he thinks he has not deserved. It is impossible that anyone should freely allow a Savior under that notion. Such a one cannot like the way of salvation by Christ, for if he thinks he has not deserved hell then he will think that freedom from hell is a debt, and therefore cannot willingly and heartily receive it as a free gift.

If a king should condemn a man to some tormenting death which the condemned person thought himself not deserving of, but looked upon the sentence as unjust and cruel, and the king, when the time of execution drew nigh, should offer him his pardon under the notion of a very great act of grace and clemency, the condemned person never could willingly and heartily allow it under that notion because he judged himself unjustly condemned.

Now by this it is evident that you are not willing to accept Christ as your Savior, because you never yet had such a sense of your own sinfulness and such a conviction of your great guilt in God's sight as to be indeed convinced that you lay justly condemned to the punishment of hell. You never were convinced that you had forfeited all favor, and were in God's hands, and at His sovereign and arbitrary disposal to be either destroyed or saved, just as He pleased. You never yet were convinced of the sovereignty of God. Hence are there so many objections arising against the justice of your punishment from original sin, and from God's decrees, from mercy shown to others, and the like.

(2) That you are not sincerely willing to accept Christ as your Savior appears also in that you never have been convinced that He is sufficient for the work of your salvation. You never had a sight or sense of any such excellency or worthiness in Christ as should give such great value to His blood and His mediation with God, as that it was sufficient to be accepted for such exceedingly guilty creatures who have so provoked God and exposed themselves to such amazing wrath. Saying it is so, and allowing it to be as others say, is a very different thing from being really convinced of it and being made sensible of it in your own heart. The sufficiency of Christ depends upon, or rather consists in, His excellency. It is because He is so excellent a person that His blood is of sufficient value to atone for sin, and it is hence that His obedience is so worthy in God's sight. It is also hence that His intercession is so prevalent; and therefore those who never had any spiri-

tual sight or sense of Christ's excellency cannot be sensible of His sufficiency. The fact that sinners are not convinced that Christ is sufficient for the work He has undertaken appears most manifestly when they are under great convictions of their sin and the danger of God's wrath. Though, it may be, before they thought they could allow Christ to be sufficient (for it is easy to allow anyone to be sufficient for our defense at a time when we see no danger), yet when they come to be sensible of their guilt and God's wrath, what discouraging thoughts they entertain! How are they ready to draw towards despair, as if there were no hope or help for such wicked creatures as they! The reason is that they have no apprehension or sense of any other way that God's majesty can be vindicated, but only in their misery. To tell them of the blood of Christ signifies nothing; it does not relieve their sinking, despairing hearts. This makes it most evident that they are not convinced that Christ is sufficient to be their Mediator. And as long as they are unconvinced of this, it is impossible that they should be willing to accept Him as their Mediator and Savior. A man in distressing fear will not willingly take himself to a fort that he judges not sufficient to defend him from the enemy. A man will not willingly venture out into the ocean in a ship that he suspects is leaky, and will sink before he gets through his voyage.

(3) It is evident that you are not willing to have Christ for your Savior because you have so mean an opinion of Him that you do not trust His faithfulness. One who undertakes to be the Savior of souls needs to be faithful; for if he fails in such a trust, how great is the loss! But you are not convinced of Christ's faithfulness, as is evident because at such times as you are, in a considerable measure,

sensible of your guilt and God's anger, you cannot be convinced that Christ is willing to accept you, or that He stands ready to receive you if you should come to him, though Christ so much invites you to come to Him, and has so fully declared that He will not reject you if you *do* come. John 6:37: "Him that cometh to Me, I will in no wise cast out." Now, there is no man can be heartily willing to trust his eternal welfare in the hands of an unfaithful person, or one whose faithfulness he suspects.

(4) You are not willing to be saved in that way by Christ, as is evident because you are not willing that your own goodness should be set at naught. In the way of salvation by Christ, men's own goodness is wholly set at naught; there is no account at all made of it. Now you cannot be willing to be saved in a way wherein your own goodness is set at naught, as is evident since you make much of it yourself. You make much of your prayers and pains in religion, and are often thinking of them; how considerable do they appear to you when you look back upon them! And some of you are thinking how much more you have done than others, and expecting some respect or regard that God should manifest to what you do. Now, if you make so much of what you do yourself, it is impossible that you should be freely willing that God would make nothing of it. We may see this in other things: if a man is proud of a great estate, or if he values himself much upon his honorable office or his great abilities, it is impossible that he should like it, and heartily approve of it, that others should make light of these things and despise them.

Seeing therefore it is so evident that you refuse to accept Christ as your Savior, why is Christ to be blamed that He does not save you? Christ has offered Himself to you to be your Savior in time past, and He continues offering

Himself still, and you continue to reject Him, and yet complain that He does not save you. So strangely unreasonable, and inconsistent with themselves are gospel sinners!

OBJECTION 2. But I expect there are many of you who still object. Such an objection as this is probably now in the hearts of many here present: If I am not willing to have Christ for my Savior, I cannot make myself willing.

But I would give an answer to this objection by laying down two things that must be acknowledged to be exceedingly evident.

(1) It is no excuse that you cannot receive Christ of yourself, unless you would if you could. This is so evident of itself that it scarcely needs any proof. Certainly if persons would not if they could, it is just the same thing as to the blame that lies upon them whether they can or cannot. If you were willing, and then found that you *could* not, your being unable would alter the case and might be some excuse; because then the defect would not be in your will, but only in your ability. But as long as you *will* not, it is no matter whether you have ability or no ability.

If you are not willing to accept Christ, it follows that you have no sincere willingness to be willing, because the will always necessarily approves of and rests in its own acts. To suppose the contrary would be to suppose a contradiction; it would be to suppose that a man's will is contrary to itself, or that he wills contrary to what he himself wills. As you are not willing to come to Christ, and cannot make yourself willing, so you have no sincere desire to be willing, and therefore may most justly perish without a Savior. There is no excuse at all for you; for say what you will about your inability, the seat of your blame lies in your perverse will that is an enemy to the Savior. It is in vain for you to tell of your want of power as long as your will is found defective. If a man should hate you and smite you in the face, but should tell you at the same time that he hated you so much that he could not help choosing and willing so to do, would you take it the more patiently for that? Would not your indignation be rather stirred up the more?

(2) If you would be willing if you could, that is no excuse unless your willingness to be willing is sincere. That which is hypocritical and does not come from the heart, but is merely forced, ought wholly to be set aside as worthy of no consideration, because common sense teaches that what is not hearty, but hypocritical, is indeed nothing, being only a show of what is not. But that which is good for nothing, ought to go for nothing. But if you set aside all that is not free and call nothing a willingness but a free hearty willingness, then see how the case stands, and whether or not you have not lost all your cause for standing out against the calls of the gospel. You say you would make yourself willing to accept if you could; but it is not from any good principle that you are willing for that. It is not from any free inclination or true respect to Christ, or any love to your duty or any spirit of obedience. It is not from the influence of any real respect or tendency in your heart, towards anything good, or from any other principle than such as is in the hearts of devils, and would make them have the same sort of willingness in the same circumstances. It is therefore evident that there can be no goodness in that "would" be willing to come to Christ: and that which has no goodness cannot be an excuse for any badness. If there is no good in it, then it signifies nothing, and weighs nothing when put into the scales to counterbalance that which is bad.

Sinners therefore spend their time in foolish arguing and objecting, making much of that which is good for nothing, making those excuses that are not worth offering. It is in vain to keep making objections. You stand justly condemned. The blame lies at your door: Thrust it off from you as often as you will, it will return upon you. Sew fig leaves as long as you will, your nakedness will appear. You continue willfully and wickedly rejecting Jesus Christ, and will not have Him for your Savior; and therefore it is sottish madness in you to charge Christ with injustice that He does not save you.

Here is the sin of unbelief! Thus the guilt of that great sin lies upon you! If you never had thus treated a Savior, you might most justly have been damned to all eternity: it would but be exactly agreeable to your treatment of God. But, besides this, when God, notwithstanding, has offered you His own dear Son to save you from this endless misery you had deserved, and not only so, but to make you happy eternally in the enjoyment of Himself, you have refused Him and would not have Him for your Savior, and still refuse to comply with the offers of the gospel. What can render any person more inexcusable? If you should now perish forever, what can you have to say?

Hereby the justice of God in your destruction appears in two respects:

(1) It is more abundantly manifest that it is just that you should be destroyed. Justice never appears so conspicuous as it does after refused and abused mercy. Justice in damnation appears abundantly the more clear and bright, after a willful rejection of offered salvation. What can an offended prince do more than freely offer pardon to a condemned malefactor? And if he refuses to accept it, will anyone say that his execution is unjust?

(2) God's justice will appear in your greater destruction. Besides the guilt that you would have had if a Savior

never had been offered, you bring that great additional guilt upon you of most ungratefully refusing offered deliverance. What more base and vile treatment of God can there be than for you, when justly condemned to eternal misery and ready to be executed, and God graciously sends His own Son who comes and knocks at your door with a pardon in His hand, and not only a pardon, but a deed of eternal glory—I say, what can be worse than for you, out of dislike and enmity against God and His Son, to refuse to accept those benefits at his hands? How justly may the anger of God be greatly incensed and increased by it! When a sinner thus ungratefully rejects mercy, his last error is worse than the first; this is more heinous than all his former rebellion, and may justly bring down more fearful wrath upon him.

The heinousness of this sin of rejecting a Savior especially appears in two things:

First, the greatness of the benefits offered, which appears in the greatness of the deliverance which is from inexpressible degrees of corruption and wickedness of heart and life, the least degree of which is infinitely evil, and from misery that is everlasting, and in the greatness and glory of the inheritance purchased and offered. Hebrews 2:3: "How shall we escape if we neglect so great salvation?"

Second, the wonderfulness of the way in which these benefits are procured and offered. That God should lay help on His own Son when our case was so deplorable that help could be had in no mere creature, and that He should undertake for us, and should come into the world and take upon Him our nature, and should not only appear in a low state of life, but should die such a death, and endure such torments and contempt for sinners while enemies, how wonderful is it! And what tongue or pen can set forth the greatness of the ingratitude, baseness, and perverseness there is in it when a perishing sinner, who is in the most extreme necessity of salvation, rejects it after it is procured in such a way as this! That so glorious a person should be thus treated, and that when He comes on so gracious an errand! That He should stand so long offering Himself and calling and inviting, as He has done to many of you, and all to no purpose, but all the while be set at naught! Surely you might justly be cast into hell without one more offer of a Savior, yea, and thrust down into the lowest hell! Herein you have exceeded the very devils, for they never rejected the offers of such glorious mercy; no, nor of any mercy at all. This will be the distinguishing condemnation of gospel-sinners: "He that believeth not is condemned already, because he hath not believed in the name of the only begotten Son of God" (John 3:18). That outward smoothness of your carriage towards Christ, and that appearance of respect to Him in your looks, your speeches, and gestures, do not argue but that you set Him at naught in your heart. There may be much of these outward shows of respect, and yet you are like Judas, who betrayed the Son of man with a kiss, and like those mockers who bowed the knee before Him and at the same time spat in His face.

3. If God should forever cast you off and destroy you, it would be agreeable to your treatment of others. It would be no other than what would be exactly answerable to your behavior towards your fellow creatures who have the same human nature and are naturally in the same circumstances with you, and whom you ought to love as yourself. And that appears especially in two things:

(1) You have, many of you, been opposed in your spirit to the salvation of others. There are several ways that natural men manifest a spirit of opposition against the sal-

vation of souls. It sometimes appears by a fear that their companions, acquaintances, and equals will obtain mercy, and so become unspeakably happier than they. It is sometimes manifested by an uneasiness at the news of what others have hopefully obtained. It appears when persons envy others for it, and dislike them the more, disrelish their talk, avoid their company, and cannot bear to hear their religious discourse, and especially to receive warnings and counsels from them. And it oftentimes appears by their backwardness to entertain charitable thoughts of them, and by their being brought with difficulty to believe that they have obtained mercy, and a forwardness to listen to anything that seems to contradict it.

The devil hated to own Job's sincerity (Job 1:7 and 2:3–5). There appears very often much of this spirit of the devil in natural men. Sometimes they are ready to make a ridicule of others' pretended godliness. They speak of the ground of others' hopes as the enemies of the Jews did of the wall that they built. Nehemiah 4:3: "Now Tobiah the Ammonite was by him, and he said, That which they build, if a fox go up, he shall even break down their stone wall." There are many who join with Sanballat and Tobiah and are of the same spirit with them. There always was, and always will be, an enmity between the seed of the serpent and the seed of the woman. It appeared in Cain, who hated his brother because he was more acceptable to God than himself; and it appears still in these times, and in this place. There are many who are like the elder brother who could not bear that the prodigal, when he returned, should be received with such joy and good entertainment, and was put into a fret by it both against his brother who had returned and his father who made him so welcome (Luke 15).

The Justice of God in the Damnation of Sinners

Thus have many of you been opposed to the salvation of others, who stand in as great necessity of it as you. You have been against their being delivered from everlasting misery, who can bear it no better than you; not because their salvation would do you any hurt, or their damnation help you, any otherwise than as it would gratify that vile spirit that is so much like the spirit of the devil who, because he is miserable himself, is unwilling that others should be happy. How just therefore is it that God should be opposed to your salvation!

If you have so little love or mercy in you as to begrudge your neighbor's salvation, whom you have no cause to hate, but the laws of God and nature require you to love, why is God bound to exercise such infinite love and mercy to you as to save you at the price of His own blood, you, whom He is in no way bound to love, but who have deserved His hatred a thousand and a thousand times? You are not willing that others' souls be converted who have behaved themselves injuriously towards you; and yet, will you count it hard if God does not bestow converting grace upon you who have deserved ten thousand times as ill of God as ever any of your neighbors have of you? You are opposed to God's showing mercy to those whom you think have been vicious persons, and are very unworthy of such mercy. Is others' unworthiness a just reason why God should not bestow mercy on them? And yet will God be hard if, notwithstanding all your unworthiness, and the abominableness of your spirit and practice in His sight, he does not show you mercy? You would have God bestow liberally on you and upbraid not; but yet when He shows mercy to others you are ready to upbraid as soon as you hear of it. You immediately are thinking with yourself how ill they have behaved themselves; and, it may be, your mouths on this occasion are open, enumerating and aggravating the sins they have been guilty of. You would have God bury all your faults and wholly blot out all your transgressions; but yet, if He bestows mercy on others, it may be you will take that occasion to rake up all their old faults that you can think of. You do not much reflect on and condemn yourself for your baseness and unjust spirit towards others in your opposition to their salvation; you do not quarrel with yourself and condemn yourself for this; but yet you, in your heart, will quarrel with God and fret at His dispensations, because you think He seems opposed to showing mercy to you. One would think that the consideration of these things should forever stop your mouth.

(2) Consider how you have promoted others' damnation. Many of you, by the bad examples you have set, by corrupting the minds of others, by your sinful conversation, by leading them into or strengthening them in sin and by the mischief you have done in human society in other ways that might be mentioned, have been guilty of those things that have tended to others' damnation. You have heretofore appeared on the side of sin and Satan, have strengthened their interest, have been many ways accessory to others' sins, have hardened their hearts, and thereby have done what has tended to the ruin of their souls. Without doubt there are those here present who have been in a great measure the means of others' damnation. One man may really be a means of others' damnation as well as salvation. Christ charged the scribes and Pharisees with this in Matthew 23:13: "Ye shut up the kingdom of heaven against men; for ye neither go in yourselves, neither suffer ye them that are entering to go in." We have no reason to think that this congregation has none in it who are cursed from day to day by poor souls who are roaring out in hell,

whose damnation they have been the means of, or have greatly contributed to. There are many who contribute to their own children's damnation by neglecting their education, by setting them bad examples, and bringing them up in sinful ways. They take some care of their bodies, but take little care of their poor souls; they provide for them bread to eat, but deny them the bread of life that their famishing souls stand in need of. And are there no such parents here who have thus treated their children? If their children are not gone to hell, it is no thanks to them; it is not because they have not done what has tended to their destruction. Seeing therefore you have had no more regard to others' salvation, and have promoted their damnation, how justly might God leave you to perish yourself!

4. If God would eternally cast you off, it would but be agreeable to your own behavior towards yourself; and that in two respects:

(1) In being so careless of your own salvation. You have refused to take care for your salvation, as God has counseled and commanded you from time to time; and why may not God neglect it, now you seek it of Him? Is God obliged to be more careful of your happiness than you are, either of your own happiness or His glory? Is God bound to take that care for you, out of love to you, that you will not take for yourself, either from love to yourself or regard to His authority? How long and how greatly have you neglected the welfare of your precious soul, refusing to take pains and deny yourself, or put yourself a little out of your way for your salvation, while God has been calling upon you! Neither your duty to God nor love to your own souls would be enough to induce you to do little things for your own eternal welfare; and yet do you now expect that God should do great things, putting forth almighty power, and exercising infinite mercy for it? You were urged to take

care for your salvation, and not to put it off. You were told that was the best time before you grew older, and that, it might be, if you would put it off God would not hear you afterwards; but yet you would not hearken; you would run the venture of it. Now how justly might God order it so that it should be too late, leaving you to seek in vain! You were told that you would repent of it if you delayed; but you would not hear. How justly therefore may God give you cause to repent of it by refusing to show you mercy now! If God sees you going on in ways contrary to His commands and His glory, and requires you to forsake them, and tells you that they tend to the destruction of your own soul, and therefore counsels you to avoid them, and you refuse, how just would it be if God would be provoked by it, henceforward to be as careless of the good of your soul as you are yourself!

(2) You have not only neglected your salvation, but you have willfully taken direct courses to undo yourself. You have gone on in those ways and practices which have directly tended to your damnation, and have been perverse and obstinate in it. You cannot plead ignorance; you had all the light set before you that you could desire. God told you that you were undoing yourself; but yet you would do it. He told you that the path you were going in led to destruction and counseled you to avoid it; but you would not hearken. How justly therefore may God leave you to be undone! You have obstinately persisted to travel in the way that leads to hell for a long time, contrary to God's continual counsels and commands, till, it may be, at length you are almost at your journey's end, and have come near to hell's gate, and so begin to be sensible of your danger and misery. And now you account it unjust and hard if God will not deliver you! You have destroyed yourself, and destroyed

yourself willfully, contrary to God's repeated counsels, yea, and destroyed yourself in fighting against God. Now therefore, why do you blame any but yourself if you are destroyed? If you will undo yourself in opposing God, and while God opposes you by His calls and counsels, and, it may be, too, by the convictions of His Spirit, what can you object against it if God now leaves you to be undone? You would have your own way, and did not like that God should oppose you in it, and your way was to ruin your own soul. How just therefore is it if, now at length, God ceases to oppose you, and falls in with you and lets your soul be ruined. And as you would destroy yourself, so He should put His hand to destroy you too! The ways you went on in had a natural tendency to your misery. If you would drink poison in opposition to God, and in contempt of Him and His advice, who can you blame but yourself if you are poisoned and so perish? If you would run into the fire against all restraints both of God's mercy and authority, you must ever blame yourself if you are burnt.

Thus I have proposed some things to your consideration which, if you are not exceedingly blind, senseless, and perverse, will stop your mouth and convince you that you stand justly condemned before God; and that He would in no wise deal hardly with you, but altogether justly, in denying you any mercy and in refusing to hear your prayers, though you pray never so earnestly and never so often and continue in it never so long. God may utterly disregard your tears and moans, your heavy heart, your earnest desires and great endeavors; and He may cast you into eternal destruction without any regard to your welfare, denying you converting grace and giving you over to Satan, and at last casting you into the lake that burns with fire and brimstone, to be there to eternity having no rest day or night, forever glorifying His justice upon you in the presence of the holy angels, and in the presence of the Lamb.

OBJECTION. But here many may still object (for I am sensible it is a hard thing to stop sinners' mouths): "God shows mercy to others who have done these things as well as I, yea, who have done a great deal worse than I."

ANSWER 1. That does not prove that God is in any way bound to show mercy to you or them either. If God bestows it on others, He does not so because He is bound to bestow it. He might, if He had pleased, with glorious justice have denied it to them. If God bestows it on some, that does not prove that He is bound to bestow it on any; and if He is bound to bestow it on none, then He is not bound to bestow it on you. God is in debt to none; and if He gives to some that He is not in debt to, because it is His pleasure, that does not bring Him into debt to others. It alters not the case to you whether others have it or have it not: you do not deserve damnation the less than if mercy never had been bestowed on any at all. Matthew 20:15: "Is thine eye evil, because I am good?"

ANSWER 2. If this objection is good, then the exercise of God's mercy is not in His own right, and His grace is not His own to give. That which God may not dispose of as He pleases is not His own; for that which is one's own is at his own disposal. But if it is not God's own, then He is not capable of making a gift or present of it to anyone. It is impossible to give what is a debt.

What is it that you would make of God? Must the great God be tied up that He must not use His own pleasure in bestowing His own gifts? But if He bestows them on one, must He be looked upon as obliged to bestow them on another? Is not God worthy to have the same right, with respect to the gifts of His grace, that a man has to his money

The Justice of God in the Damnation of Sinners

or goods? Is it because God is not so great, and should be more in subjection than man, that this cannot be allowed Him? If any of you see cause to show kindness to a neighbor, do all the rest of your neighbors come to you and tell you that you owe them so much as you have given to such a man? But this is the way that you deal with God, as though God were not worthy to have as absolute a property in His goods as you have in yours.

At this rate God cannot make a present of anything. He has nothing of His own to bestow. If He has a mind to show peculiar favor to some, or to lay some particular persons under peculiar obligations to Him, He cannot do it because He has no special gift at His own disposal. If this is the case, why do you pray to God to bestow saving grace upon you? If God does not do fairly to deny it to you because He bestows it on others, then it is not worth your while to pray for it, but you may go and tell Him that he has bestowed it on others as bad or worse than you and so demand it of Him as a debt. And at this rate persons never need to thank God for salvation when it is bestowed, for what occasion is there to thank God for that which was not at His own disposal, and that He could not fairly have denied? The thing at bottom is that men have low thoughts of God and high thoughts of themselves, and therefore it is that they look upon God as having so little right and they so much. Matthew 20:15: "Is it not lawful for me to do what I will with mine own?"

ANSWER 3. God may justly show greater respect to others than to you, for you have shown greater respect to others than to God. You have rather chosen to offend God than men. God only shows a greater respect to others who are by nature your equals than to you; but you have shown a greater respect to those who are infinitely inferior to God than to Him. You have shown a greater regard to wicked men than to God: you have honored them more, loved them better, and adhered to them rather than to Him. Yea, you have honored the devil, in many respects, more than God: you have chosen his will and his interest rather than God's will and His glory. You have chosen a little worldly self rather than God; you have set more by a vile lust than by him. You have chosen these things and rejected God. You have set your heart on these things and cast God behind your back: and where is the injustice if God is pleased to show greater respect to others than to you, or if He chooses others and rejects you? You have shown great respect to vile and worthless things, and no respect to God's glory; and why may not God set His love on others and have no respect to your happiness? You have shown great respect to others and not to God, whom you are laid under infinite obligations to respect above all; and why may not God show respect to others and not to you, who never have laid Him under the least obligation?

    And will you not be ashamed, notwithstanding all these things, and still open your mouth to object and cavil about the decrees of God and other things that you cannot fully understand. Let the decrees of God be what they will, that alters not the case as to your liberty any more than if God had only foreknown. And why is God to blame for decreeing things?—especially since He decrees nothing but good. How unbecoming an infinitely wise Being would it have been to have made a world and let things run at random, without disposing events, or fore-ordering how they should come to pass? And what is that to you how God has fore-ordered things, as long as your constant experience teaches you that it does not hinder your doing what you choose to do? This you know, and your daily practice and behavior among men declare that you are fully sensible of it with respect to yourself and others. Still to object because there are some things in God's dispensations above your understanding is exceedingly unreasonable. Your own conscience charges you with great guilt, and with those things that have been mentioned, let the secret things of God be what they will. Your conscience charges you with those vile dispositions, and that base behavior towards God, that you would at any time most highly resent in your neighbor towards you, and that not a whit the less for any concern those secret counsels and mysterious dispensations of God may have in the matter. It is in vain for you to exalt yourself against an infinitely great and holy and just God. If you continue in it, it will be to your eternal shame and confusion when hereafter you shall see at whose door all the blame of your misery lies.

I will finish what I have to say to natural men in the application of this doctrine with a caution not to improve the doctrine to discouragement. For though it would be righteous in God forever to cast you off and destroy you, yet it would also be just in God to save you in and through Christ, who has made complete satisfaction for all sin. Romans 3:25–26: "Whom God hath set forth to be a propitiation, through faith in His blood, to declare His righteousness for the remission of sins that are past, through the forbearance of God; to declare, I say, at this time His righteousness, that He might be just, and the justifier of him which believeth in Jesus." Yea, God may, through this Mediator, not only justly, but honorably, show you mercy. The blood of Christ is so precious that it is fully sufficient to pay the debt you have contracted, and perfectly to vindicate the Divine Majesty from all the dishonor cast upon it, by those many great sins of yours that have been mentioned. It was as great, and indeed a much greater thing, for Christ to die than it would have been for you and all mankind to have burnt in hell to all eternity. Of such dignity and excellency is Christ in the eyes of God that, seeing He has suffered so much for poor sinners, God is willing to be at peace with them, however vile and unworthy they have been, and on however many accounts the punishment would be just. So that you need not be at all discouraged from seeking mercy, for there is enough in Christ.

Indeed, it would not become the glory of God's majesty to show mercy to you, so sinful and vile a creature, for anything that you have done, for such worthless and despicable things as your prayers and other religious performances. It would be very dishonorable and unworthy of God so to do, and it is in vain to expect it. He will show mercy only on Christ's account, and that, according to His sovereign pleasure, on whom He pleases, when He pleases, and in what manner He pleases. You cannot bring Him under obligation by your works. Do what you will, He will not look on Himself as obliged. But if it is His pleasure, He can honorably show mercy through Christ to any sinner of you all, not one in this congregation excepted. Therefore, here is encouragement for you still to seek and wait, notwithstanding all your wickedness. This is agreeable to Samuel's speech to the children of Israel, when they were terrified with the thunder and rain that God sent, and when guilt stared them in the face. 1 Samuel 12:20: "Fear not; ye have done all this wickedness, yet turn not aside from following the Lord, but serve the Lord with all your heart."

I would conclude this discourse by putting the godly in mind of the freeness and wonderfulness of the grace of God towards them. For such were some of you. The case

The Justice of God in the Damnation of Sinners 137

was just so with you as you have heard: you had such a wicked heart; you lived such a wicked life; and it would have been most just with God forever to have cast you off; but He has had mercy upon you. He has made His glorious grace appear in your everlasting salvation. You had no love to God, but yet He has exercised unspeakable love to you. You have condemned God and set light by Him; but so great a value has God's grace set on you and your happiness that you have been redeemed at the price of the blood of His own Son. You chose to be with Satan in his service; but yet God has made you a joint heir with Christ of His glory. You were ungrateful for past mercies, yet God not only continued those mercies, but bestowed unspeakably greater mercies upon you. You refused to hear when God called, yet God heard you when you called. You abused the infiniteness of God's mercy to encourage yourself in sin against Him, yet God has manifested the infiniteness of that mercy in the exercises of it towards you. You have rejected Christ and set Him at naught; and yet He has become your Savior. You have neglected your own salvation, but God has not neglected it. You have destroyed yourself, but yet God has been your help. God has magnified His free grace towards you and not to others, because He has chosen you, and it has pleased Him to set His love upon you.

Oh, what cause is here for praise! What obligations you are under to bless the Lord who has dealt bountifully with you, and magnify His holy name! What cause for you to praise God in humility, to walk humbly before Him. Ezekiel 16:63: "That thou mayest remember and be confounded, and never open thy mouth any more, because of thy shame, when I am pacified toward thee for all that thou hast done, saith the Lord God." You shall never open your mouth in boasting or self-justification, but lie the lower before God for His mercy to you. You have reason the more abundantly to open your mouth in God's praises, that they may be continually in your mouth both here and to all eternity, for His rich, unspeakable, and sovereign mercy to you whereby He, and He alone, has made you to differ from others.

The Final Judgment
or
The World Judged Righteously by Jesus Christ

"Because He hath appointed a day, in the which He will judge the world in righteousness by that man whom He hath ordained." Acts 17:31

Introduction

These words are a part of the speech which Paul made in Mars hill, a place of concourse of the judges and learned men of Athens. Athens was the principal city of that part of Greece which was formerly a commonwealth by itself, and was the most noted place in the whole world for learning, philosophy, and human wisdom; and it continued so for many ages, till at length the Romans, having conquered Greece, its renown from that time began to diminish; and Rome, having borrowed learning of it, began to rival it in science, and in the polite and civil arts. However, it was still very famous in the days of Christ and the apostles, and was a place of concourse for wise and learned men.

Therefore, when Paul came there and began to preach concerning Jesus Christ, a man who had lately been crucified at Jerusalem (as in the 18th verse), the philosophers thronged about him to hear what he had to say. The strangeness of his doctrine excited their curiosity, for they spent their time in endeavoring to find out new things, and valued themselves greatly upon their being the authors of new discoveries, as we are informed in verse 21. They despised his doctrine in their hearts and esteemed it very ridiculous, calling the apostle a babbler, for the preaching of Christ crucified was to the Greeks foolishness (1 Corinthians 1:23), yet the Epicurean and Stoic philosophers, two different sects, had a mind to hear what the babbler had to say.

Upon this Paul rises up in the midst of them and makes a speech; and as he speaks to philosophers and men of learning he speaks quite differently from his common mode of address. There is evidently in his discourse a greater depth of thought, more philosophical reasoning, and a more elevated style than are to be found in his ordinary discourses to common men. His speech is such as was likely to draw the attention and gain the assent of philosophers. He shows himself to be no babbler, but a man who could offer such reason as they, however they valued themselves upon their wisdom, were not able to gainsay. His practice here is agreeable to what he said of himself in 1 Corinthians 9:22, that he became "all things to all men, that I might by all means save some." He not only to the weak became as weak that he might gain the weak, but to the wise he became as wise that he might gain the wise.

In the first place, he reasons with them concerning their worship of idols. He declares to them the true God, and points out how unreasonable it is to suppose that He delights in such superstitious worship. He begins with this because they were most likely to hearken to it, as being so evidently agreeable to the natural light of human reason, and also agreeable to what some of their own poets and philosophers had said (verse 28). He begins not immediately to tell them about Jesus Christ, His dying for sinners, and His resurrection from the dead, but first draws their attention with that to which they were more likely to hearken; and then, having thus introduced himself, he proceeds to speak concerning Jesus Christ.

He tells them that the times of this ignorance concerning the true God, in which they had hitherto been, God winked at. He suffered the world to lie in heathenish darkness, but now the appointed time was come, when He expected men should everywhere repent, "because He had appointed a day, in the which He will judge the world in righteousness by that man whom He hath ordained." As an enforcement to the duty of turning to God from their ignorance, superstition, and idolatry, the apostle brings in this, that God had appointed such a day of judgment. And as a proof of this he brings the resurrection of Christ from the dead.

Concerning the words of the text, we may observe that in them the apostle speaks of:

The general judgment: "He will judge the world."

The time when this shall be, on the appointed day: "He hath appointed a day."

How the world is to be judged: "in righteousness."

The man by whom it is to be judged: "Christ Jesus whom God raised from the dead."

DOCTRINE. There is a day coming in which there will be a general righteous judgment of the whole world by Jesus Christ.

In speaking upon this subject I shall show that God is the supreme Judge of the world; that there is a time coming when God will, in the most public and solemn manner, judge the whole world; that the person by whom He will judge it is Jesus Christ; that the transactions of that day will be greatly interesting and truly awful; that all shall be done in righteousness; and, finally, I shall take notice of those things which shall be immediately consequent upon the judgment.

Section I. God is the supreme Judge of the world.

1. God is so by right. He is by right the supreme and abso-

lute Ruler and Disposer of all things, both in the natural and moral world. The rational understanding part of the creation is indeed subject to a different sort of government from that to which irrational creatures are subject. God governs the sun, moon, and stars. He governs even the mites of dust which fly in the air. Not a hair of our heads falls to the ground without our heavenly Father. God also governs the brute creatures; by His providence He orders, according to His own decrees, all events concerning those creatures. And rational creatures are subject to the same sort of government: all their actions (except as they are sinful; for the sinfulness of actions is not included in the decrees of God, who is pure act from eternity to eternity), and all events relating to them, being ordered by superior providence, according to absolute decrees; so that no event that relates to them ever happens without the disposal of God, according to His own decrees. The rule of this government is God's wise decree and nothing else.

But rational creatures, because they are intelligent and voluntary agents, are the subjects of another kind of government. They are so only with respect to those of their actions in which they are causes by counsel, or with respect to their voluntary actions. The government of which I now speak is called moral government, and consists in two things: in giving laws and in judging.

God is, with respect to this sort of government, by right the sovereign Ruler of the world. He is possessed of this right by reason of His infinite greatness and excellency, by which He merits, and is perfectly and solely fit for, the office of supreme Ruler. He who is so excellent as to be infinitely worthy of the highest respect of the creature has thereby a right to that respect. He deserves it by a merit of condignity, so that it is injustice to deny it to Him. And He who is perfectly wise and true, and is only so regarded, has a right in everything to be regarded, and to have His determinations attended to and obeyed.

God has also a right to the character of supreme Ruler by reason of the absolute dependence of every creature on Him. All creatures, and rational creatures no less than others, are wholly derived from Him, and every moment are wholly dependent upon Him for being and for all good, so that they are properly His possession. And as, by virtue of this, He has a right to give His creatures whatever rules of conduct He pleases, or whatever rules are agreeable to His own wisdom, so the mind and will of the creature ought to be entirely conformed to the nature and will of the Creator, and to the rules He gives that are expressive of it.

For the same reason He has a right to judge their actions and conduct, and to fulfill the sanction of His law. He who has an absolute and independent right to give laws has evermore the same right to judge those to whom the laws are given. It is absolutely necessary that there should be a judge of reasonable creatures, and sanctions, or rewards and punishments, annexed to rules of conduct are necessary to the being of laws. A person may instruct another without sanctions, but not give laws. However, these sanctions themselves are vain, are as good as none, without a judge to determine the execution of them. As God has a right to be Judge, so has He a right to be the supreme Judge; and none has a right to reverse His judgments, to receive appeals from Him, or to say to Him, "Why judgest Thou thus?"

2. God is, in fact, the supreme Judge of the world. He has power sufficient to vindicate His own right. As He has a right which cannot be disputed, so He has power which cannot be controlled. He is possessed of omnipotence, wherewith to maintain His dominion over the world; and He maintains His dominion in the moral as well as the natural world. Men may

refuse subjection to God as a Lawgiver; they may shake off the yoke of His laws by rebellion; yet they cannot withdraw themselves from His judgment. Although they will not have God for their Lawgiver, yet they shall have Him for their Judge. The strongest of creatures can do nothing to control God or to avoid Him while acting in His judicial capacity. He is able to bring them to His judgment seat, and is also able to execute the sentence which He shall pronounce.

There was once a notable attempt made by opposition of power entirely to shake off the yoke of the moral government of God, both as Lawgiver and as Judge. This attempt was made by the angels, the most mighty of creatures, but they miserably failed in it. God notwithstanding acted as their Judge in casting those proud spirits out of heaven and binding them in chains of darkness unto a further judgment and a further execution. "God is wise in heart and mighty in strength; who hath hardened himself against Him, and hath prospered?" (Job 9:4). Wherein the enemies of God deal proudly, He is above them. He ever has acted as Judge in bestowing what rewards, and inflicting what punishments, He pleased on the children of men. And so He does still: He is daily fulfilling the promises and threatenings of the law in disposing of the souls of the children of men, and so He evermore will act.

God acts as Judge towards the children of men more especially:

(1) In man's particular judgment at death. Then the sentence is executed and the reward bestowed in part, which is not done without a judgment. The soul, when it departs from the body, appears before God to be disposed of by Him according to His law. But by this appearing no more is signified than this: that he should be made immediately sensible of the presence of God, God manifesting Himself immediately

to the soul with the glory and majesty of a Judge; that the sins of the wicked and the righteousness of the saints are brought by God to the view of their consciences, so that they know the reason of the sentence given, and their consciences are made to testify to the justice of it; and that thus the will of God for the fulfillment of the law, in their reward or punishment, is made known to them and executed. This is undoubtedly done at every man's death.

(2) In the great and general judgment, when all men shall together appear before the judgment seat to be judged: and which judgment will be much more solemn, and the sanctions of the law will to a further degree be fulfilled. But this brings me to another branch of the subject.

Section II. There is a time coming when God will, in the most public and solemn manner, judge the whole world of mankind.
The doctrine of a general judgment is not sufficiently discoverable by the light of nature. Indeed, some of the heathens had some obscure notions concerning a future judgment. But the light of nature, or mere unassisted reason, was not sufficient to instruct the world of fallen men in this doctrine. It is one of the peculiar doctrines of revelation, a doctrine of the gospel of Jesus Christ. There were indeed some hints of it in the Old Testament, as in Psalm 96:13: "The Lord cometh to judge the world with righteousness, and the people with His truth." Also Ecclesiastes 12:14: "For God will bring every work into judgment, with every secret thing, whether it be good, or whether it be evil." And there are some other such like passages. But this doctrine is, with abundantly the greatest clearness, revealed in the New Testament; there we have it frequently and particularly declared and described with its circumstances.

However, although it is a doctrine of revelation, and is

brought to light by the gospel, the brightest and most glorious revelation that God has given to the world, yet it is a doctrine which is entirely agreeable to reason, and of which reason gives great confirmation. That there will be a time before the dissolution of the world when the inhabitants of it shall stand before God and give an account of their conduct, and that God will, in a public manner, by a general and just judgment, set all things to rights respecting their moral behavior, is a doctrine entirely agreeable to reason, which I shall now endeavor to make appear. But I would premise that what we would inquire into is not whether all mankind shall be judged by God—for that is a thing that the light of nature clearly teaches, and we have already spoken something of it—but whether it is rational to think that there will be a public judgment of all mankind together. This I think will appear very rational from the following considerations.

1. Such a judgment will be a more glorious display of God's majesty and dominion; it will be more glorious because it will be more open, public, and solemn. Although God now actually exercises the most sovereign dominion over the earth; although He reigns and does all things according to His own will, ordering all events as seemeth to Himself good; and although He is actually Judge in the earth, continually disposing of men's souls according to their works; yet He rules after a more hidden and secret manner, insomuch that it is common among the proud sons of men to refuse acknowledging His dominion. Wicked men question the very existence of a God who takes care of the world, who orders the affairs of it, and judges in it; and therefore they cast off the fear of Him. Many of the kings and great men of the earth do not suitably acknowledge the God who is above them, but seem to look upon themselves as supreme, and therefore tyrannize over mankind as if they were in no wise accountable

for their conduct. There have been, and now are, many atheistic persons who acknowledge not God's moral dominion over mankind; and therefore they throw off the yoke of His laws and government. And how great a part of the world is there now, and has there always been, that has not acknowledged that the government of the world belongs to the God of Israel or to the God of Christians, but has paid homage to other imaginary deities as though they were their sovereign lords and supreme judges. Over how great a part of the world has Satan usurped the dominion, and set up himself for god in opposition to the true God!

Now, how agreeable to reason is it that God, in the winding up of things, when the present state of mankind shall come to a conclusion, should, in the most open and public manner, manifest His dominion over the inhabitants of the earth by bringing them all, high and low, rich and poor, kings and subjects, together before Him to be judged with respect to all that they ever did in the world! that He should thus openly discover His dominion in this world, where His authority has been so much questioned, denied, and proudly opposed! that those very persons who have thus denied and opposed the authority of God should be themselves, with the rest of the world, brought before the tribunal of God! that however God is not now visibly present upon earth, disposing and judging in that visible manner that earthly kings do, yet at the conclusion of the world He should make His dominion visible to all, and with respect to all mankind, so that every eye shall see Him, and even they who have denied Him shall find that God is supreme Lord of them, and of the whole world!

2. The end of judgment will be more fully answered by a public and general than only by a particular and private judgment. The end of which there is any judgment at all is to display and glorify the righteousness of God; which end is

more fully accomplished by calling men to an account, bringing their actions to the trial, and determining their state according to them, the whole world, both angels and men, being present to behold, than if the same things should be done in a more private way. At the day of judgment there will be the most glorious display of the justice of God that ever was made. Then God will appear to be entirely righteous towards everyone; the justice of all His moral government will on that day be at once discovered. Then all objections will be removed; the conscience of every man shall be satisfied; the blasphemies of the ungodly will be forever put to silence, and argument will be given for the saints and angels to praise God forever. Revelation 19:1-2: "And after these things I heard a great voice of much people in heaven, saying, Alleluia; salvation, and glory, and honor, and power be to the Lord our God: for true and righteous are His judgments."

3. It is very agreeable to reason that the irregularities which are so open and manifest in the world should, when the world comes to an end, be publicly rectified by the supreme Governor. The infinitely wise God, who made this world to be a habitation of men, and placed mankind to dwell here, and has appointed man His end and work, must take care of the order and good government of the world which He has thus made. He is not regardless how things proceed here on earth. It would be a reproach to His wisdom, and to the perfect rectitude of His nature, to suppose so. This world is a world of confusion; it has been filled with irregularity and confusion ever since the fall, and the irregularities of it are not only private, relating to the actions of particular persons, but states, kingdoms, nations, churches, cities, and all societies of men in all ages have been full of public irregularities. The affairs of the world, so far as they are in the hands of men, are carried on in the most irregular and confused

manner.

Though justice sometimes takes place, yet how often do injustice, cruelty, and oppression prevail! How often are the righteous condemned and the wicked acquitted and rewarded! How common is it for the virtuous and pious to be depressed and the wicked to be advanced! How many thousands of the best men have suffered intolerable cruelties, merely for their virtue and piety, and in this world have had no help, no refuge to fly to! The world is very much ruled by the pride, covetousness, and passions of men. Solomon takes much notice of such like irregularities in the present state (in his book of Ecclesiastes), whereby he shows the vanity of the world.

Now, how reasonable is it to suppose that God, when He shall come and put an end to the present state of mankind, will, in an open, public manner, the whole world being present, rectify all these disorders! and that He will bring all things to a trial by a general judgment in order that those who have been oppressed may be delivered; that the righteous cause may be pleaded and vindicated, and wickedness, which has been approved, honored, and rewarded, may receive its due disgrace and punishment; that the proceedings of kings and earthly judges may be inquired into by Him, whose eyes are as a flame of fire; and that the public actions of men may be publicly examined and recompensed according to their desert! How agreeable is it to divine wisdom thus to order things, and how worthy of the supreme Governor of the world!

4. By a public and general judgment, God more fully accomplishes the reward He designs for the godly, and the punishment He designs for the wicked. One part of the reward which God intends for His saints is the honor which He intends to bestow upon them. He will honor them in the most

public and open manner before the angels, before all mankind, and before those who hated them. And it is most suitable that it should be so: it is suitable that those holy, humble souls who have been hated by wicked men, have been cruelly treated and put to shame by them, and who have been haughtily domineered over, should be openly acquitted, commended, and crowned before all the world.

So one part of the punishment of the ungodly will be the open shame and disgrace which they shall suffer. Although many of them have proudly lifted up their heads in this world, have had a very high thought of themselves, and have obtained outward honor among men, yet God will put them to open shame by showing all their wickedness and moral filthiness before the whole assembly of angels and men; by manifesting His abhorrence of them, in placing them upon his left hand, among devils and foul spirits; and by turning them away into the most loathsome, as well as most dreadful, pit of hell to dwell there forever. These ends may be much more fully accomplished in a general than in a particular judgment.

Section III. The world will be judged by Jesus Christ.
The person by whom God will judge the world is Jesus Christ, God-man. The second person in the Trinity, that same person of whom we read in our Bibles, who was born of the Virgin Mary, lived in Galilee and Judea, and was at last crucified outside the gates of Jerusalem, will come to judge the world both in His divine and human nature, in the same human body that was crucified and rose again and ascended up into heaven. Acts 1:11: "This same Jesus, that is taken up from you into heaven, shall come in like manner as ye have seen Him go into heaven." It will be His human nature which will then be seen by the bodily eyes of men. However, His divine nature, which is united to the human, will then also be pre-

The Final Judgment

sent; and it will be by the wisdom of that divine nature that Christ will see and judge.

QUESTION. Here naturally arises an inquiry, "Why is Christ appointed to judge the world rather than the Father or the Holy Ghost?"

We cannot pretend to know all the reasons of the divine dispensations. God is not obliged to give us an account of them. But so much may we learn by divine revelations as to discover marvelous wisdom in what He determines and orders with respect to this matter. We learn that:

1. God sees fit that He who is *in* the human nature should be the Judge of those who are *of* the human nature. John 5:27: "And hath given Him authority to execute judgment also, because He is the Son of man." Seeing there is one of the persons of the Trinity united to the human nature, God chooses, in all His transactions with mankind, to transact by Him. He did so of old in His discoveries of Himself to the patriarchs, in giving the law, in leading the children of Israel through the wilderness, and in the manifestations He made of Himself in the tabernacle and temple, when, although Christ was not actually incarnate, yet He was so in design, it was ordained and agreed in the covenant of redemption that He should become incarnate. And since the incarnation of Christ, God governs both the church and the world by Christ. So He will also at the end judge the world by Him. All men shall be judged by God, and yet at the same time by one invested with their own nature.

God sees fit that those who have bodies, as all mankind will have at the day of judgment, should see their Judge with their bodily eyes, and hear Him with their bodily ears. If one of the other persons of the Trinity had been appointed to be Judge, there must have been some extraordinary outward appearance made on purpose to be a token of the divine presence, as it was of old before Christ was incarnate. But now there is no necessity of that. Now one of the persons of the Trinity is actually incarnate, so that God, by Him, may appear to bodily eyes without any miraculous visionary appearance.

2. Christ has this honor of being the Judge of the world given Him as a suitable reward for His sufferings. This is a part of Christ's exaltation. The exaltation of Christ is given Him in reward for His humiliation and sufferings. This was stipulated in the covenant of redemption; and we are expressly told that it was given Him in reward for His sufferings in Philippians 2:8–12: "And being found in fashion as a man, He humbled Himself, and became obedient unto death, even the death of the cross. Wherefore God also hath highly exalted Him, and given Him a name which is above every name, that at the name of Jesus every knee should bow, of things in heaven, and things in earth, and things under the earth; and that every tongue should confess that Jesus Christ is Lord, to the glory of God the Father."

God sees fit that He who appeared in such a low estate among mankind, without form or comeliness, having His divine glory veiled, should appear among men a second time, in His own proper majesty and glory, without a veil, to the end that those who saw Him here at the first as a poor, frail man, not having anywhere to lay His head, subject to much hardship and affliction, may see Him the second time in power and great glory, invested with the glory and dignity of the absolute Lord of heaven and earth; and that He who once tabernacled with men, and was despised and rejected of them, may have the honor of arraigning all men before His throne, and judging them with respect to their eternal state (John 5:21–24).

God sees fit that He who was once arraigned before the judgment seat of men, and was there most vilely treated, being mocked, spat upon, and condemned, and who was at last crucified, should be rewarded by having those very persons brought to His tribunal, that they may see Him in glory and be confounded; and that He may have the disposal of them for all eternity; as Christ said to the high priest while arraigned before him (Matthew 26:64): "Hereafter ye shall see the Son of man sitting on the right hand of power, and coming in the clouds of heaven."

3. It is needful that Christ should be the Judge of the world in order that He may finish the work of redemption. It is the will of God that He who is the Redeemer of the world should be a complete Redeemer, and that therefore He should have the whole work of redemption left in His hands. Now the redemption of fallen man consists not merely in the petition of redemption, by obeying the divine law and making atonement for sinners, or in preparing the way for their salvation, but it consists in a great measure, and is actually fulfilled, in converting sinners to the knowledge and love of the truth, in carrying them on in the way of grace and true holiness through life, and in finally raising their bodies to life, in glorifying them, in pronouncing the blessed sentence upon them, in crowning them with honor and glory in the sight of men and angels, and in completing and perfecting their reward. Now, it is necessary that Christ should do this in order to His finishing the work which He has begun. Raising the saints from the dead, judging them, and fulfilling the sentence is part of their salvation; and therefore it was necessary that Christ should be appointed Judge of the world in order that He might finish His work (John 6:39–40, 5:25–31). The redemption of the bodies of the saints is part of the work of redemption; the resurrection to life is called a redemption of their bodies (Romans 8:23).

It is the will of God that Christ Himself should have the

fulfilling of that for which He died, and for which He suffered so much. Now the end for which He suffered and died was the complete salvation of His people; and this shall be obtained at the last judgment, and not before. Therefore it was necessary that Christ be appointed Judge in order that He Himself might fully accomplish the end for which He had both suffered and died. When Christ had finished His appointed sufferings, God did, as it were, put the purchased inheritance into His hands to be kept for believers, and be bestowed upon them at the day of judgment.

4. It was proper that He who is appointed King of the Church should rule till He should have put all His enemies under His feet, in order to which He must be the Judge of His enemies as well as of His people. One of the offices of Christ as Redeemer is that of a King. He is appointed King of the Church, and Head over all things to the Church. And in order that His kingdom be complete, and the design of His reign be accomplished, He must conquer all His enemies, and then He will deliver up the kingdom to the Father. 1 Corinthians 15:24–25: "Then cometh the end, when He shall have delivered up the kingdom to God, even the Father; when He shall have put down all rule, and all authority and power. For He must reign till He hath put all enemies under His feet." Now when Christ shall have brought His enemies, who had denied, opposed, and rebelled against Him, to His judgment seat, and shall have passed and executed sentence upon them, this will be a final and complete victory over them, a victory which shall put an end to the war. And it is proper that He who at present reigns, and is carrying on the war against those who are of the opposite kingdom, should have the honor of obtaining the victory and finishing the war.

5. It is for the abundant comfort of the saints that Christ is appointed to be their Judge. The covenant of grace, with all

The Final Judgment

its circumstances and all those events to which it has relation, is in every way so contrived of God as to give strong consolation to believers: for God designed the gospel for a glorious manifestation of His grace to them; and therefore everything in it is so ordered as to manifest the most grace and mercy.

Now it is for the abundant consolation of the saints that their own Redeemer is appointed to be their Judge, that the same person who spilled His blood for them has the determination of their state left with Him; so that they need not doubt but that they shall have what He was at so much cost to procure.

What matter of joy to them will it be at the last day to lift up their eyes and behold the person in whom they have trusted for salvation, to whom they have fled for refuge, upon whom they have built as their foundation for eternity, and whose voice they have often heard inviting them to Himself for protection and safety, coming to judge them.

6. That Christ is appointed to be the Judge of the world will be for the more abundant conviction of the ungodly. It will be for their conviction that they are judged and condemned by that very person whom they have rejected, by whom they might have been saved, who shed His blood to give them an opportunity to be saved, who was wont to offer His righteousness to them when they were in their state of trial, and who many a time called and invited them to come to Him that they might be saved. How justly will they be condemned by Him whose salvation they have rejected, whose blood they have despised, whose many calls they have refused, and whom they have pierced by their sins!

How much will it be for their conviction, when they shall hear the sentence of condemnation pronounced, to reflect with themselves, "How often has this same person, who now passes sentence of condemnation upon me, called me in His

Word and by His messengers to accept Him, and to give myself to Him! How often has He knocked at the door of my heart! And had it not been for my own folly and obstinacy, how might I have had Him for my Savior, who is now my incensed Judge!"

Section IV. Christ's coming, the resurrection, the judgment prepared, the books opened, the sentence pronounced and executed.
1. Christ Jesus will, in a most magnificent manner, descend from heaven with all the holy angels. The man Christ Jesus is now in the heaven of heavens, or, as the apostle expresses it, far above all heavens (Ephesians 4:10). And there He has been ever since His ascension, being there enthroned in glory in the midst of millions of angels and blessed spirits. But when the time appointed for the day of judgment shall have come, notice will be given in those happy regions, and Christ will descend to the earth, attended with all those heavenly hosts, in a most solemn, awful, and glorious manner. Christ will come with divine majesty. He will come in the glory of the Father. Matthew 16:27: "For the Son of man shall come in the glory of His Father, with His angels."

We can now conceive but little of the holy and awful magnificence in which Christ will appear as He shall come in the clouds of heaven, or of the glory of his retinue. How mean and despicable, in comparison with it, is the most splendid appearance that earthly princes can make! A glorious visible light will shine round about Him, and the earth, with all nature, will tremble at His presence. How vast and innumerable will that host be which will appear with Him! Heaven will be, for the time, deserted of its inhabitants.

We may argue the glory of Christ's appearance from His appearance at other times. When He appeared in transfiguration, His face did shine as the sun and His raiment was white

The Final Judgment

as the light. The apostle Peter long after spoke of this appearance in magnificent terms in 2 Peter 1:16–17: "We were eyewitnesses of His majesty; for He received from God the Father honor and glory, when there came such a voice to Him from the excellent glory." And His appearance to St. Paul at his conversion, and to St. John as related in Revelation 1:13, were very grand and magnificent. But we may conclude that His appearance at the day of judgment will be vastly more so than either of these as the occasion will be so much greater. We have good reason to think that our nature, in the present frail state, could not bear the appearance of the majesty in which He will then be seen.

We may argue the glory of His appearance from the appearances of some of the angels to men; as of the angel that appeared at Christ's sepulcher after His resurrection. Matthew 28:3: "His countenance was like lightning, and his raiment white as snow." The angels will doubtless, all of them, make as glorious an appearance at the day of judgment as ever any of them have made on former occasions. How glorious, then, will be the retinue of Christ made up of so many thousands of such angels! And how much more glorious will Christ, the Judge Himself, appear than those His attendants! Doubtless their God will appear immensely more glorious than they. Christ will thus descend into our air, to such a distance from the surface of the earth that everyone, when all shall be gathered together, shall see Him. Revelation 1:7: "Behold, He cometh with clouds, and every eye shall see Him."

Christ will make this appearance suddenly, and to the great surprise of the inhabitants of the earth. It is therefore compared to a cry at midnight by which men are awakened in a great surprise.

2. At the sound of the last trumpet, the dead shall rise and

the living shall be changed. As soon as Christ is descended, the last trumpet shall sound as a notification to all mankind to appear; at which mighty sound shall the dead be immediately raised and the living changed. 1 Corinthians 15:52: "For the trumpet shall sound, and the dead shall be raised incorruptible, and we shall be changed." Matthew 24:31: "And He shall send His angels with a great sound of a trumpet." 1 Thessalonians 4:16: "For the Lord Himself shall descend from heaven with a shout, with the voice of the archangel, and with the trump of God." There will be some great and remarkable signal given for the rising of the dead, which it seems will be some mighty sound, caused by the angels of God who shall attend on Christ.

Upon this all the dead shall rise from their graves—all, both small and great, who shall have lived upon earth since the foundation of the world, those who died before the flood, and those who were drowned in the flood, all who have died since that time and who shall die to the end of the world. There will be a great moving upon the face of the earth and in the waters in bringing bone to bone, in opening graves, and bringing together all the scattered particles of dead bodies. The earth shall give up the dead who are in it, and the sea shall give up the dead who are in it.

However the parts of the bodies of many are divided and scattered; however many have been burnt and their bodies have been turned to ashes and smoke and driven to the four winds; however many have been eaten of wild beasts, of the fowls of heaven, and the fishes of the sea; however many have consumed away upon the face of the earth, and great parts of their bodies have ascended in exhalations, yet the all-wise and all-powerful God can immediately bring every part to his part again.

Of this vast multitude some shall rise to life and others to condemnation. John 5:28-29: "All that are in the graves shall hear His voice, and shall come forth: they that have done good, unto the resurrection of life; and they that have done evil, unto the resurrection of damnation."

When the bodies are prepared, the departed souls shall again enter into their bodies, and be reunited to them, never more to be separated. The souls of the wicked shall be brought up out of hell, not out of misery, and shall very unwillingly enter into their bodies which will be but eternal prisons to them. Revelation 20:13: "And death and hell delivered up the dead that were in them." They shall lift their eyes full of the utmost amazement and horror to see their awful Judge. And perhaps the bodies with which they shall be raised will be most filthy and loathsome, thus properly corresponding to the inward, moral turpitude of their souls.

The souls of the righteous shall descend from heaven together with Christ and His angels. 1 Thessalonians 4:14: "Them also which sleep in Jesus will God bring with Him." They also shall be reunited to their bodies that they may be glorified with them. They shall receive their bodies prepared by God to be mansions of pleasure to all eternity. They shall be in every way fitted for the uses, exercises, and delights of perfectly holy and glorified souls. They shall be clothed with a superlative beauty, similar to that of Christ's glorious body. Philippians 3:21: "Who shall change our vile body, that it may be fashioned like unto His glorious body." Their bodies shall rise incorruptible, no more liable to pain or disease, and with an extraordinary vigor and vivacity, like that of those spirits that are as a flame or fire. 1 Corinthians 15:43-44: "It is sown in dishonor, it is raised in glory; it is sown in weakness, it is raised in power; it is sown a natural body, it is raised a spiritual body." With what joy will the souls and bodies of the saints meet, and with what joy will they lift up their heads out of their graves to behold the glorious sight of the appearing of Christ! And it will be a glorious sight to see those saints arising out of their graves, putting off their corruption, and putting on incorruption and glory.

At the same time, those who shall then be alive upon the earth shall be changed. Their bodies shall pass through a great change in a moment, in the twinkling of an eye. 1 Corinthians 15:51–52: "Behold, I show you a mystery: We shall not all sleep, but we shall all be changed, in a moment, in the twinkling of an eye, at the last trump." The bodies of the wicked then living will be changed into such hideous things as shall be answerable to the loathsome souls that dwell in them, and such as shall be prepared to receive and administer eternal torments without dissolution. But the bodies of the righteous shall be changed into the same glorious and immortal form in which those that shall be raised will appear.

3. They shall all be brought to appear before Christ, the godly being placed on the right hand, the wicked on the left (Matthew 25:31–33). The wicked, however unwilling, however full of fear and horror, shall be brought or driven before the judgment seat. However they may try to hide themselves, and for this purpose creep into dens and caves of the mountains, and cry to the mountains to fall on them and hide them from the face of Him who sits on the throne, and from the wrath of the Lamb, yet there shall not one escape. To the Judge they must come, and stand on the left hand with the devils. On the contrary, the righteous will be joyfully conducted to Jesus Christ, probably by the angels. Their joy will, as it were, give them wings to carry them there. They will with ecstasies and raptures of delight meet their friend and Savior, come into His presence, and stand at His right hand.

Besides the one standing on the right hand and the other on the left, there seems to be this difference between them:

The Final Judgment

when the dead in Christ shall be raised, they will all be caught up into the air where Christ shall be, and shall be there at His right hand during the judgment, never more to set their feet on this earth. The wicked shall be left standing on the earth, there to abide the judgment. 1 Thessalonians 4:16–17: "The dead in Christ shall rise first; then we which are alive and remain shall be caught up together with them in the clouds to meet the Lord in the air; and so shall we ever be with the Lord."

And what a vast congregation will there be of all the men, women, and children that shall have lived upon earth from the beginning to the end of the world! Revelation 20:12: "And I saw the dead, small and great, stand before God."

4. The next thing will be that the books shall be opened. Revelation 20:12: "I saw the dead, great and small, stand before God; and the books were opened." These books seem to be the book of God's remembrance and the book of Scripture; the former as the evidence of their deeds which are to be judged, the latter as the rule of judgment. The works both of the righteous and of the wicked will be brought forth that they may be judged according to them, and those works will be tried according to the appointed and written rule.

(1) The works of both righteous and wicked will be rehearsed. The book of God's remembrance will be opened first. The various works of the children of men are, as it were, written by God in a book of remembrance. Malachi 3:16: "A book of remembrance was written before Him." However ready ungodly men may be to make light of their own sins and to forget them, yet God never forgets any of them: neither does God forget any of the good works of the saints. If they give but a cup of cold water with a spirit of charity, God remembers it.

The evil works of the wicked shall then be brought forth

to light. They must then hear of all their profaneness, their impenitence, their obstinate unbelief, their abuse of ordinances, and various other sins. The various aggravations of their sins will also be brought to view, as how this man sinned after such and such warnings, that after the receipt of such and such mercies; one after being so and so favored with outward light, another after having been the subject of inward conviction, excited by the immediate agency of God. Concerning these sins, they shall be called to account to see what answer they can make for themselves. Matthew 12:36: "But I say unto you that every idle word that men shall speak, they shall give account thereof in the day of judgment." Romans 14:12: "So then every one of us shall give account of himself to God."

The good works of the saints will also be brought forth as evidences of their sincerity, and of their interest in the righteousness of Christ. As to their evil works, they will not be brought forth against them on that day, for the guilt of them will not lie upon them, they being clothed with the righteousness of Jesus Christ. The Judge Himself will have taken the guilt of their sins upon Him; therefore their sins will not stand against them in the book of God's remembrance. The account of them will appear to have been canceled before that time. The account that will be found in God's book will not be of debt, but of credit. God cancels their debts and sets down their good works, and is pleased, as it were, to make Himself a debtor for them by His own gracious act.

Both good and bad will be judged according to their works. Revelation 20:12: "And the dead were judged out of those things that were found written in the books, according to their works." And verse 13: "And they were judged every man according to their works." Though the righteous are justified by faith and not by their works, yet they shall be judged according to their works: then works shall be brought forth as the evidence of their faith. Their faith on that great day shall be tried by its fruits. If the works of any man shall have been bad, if his life shall appear to have been unchristian, that will condemn him without any further inquiry. But if his works, when they shall be examined, prove good and of the right sort, he shall surely be justified. They will be declared as a sure evidence of his having believed in Jesus Christ, and of his being clothed with His righteousness.

But by works we are to understand all voluntary exercises of the faculties of the soul; as, for instance, the words and conversation of men as well as what is done with their hands. Matthew 12:37: "By thy words thou shalt be justified, and by thy words thou shalt be condemned." Nor are we to understand only outward acts or the thoughts outwardly expressed, but also the thoughts themselves and all the inward workings of the heart. Man judges according to the outward appearance, but God judges the heart. Revelation 2:23: "I am He that searcheth the reins and the hearts, and I will give unto every one of you according to his works." Nor will only positive sins be brought into judgment, but also omissions of duty, as is manifest by Matthew 25:42: "For I was an hungred, and ye gave me no meat; I was thirsty, and ye gave Me no drink."

On that day, secret and hidden wickedness will be brought to light. All the uncleanness, injustice, and violence of which men have been guilty in secret shall be manifest both to angels and men. Then it will be made to appear how this and that man indulged themselves in wicked imaginations, in lascivious, covetous, malicious, or impious desires and wishes, and how others have harbored in their hearts enmity against God and His law—also impenitence and unbelief, notwithstanding all the means used with them, and motives set before them, to induce them to repent, return, and live.

The good works of the saints also, which were done in secret, shall then be made public, and even the pious and benevolent affections and designs of their hearts; so that the real and secret characters of both saints and sinners shall then be most clearly and publicly displayed.

(2) The book of Scripture will be opened, and the works of men will be tried by that touchstone. Their works will be compared with the Word of God. That which God gave men for the rule of their action while in this life shall then be made the rule of their judgment. God has told us beforehand what will be the rule of judgment. We are told in the Scriptures upon what terms we shall be justified and upon what terms we shall be condemned. That which God has given us to be our rule in our lives He will make His own rule in judgment.

The rule of judgment will be twofold. The primary rule of judgment will be the law. The law ever has stood, and ever will stand, in force as a rule of judgment for those to whom the law was given. Matthew 5:18: "For verily I say unto you, Till heaven and earth pass, one jot or one tittle shall in no wise pass from the law, till all be fulfilled." The law will so far be made the rule of judgment that no one person at that day shall by any means be justified or condemned in a way inconsistent with that which is established by the law. As to the wicked, the law will be so far the rule of judgment respecting them that the sentence denounced against them will be the sentence of the law. The righteous will be so far judged by the law that, although their sentence will not be the sentence of the law, yet it will by no means be such a sentence as shall be inconsistent with the law, but such as it allows; for it will be by the righteousness of the law that they shall be justified.

It will be inquired concerning everyone, both righteous and wicked, whether the law stands against him or whether he has a fulfillment of the law to show. As to the righteous, they will have fulfillment to show; they will have it to plead that the Judge Himself has fulfilled the law for them; that He has both satisfied for their sins and fulfilled the righteousness of the law for them. Romans 10:4: "Christ is the end of the law for righteousness to every one that believeth." But as to the wicked, when it shall be found by the book of God's remembrance that they have broken the law, and have no fulfillment of it to plead, the sentence of the law shall be pronounced upon them.

A secondary rule of judgment will be the gospel, or the covenant of grace, wherein it is said, "He that believeth shall be saved, and he that believeth not shall be damned." Romans 2:16: "In the day when God shall judge the secrets of men by Jesus Christ according to my gospel." By the gospel, or covenant of grace, eternal blessedness will be adjudged to believers. When it shall be found that the law hinders not, and that the curse and condemnation of the law stands not against them, the reward of eternal life shall be given them according to the glorious gospel of Jesus Christ.

5. The sentence will be pronounced. Christ will say to the wicked on the left hand, "Depart, ye cursed, into everlasting fire, prepared for the devil and his angels." How dreadful will these words of the Judge be to the poor, miserable, despairing wretches on the left hand! How amazing will every syllable of them be! How will they pierce them to the soul! These words show the greatest wrath and abhorrence. Christ will bid them depart. He will send them away from His presence. He will remove them forever far out of His sight into an everlasting separation from God, as being most loathsome and unfit to dwell in His presence and enjoy communion with Him.

Christ will call them "cursed": "Depart, ye cursed, to whom everlasting wrath and ruin belong; who are by your own wickedness prepared for nothing else but to be firebrands of hell; who are the fit objects and vessels of the vengeance and fury of the Almighty."

He will send them into fire. He will not send them away merely into a loathsome prison, the receptacle of the filth and rubbish of the universe, but into a furnace of fire. That must be their dwelling place; there they must be tormented with the most racking pain and anguish.

It is everlasting fire. There is eternity in the sentence, which infinitely aggravates the doom, and will make every word of it immensely more dreadful, sinking, and amazing to the souls that receive it.

It is prepared for the devil and his angels. This sets forth the greatness and intenseness of the torments, as the preceding part of the sentence does the duration. It shows the dreadfulness of that fire to which they shall be condemned, that it is the same that is prepared for the devils, those foul spirits and great enemies of God. Their condition will be the same as that of the devils, in many respects; particularly as they must burn in the fire forever.

This sentence will doubtless be pronounced in such an awful manner as shall be a terrible manifestation of the wrath of the Judge. There will be divine, holy, and almighty wrath manifested in the countenance and voice of the Judge, and we know not what other manifestations of anger will accompany the sentence. Perhaps it will be accompanied with thunders and lightnings far more dreadful than were on Mount Sinai at the giving of the law. Correspondent to these exhibitions of divine wrath will be the appearances of terror and most horrible amazement in the condemned. How will all their faces look pale! How will death sit upon their countenances when those words shall be heard! What dolorous cries, shrieks, and groans, what trembling, wringing of hands, and

The Final Judgment 167

gnashing of teeth will there then be!

But with the most benign aspect, in the most endearing manner, and with the sweetest expressions of love, will Christ invite His saints on his right hand to glory, saying, "Come, ye blessed of My Father, inherit the kingdom prepared for you from the foundation of the world." He will not bid them to go *from* Him, but to come *with* Him; to go where He goes; to dwell where He dwells; to enjoy Him and to partake with Him. He will call them blessed, blessed of His Father, blessed by Him whose blessing is infinitely the most desirable, namely God.

"Inherit the kingdom." They are not only invited to go with Christ and to dwell with Him, but to inherit a kingdom with Him; to sit down with Him on His throne, and to receive the honor and happiness of a heavenly kingdom.

"Prepared for you from the foundation of the world." This denotes the sovereign and eternal love of God as the source of their blessedness. He puts them in mind that God was pleased to set His love upon them long before they had a being, even from eternity; that therefore God made heaven on purpose for them and fitted it for their delight and happiness.

6. Immediately after this, the sentence will be executed, as we are informed in Matthew 25:46: "These shall go away into everlasting punishment; but the righteous into life eternal." When the words of the sentence shall have once proceeded out of the mouth of the Judge, then that vast and innumerable throng of ungodly men shall go away, shall be driven away, shall be necessitated to go away with devils, and shall with dismal cries and shrieks be cast into the great furnace of fire prepared for the punishment of devils, the perpetual thunders and lightnings of the wrath of God following them. Into this furnace they must in both soul and body enter, never more to come out. Here they must spend eternal ages

wrestling with the most excruciating torments, and in crying out in the midst of the most dreadful flames, and under the most insupportable wrath.

On the other hand, the righteous shall ascend to heaven with their glorified bodies, in company with Christ, His angels, and all that host which descended with Him. They shall ascend in the most joyful and triumphant manner, and shall enter with Christ into that glorious and blessed world which had for the time been empty of its creature inhabitants. Christ having given His Church that perfect beauty, and crowned it with that glory, honor, and happiness which were stipulated in the covenant of redemption before the world was, and which He died to procure for them. And having made it a truly glorious church, in every way complete, He will present it before the Father without spot or wrinkle or any such thing. Thus shall the saints be instated in everlasting glory, to dwell there with Christ, who shall feed them and lead them to living fountains of water, to the full enjoyment of God and to an eternity of the most holy, glorious, and joyful employments.

Section V. All will be done in righteousness.
Christ will give to every man his due, according to a most righteous rule. Those who shall be condemned will be most justly condemned. They will be condemned to that punishment which they shall most justly deserve; and the justice of God in condemning them will be made most evident. Now the justice of God in punishing wicked men, and especially in the degree of their punishment, is often blasphemously called in question. But it will be made clear and apparent to all; their own consciences will tell them that the sentence is just, and all cavils will be put to silence.

So those who shall be justified shall be most justly adjudged to eternal life. Although they also were great sinners and deserved eternal death, yet it will not be against justice or the law to justify them; they will be in Christ. But the acquitting of them will be but giving the reward merited by Christ's righteousness. Romans 3:26: "That God may be just, and the Justifier of him that believeth in Jesus."

Christ will judge the world in righteousness, particularly as He will give to everyone a due proportion either of reward or punishment, according to the various characters of those who shall be judged. The punishments shall be duly proportioned to the number and aggravations of the sins of the wicked; and the rewards of the righteous shall be duly proportioned to the number of their holy acts and affections, and also to the degree of virtue implied in them. I would observe further that:

1. Christ cannot fail of being just in judging through mistake. He cannot take some to be sincere and godly who are not so, nor others to be hypocrites who are really sincere. His eyes are as a flame of fire, and He searches the hearts and tries the reins of the children of men. He can never err in determining what is justice in particular cases as human judges often do. Nor can He be blinded by prejudices as human judges are very liable to be. Deuteronomy 10:17: "He regardeth not persons, nor taketh reward." It is impossible that He should be deceived by the excuses, false colors, and pleas of the wicked as human judges very commonly are. It is equally impossible that He should err in assigning to everyone his proper proportion of reward or punishment, according to his wickedness or good works. His knowledge, being infinite, will effectually guard Him against all these, and other such errors.

2. He cannot fail of judging righteously through an unrighteous disposition, for He is infinitely just and holy in His nature. Deuteronomy 32:4: "He is the Rock, His work is perfect; for all His ways are judgment; a God of truth and without

iniquity, just and right is He." It is not possible that an infinitely powerful, self-sufficient Being should be under any temptation to injustice. Nor is it possible that an infinitely wise Being who knows all things should not choose justice. For He who perfectly knows all things perfectly knows how much more amiable justice is than injustice, and therefore must choose it.

Section VI. Those things which will immediately follow the day of judgment.

1. After the sentence shall have been pronounced and the saints shall have ascended with Christ into glory, this world will be dissolved by fire; the conflagration will immediately succeed the judgment. When an end shall have been put to the present state of mankind, this world, which was the place of their habitation during that state, will be destroyed, there being no further use for it. This earth, which had been the stage upon which so many scenes had been acted, upon which there had been so many great and famous kingdoms and large cities, where there had been so many wars, so much trade and business carried on for so many ages, shall then be destroyed. These continents, these islands, these seas and rivers, these mountains and valleys, shall be seen no more at all; all shall be destroyed by devouring flames. This we are plainly taught in the Word of God. 2 Peter 3:7: "But the heavens and the earth which are now, by the same word are kept in store, reserved unto fire against the day of judgment and perdition of ungodly men." Verse 10: "But the day of the Lord will come as a thief in the night, in the which the heavens shall pass away with a great noise, and the elements shall melt with fervent heat; the earth also and the works that are therein shall be burnt up." Verse 12: "Looking for and hasting unto the coming of the day of God, wherein the heavens be-

ing on fire shall be dissolved, and the elements shall melt with fervent heat."

2. Both the misery of the wicked and the happiness of the saints will be increased beyond what shall be before the judgment. The misery of the wicked will be increased as they will be tormented not only in their souls, but also in their bodies, which will be prepared both to receive and administer torment to their souls. There will doubtless then be the like connection between soul and body as there is now; and therefore the pains and torments of the one will affect the other. And why may we not suppose that their torments will be increased as well as those of the devils? Concerning them we are informed (James 2:19) that they believe there is one God and tremble in the belief; expecting, no doubt, that He will inflict upon them, in due time, more severe torments than even those which they now suffer. We are also informed that they are bound "in chains of darkness, to be reserved unto judgment; and unto the judgment of the great day" (2 Peter 2:4 and Jude 6). This implies that their full punishment is not yet executed upon them, but that they are now reserved as prisoners in hell to receive their just recompense on the day of judgment. Hence it was that they thought Christ had come to torment them before the time (Matthew 8:29). Thus the punishment neither of wicked men nor devils will be complete before the final judgment.

No more will the happiness of the saints be complete before that time. Therefore we are in the New Testament so often encouraged with promises of the resurrection of the dead, and of the day when Christ shall come the second time. These things are spoken of as the great objects of the expectation and hope of Christians. A state of separation of soul and body is to men an unnatural state. Therefore, when the bodies of the saints shall be raised from the dead and their souls shall be again united to them, as their state will be more natural, so doubtless it will be more happy. Their bodies will be glorious bodies, and prepared to administer as much to their happiness as the bodies of the wicked will be to administer to their misery.

We may with good reason suppose the accession of happiness to the souls of the saints will be great, since the occasion is represented as the marriage of the Church and the Lamb. Revelation 19:7: "The marriage of the Lamb is come, and His wife hath made herself ready." Their joy will then be increased because they will have new arguments of joy. The body of Christ will then be perfect; the Church will be complete; all the parts of it will have come into existence, which will not be the case before the end of the world. No parts of it will be under sin or affliction: all the members of it will be in a perfect state; and they shall all be together by themselves, none being mixed with ungodly men. Then the Church will be as a bride adorned for her husband, and therefore she will exceedingly rejoice.

Then also the Mediator will have fully accomplished His work. He will then have destroyed, and will triumph over, all His enemies. Then Christ will have fully obtained His reward, and fully accomplished the design which was in His heart from all eternity. For these reasons Christ Himself will greatly rejoice, and His members must proportionally rejoice with Him. Then God will have obtained the end of all the great works which He has been doing from the beginning of the world. All the designs of God will be unfolded in their events; then His marvelous contrivance in His hidden, intricate, and inexplicable works will appear, the ends being obtained. Then, the works of God being perfected, the divine glory will more abundantly appear. These things will cause a great accession of happiness to the saints who shall behold them.

The Final Judgment

Then God will have fully glorified Himself, His Son, and His elect. Then He will see that all is very good, and will entirely rejoice in His own works. At the same time the saints also, viewing the works of God brought thus to perfection, will rejoice in the view, and receive from it a large accession of happiness. Then God will make more abundant manifestations of His glory, and of the glory of His Son. Then He will more plentifully pour out His Spirit and make answerable additions to the glory of the saints, and by means of all these will so increase the happiness of the saints as shall be suitable to the commencement of the ultimate and most perfect state of things and, to such a joyful occasion, the completion of all things. In this glory and happiness will the saints remain forever and ever.

Application

I. The first proper use to be made of this doctrine is of instruction. Hence many of the mysteries of divine Providence may be unfolded. There are many things in the dealings of God towards the children of men which appear very mysterious if we view them without having an eye to this last judgment, which yet, if we consider this judgment, have no difficulty in them. As:

1. God suffers the wicked to live and prosper in the world. The infinitely holy and wise Creator and Governor of the world must necessarily hate wickedness, yet we see many wicked men spreading themselves as a green bay tree. They live with impunity; things seem to go well with them, and the world smiles upon them. Many who have not been fit to live, who have held God and religion in the greatest contempt, who have been open enemies to all that is good, who by their

wickedness have been the pests of mankind; many cruel tyrants, whose barbarities have been such as would even fill one with horror to hear or read of them, yet have lived in great wealth and outward glory, have reigned over great and mighty kingdoms and empires, and have been honored as a sort of earthly gods.

Now, it is very mysterious that the holy and righteous Governor of the world, whose eye beholds all the children of men, should suffer it so to be, unless we look forward to the day of judgment and then the mystery is unraveled. For although God for the present keeps silence and seems to let them alone, yet then He will give suitable manifestations of His displeasure against their wickedness. They shall then receive condign punishment. The saints under the Old Testament stumbled much at these dispensations of Providence, as you may see in Job 21, Psalm 88, and Jeremiah 12. The difficulty to them was so great because then a future state and a day of judgment were not revealed with that clearness with which they are now.

2. God sometimes suffers some of the best of men to be in great affliction, poverty, and persecution. The wicked rule while they are subject; the wicked are the head, and they are the tail; the wicked domineer while they serve and are oppressed, yea, are trampled under their feet as the mire of the streets. These things are very common, yet they seem to imply great confusion. When the wicked are exalted to power and authority, and the godly are oppressed by them, things are quite out of joint. Proverbs 25:26: "A righteous man falling down before the wicked is as a troubled fountain, and a corrupt spring." Sometimes one wicked man makes many hundreds, yea, thousands of precious saints a sacrifice to his lust and cruelty, or to his enmity against virtue and the truth, and puts them to death for no other reason but that for which

they are especially to be esteemed and commended.

Now, if we look no further than the present state, these things appear strange and unaccountable. But we ought not to confine our views within such narrow limits. When God shall have put an end to the present state, these things shall all be brought to rights. Though God suffers things to be so for the present, yet they shall not proceed in this course always; comparatively speaking, the present state of things is but for a moment. When all shall be settled and fixed by a divine judgment, the righteous shall be exalted, honored, and rewarded, and the wicked shall be depressed and put under their feet. However the wicked now prevail against them, the righteous shall at last have the ascendant, shall come off as conquerors, and shall see the just vengeance of God executed upon those who now hate and persecute them.

3. It is another mystery of Providence that God suffers so much public injustice to take place in the world. There are not only private wrongs, but wrongs done by men acting in a public character, and wrongs which affect nations, kingdoms, and other public bodies of men. Many suffer by men in public offices from whom there is no refuge, from whose decisions there is no appeal. Now it seems a mystery that these things are tolerated when He who is rightfully the supreme Judge and Governor of the world is perfectly just. But at the final judgment all these wrongs shall be adjusted, as well as those of a more private nature.

II. Our second use of this subject shall be to apply it to the awakening of sinners. You who have not the fear of God before your eyes, who are not afraid to sin against Him, consider seriously what you have heard concerning the day of judgment. Although these things are now future and unseen, yet they are real and certain. If you now are left to yourselves, if

God keeps silent and judgment is not speedily executed, it is not because God does not regard how you live and how you behave yourselves. Now, indeed, God is invisible to you, and His wrath is invisible; but at the day of judgment you yourselves shall see Him with your bodily eyes. You shall not then be able to keep out of His sight or avoid seeing Him. Revelation 1:7: "Behold He cometh with clouds; and every eye shall see Him, and they also which pierced Him: and all kindreds of the earth shall wail because of Him." You shall see Him coming in the clouds of heaven; your ears shall hear the last trumpet, that dreadful sound, the voice of the archangel; your eyes shall see your Judge sitting on the throne. They shall see those manifestations of wrath which there will be in His countenance; your ears shall hear Him pronounce the sentence.

Seriously consider, if you live in the ways of sin, and appear at that day with the guilt of it upon you, how you will be able to endure the sight or the hearing of these things, and whether horror and amazement will not be likely to seize you when you shall see the Judge descending and hear the trump of God. What account will you be able to give when it shall be inquired of you why you led such a sinful, wicked life? What will you be able to say for yourselves, when it shall be asked why you neglected such and such particular duties, such as the duty of secret prayer, for instance? Or why you have habitually practiced such and such particular sins or lusts? Although you are so careless of your conduct and manner of life, make so light of sin, and proceed in it so freely with little or no dread or remorse, yet you must give an account of every sin that you commit, of every idle word that you speak, and of every sinful thought of your hearts. Every time you deviate from the rules of justice, of temperance, or of charity; every time you indulge any lust, whether secretly or openly, you must give an account of it. It will never be forgotten; it stands written in that book which will be opened on that day.

Consider the rule you will be judged by. It is the perfect rule of the divine law, which is exceedingly strict and exceedingly broad. And how will you ever be able to answer the demands of this law? Consider also that:

1. The judge will be your supreme Judge. You will have no opportunity to appeal His decision. This is often the case in this world: when we are dissatisfied with the decisions of a judge, we often may appeal to a higher, a more knowing or a more just judicatory. But no such appeal can be made from our Divine Judge; no such indulgence will be allowed; or, if it were allowed, there is no superior judge to whom the appeal should be made. By His decision, therefore, you must abide.

2. The Judge will be omnipotent. Were He a mere man like yourselves, however He might judge and determine, you might resist and, by the help of others, if not by your own strength, prevent or elude the execution of the judgment. But the Judge being omnipotent, this is utterly impossible. In vain is all resistance, either by yourselves or by whatever help you can obtain. "Though hand join in hand, the wicked shall not be unpunished" (Proverbs 11:21). As well might you "set the briers and thorns in battle against God" (Isaiah 27:4).

3. The Judge will be inexorable. Human judges may be prevailed upon to reverse their sentence, or at least to remit something of its severity. But in vain will be all your entreaties, all your cries and tears to this effect with the great Judge of the world. Now indeed He inclines His ear, and is ready to hear the prayers, cries, and entreaties of all mankind; but then the day of grace will be past and the door of mercy be shut; then although you spread forth your hands, yet the Judge will hide His eyes from you; yea, though you make many prayers, He will not hear (Isaiah 1:15). Then the Judge

will deal in fury. "His eye shall not spare, neither will He have pity: and though ye cry in His ears with a loud voice, yet will He not hear you" (Ezekiel 8:18). And you will find no place of repentance in God, though you seek it carefully with tears.

4. The Judge at that day will not mix mercy with justice. The time for mercy to be shown to sinners will then be past. Christ will then appear in another character than that of the merciful Savior. Having laid aside the inviting attributes of grace and mercy, He will clothe Himself with justice and vengeance. He will not only, in general, exact of sinners the demands of the law, but He will exact the whole without any abatement. He will exact the very uttermost farthing (Matthew 5:26). Then Christ will come to fulfill Revelation 14:10: "The same shall drink of the wine of the wrath of God, which is poured out without mixture, into the cup of his indignation." The punishment threatened to ungodly men is without any pity. Ezekiel 5:11: "Neither shall Mine eye spare, neither will I have any pity." Here all judgments have a mixture of mercy; but the wrath of God will be poured out upon the wicked without mixture, and vengeance will have its full weight.

III. I shall apply myself to several different characters of men.

1. To those who live in secret wickedness, let such consider that for all these things God will bring them into judgment. Secrecy is your temptation. Promising yourselves this, you practice many things; you indulge many lusts under the cover of darkness, and in secret corners, which you would be ashamed to do in the light of the sun and before the world. But this temptation is entirely groundless. All your secret abominations are even now perfectly known to God, and will also hereafter be made known both to angels and men. Luke

12:2–3: "For there is nothing covered that shall not be revealed; neither hid, that shall not be known. Therefore, whatsoever you have spoken in darkness shall be heard in the light, and that which ye have spoken in the ear in closets shall be proclaimed upon the housetops."

Before human judges are brought only those things which are known, but before this Judge shall be brought the most "hidden things of darkness," and "the counsels of the heart" (1 Corinthians 4:5). All your secret uncleanness, all your secret fraud and injustice, all your lascivious desires, wishes, and designs, all your inward covetousness, which is idolatry, all your malicious, envious, and vengeful thoughts and purposes, whether brought forth into practice or not, shall then be made manifest, and you shall be judged according to them. Of these things, however secret, there will be need of no other evidence than the testimony of God and your own consciences.

2. To such as are not just and upright in their dealings with their fellow men, consider that all your dealings with men must be tried, brought forth into judgment, and there compared with the rules of the Word of God. All your actions must be judged according to those things which are found written in the book of the Word of God. If your ways of dealing with men shall not agree with those rules of righteousness, they will be condemned. Now, the Word of God directs us to practice entire justice. "That which is altogether just shalt thou follow" (Deuteronomy 16:20), and to do to others as we would they should do to us. But how many are there whose dealings with their fellow men, if strictly tried by these rules, would not stand the test!

God has, in His Word, forbidden all deceit and fraud in our dealings one with another (Leviticus 11:13). He has forbidden us to oppress one another (Leviticus 25:14). But how frequent are practices contrary to those rules, and which will not bear to be tried by them! How common are fraud and trickishness in trade! How will men endeavor to lead on those with whom they trade in the dark so that they may make their advantage! Yea, lying in trading is too common a thing among us. How common are such things as that mentioned in Proverbs 20:14: "It is naught, it is naught, saith the buyer; but when he is gone his way, then he boasteth"?

Many men will take the advantage of another's ignorance to advance their own gain to his wrong; yea, they seem not to scruple such practices. Beside downright lying, men have many ways of blinding and deceiving one another in trade, which are by no means right in the sight of God, and will appear to be very unjust when they shall be tried by the rule of God's Word at the day of judgment. And how common a thing is oppression or extortion, in taking any advantage that men can by any means obtain to get the utmost possible of their neighbor for what they have to dispose of and their neighbor's needs!

Let such consider that there is a God in heaven who beholds them and sees how they conduct themselves in their daily traffic with one another. And He will try their works another day. Justice shall assuredly take place at last. The righteous Governor of the world will not suffer injustice without control. He will control and rectify it by returning the injury upon the head of the injurer. Matthew 7:2: "With what measure ye mete, it shall be measured to you again."

3. To those who plead for the lawfulness of practices generally condemned by God's people, you who do this, consider that your practices must be tried at the day of judgment. Consider whether or not they are likely to be approved by the most holy Judge at that day. Proverbs 5:21: "The ways of man are before the eyes of the Lord; and He pondereth all his go-

ings." However, by your carnal reasonings, you may deceive your own hearts, yet you will not be able to deceive the Judge. He will not hearken to your excuses, but will try your ways by the rule. He will know whether they be straight or crooked.

When you plead for these and those liberties which you take, let it be considered whether they are likely to be allowed by the Judge at the last great day. Will they bear to be tried by His eyes, which are purer than to behold evil, and cannot look on iniquity?

4. To those who are wont to excuse their wickedness, will the excuses which you make for yourselves be accepted at the day of judgment? If you excuse yourselves to your own consciences by saying that you were under such and such temptations which you could not withstand, that corrupt nature prevailed and you could not overcome it, that it would have been so and so to your damage if you had done otherwise, that if you had done such a duty you would have brought yourselves into difficulty and would have incurred the displeasure of such and such friends, or would have been deposed and laughed at; or if you say you did no more than it was the common custom to do, no more than many godly men have done, no more than certain persons of good reputation now practice; that if you had done otherwise you would have been singular—if these are your excuses for the sins which you commit, or for the duties which you neglect, let me ask you, will they appear sufficient when they shall be examined at the day of judgment?

5. This is to those who live in impenitence and unbelief. There are some persons who live in no open vice, and perhaps conscientiously avoid secret immorality, who yet live in impenitence and unbelief. They are indeed called upon to repent and believe the gospel, to forsake their evil ways and thoughts, and to return to God that He may have mercy on

them; to come unto Christ, laboring and heavy laden with sin, that they may obtain rest of Him. They are assured that if they believe they shall be saved, and that if they believe not they shall be damned; and all the most powerful motives are set before them to induce them to comply with these exhortations, especially those drawn from the eternal world. Yet they persist in sin; they remain impenitent and unhumbled; they will not come unto Christ that they may have eternal life.

Now such men shall be brought into judgment for their conduct as well as more gross sinners. Nor will they be any more able to stand in the judgment than the other. They resist the most powerful means of grace, go on in sin against the clear light of the gospel, refuse to hearken to the kindest calls and invitations, reject the most amiable Savior, the Judge Himself, and despise the free offers of eternal life, glory, and felicity. And how will they be able to answer for these things at the tribunal of Christ?

IV. If there is a day of judgment appointed, then let all be very strict in trying their own sincerity. God, on that day, will discover the secrets of all hearts. The judgment of that day will be like the fire which burns up whatsoever is not truly good; wood, hay, stubble, and dross shall be all consumed by the scorching fire of that day. The Judge will be like a refiner's fire and a fuller's soap, which will cleanse away all filthiness, however it may be colored over. Malachi 3:2: "Who may abide the day of His coming? And who shall stand when He appeareth? For He is like a refiner's fire, and like fuller's soap." And 4:1: "For behold the day cometh that shall burn as an oven, and all the proud, yea, and all that do wickedly, shall be stubble, and the day that cometh shall burn them up, saith the Lord of hosts."

There are multitudes of men who wear the guise of saints,

appear like saints, and their state, both in their own eyes and in the eyes of their neighbors, is good. They have sheep's clothing, but no disguise can hide them from the eyes of the Judge of the world. His eyes are as a flame of fire; they search the hearts and try the reins of the children of men. He will see whether they are sound at heart. He will see from what principles they have acted. A fair show will in no degree deceive Him as it does men in the present state. It will signify nothing to say, "Lord, we have eaten and drunk in Thy presence; and in Thy name have we cast out devils, and in Thy name have done many wonderful works." It will signify nothing to pretend to a great deal of comfort and joy, to the experience of great religious affections, and to your having done many things in religion and morality unless you have some greater evidences of sincerity.

Wherefore let everyone take heed that he is not deceived concerning himself, and that he depends not on that which will not bear examination at the day of judgment. Be not contented that you have the judgment of men, the judgment of godly men, or that of ministers in your favor. Consider that they are not to be your judges at last. Take occasion frequently to compare your hearts with the Word of God; that is the rule by which you are to be finally tried and judged. And try yourselves by your works, by which also you must be tried at last. Inquire whether you lead holy Christian lives, whether you perform universal and unconditional obedience to all God's commands, and whether you do it from a truly gracious respect to God.

Also frequently beg God, the Judge, that He would search you, try you now, and discover you to yourselves that you may see if you are insincere in religion, that He would lead you in the way everlasting. Beg God that if you are not upon a good foundation, He would unsettle you and fix you upon the sure foundation. The example of the psalmist in this is worthy of imitation. Psalm 26:1–2: "Judge me, O Lord, examine me, and prove me; try my reins and my heart." And Psalm 139:23–24: "Search me, O God, and know my heart: try me, and know my thoughts. And see if there be any wicked way in me, and lead me in the way everlasting." God will search us hereafter and discover what we are, both to ourselves and to all the world. Let us pray that He would search us and discover our hearts to us now. We have need of divine help in this matter, for the heart is deceitful above all things.

V. If God has appointed a day to judge the world, let us judge and condemn ourselves for our sins. This we must do if we would not be judged and condemned for them on that day. If we would escape condemnation, we must see that we justly may be condemned; we must be so sensible of our vileness and guilt as to see that we deserve all that condemnation and punishment which are threatened, and that we are in the hands of God, who is the sovereign Disposer of us, and will do with us as seems good to Himself. Let us therefore often reflect on our sins, confess them before God, condemn and abhor ourselves, be truly humbled, and repent in dust and ashes.

VI. If these things are so, let us by no means be forward to judge others. Some are forward to judge others, to judge their hearts both in general and upon particular occasions, to determine as to the principles, motives, and ends of their actions. But this is to assume the province of God and set up ourselves as lords and judges. Romans 14:4: "Who art thou that judgest another man's servant?" James 4:11: "Speak not evil one of another, brethren. He that speaketh evil of his brother, and judgeth his brother, speaketh evil of the law, and judgeth the law." To be thus disposed to judge and act censoriously towards others is the way to be judged and condemned ourselves. Matthew 7:1–2: "Judge not, that ye be not judged. For with what judgment ye judge, ye shall be judged; and with what measure ye mete, it shall be measured to you again."

VII. This doctrine affords matter of great consolation to the godly. This day of judgment, which is so terrible to ungodly men, affords no ground of terror to you, but abundant ground of joy and satisfaction. For though you now meet with more affliction and trouble than most wicked men, yet on that day you shall be delivered from all afflictions, and from all trouble. If you are unjustly treated by wicked men, and abused by them, what a comfort is it to the injured that they may appeal to God who judges righteously. The psalmist used often to comfort himself with this.

Upon these accounts the saints have reason to love the appearing of Jesus Christ. 2 Timothy 4:8: "Henceforth there is laid up for me a crown of righteousness, which the Lord, the righteous Judge, shall give me at that day; and not to me only, but to all those that love His appearing." This is to the saints a blessed hope. Titus 2:13: "Looking for that blessed hope, and the glorious appearing of the great God and our Savior Jesus Christ." This day may well be the object of their eager desire, and when they hear of Christ's coming to judgment they may well say, "Even so, come, Lord Jesus" (Revelation 22:20). It will be the most glorious day that ever the saints saw; it will be so both to those who shall die, and whose souls shall go to heaven, and to those who shall then be found alive on earth. It will be the wedding day of the Church. Surely, then, in the consideration of the approach of this day, there is ground of great consolation to the saints.

The Portion of the Wicked

"But unto them that are contentious, and do not obey the truth, but obey unrighteousness, indignation and wrath, tribulation and anguish, upon every soul of man that doeth evil, of the Jew first, and also of the Gentile." Romans 2:8–9

It is the drift of the apostle in the three first chapters of this epistle to show that both Jews and Gentiles are under sin, and therefore cannot be justified by works of the law, but only by faith in Christ. In the first chapter he had shown that the Gentiles were under sin: in this he shows that the Jews also are under sin, and that however severe they were in their censures upon the Gentiles, yet they themselves did the same things, for which the apostle very much blames them: "Therefore thou art inexcusable, O man, whosoever thou art that judgest, for wherein thou judgest another, thou condemnest thyself; for thou that judgest doest the same things" (Romans 2:1). And he warns them not to go on in such a way by forewarning them of the misery to which they will expose themselves by it, and by giving them to understand that instead of their misery being less than that of the Gentiles, it would be the greater for God's distinguishing goodness to them above the Gentiles. The Jews thought that they should be exempted from future wrath, because God had chosen them to be His peculiar people. But the apostle informs them that there should be indignation and wrath, tribulation and anguish, to every soul of man, not only to the Gentile, but to every soul, and to the Jews first and chiefly, when they did evil, because their sins were more aggravated.

In the text we find:

1. A description of wicked men, in which may be observed those qualifications of wicked men which have the nature of a cause and those which have the nature of an effect. Those qualifications of wicked men here mentioned that have the nature of a cause are their being contentious and not obeying the truth, but obeying unrighteousness. By their being contentious is meant their being contentious against the truth, their quarreling with the gospel, their finding fault with its declarations and offers. Unbelievers find many things in the ways of God at which they stumble and by which they are offended. They are always quarreling and finding fault with one thing or another whereby they are kept from believing the truth and yielding to it. Christ is to them a stone of stumbling and a rock of offense. They do not obey the truth, that is, they do not yield to it; they do not receive it with faith. That yielding to the truth and embracing it which there is in saving faith is called "obeying" in Scripture. Romans 6:17: "But God be thanked that ye were the servants of sin, but ye have obeyed from the heart that form of doctrine which was delivered you." Hebrews 5:9: "And being made perfect, He became the author of eternal salvation unto all them that obey Him." Romans 1:5: "By whom we have received grace and apostleship, for obedience to the faith among all nations for His name." But they obey unrighteousness instead of yielding to the gospel; they are under the power and dominion of sin, and are slaves to their lusts and corruptions.

It is in those qualifications of wicked men that their wickedness radically consists; their unbelief and opposition to the truth and their slavish subjection to lust are the foundation of all wickedness.

Those qualifications of wicked men which have the nature

of an effect are their doing evil. This is the least of their opposition against the gospel and of their slavish subjection to their lusts: that they do evil. Those wicked principles are the foundation and their wicked practice is the superstructure; those were the root and this is the fruit.

2. The punishment of wicked men, in which may be also noticed the cause and the effect.

Those things mentioned in their punishment that have the nature of a cause are indignation and wrath—the indignation and wrath of God. It is the anger of God that will render wicked men miserable; they will be the subjects of divine wrath, and hence will arise their whole punishment.

Those things in their punishment that have the nature of an effect are tribulation and anguish. Indignation and wrath in God will work extreme sorrow, trouble, and anguish of heart in them.

DOCTRINE. Indignation, wrath, misery, and anguish of soul are the portion that God has allotted to wicked men.

Every one of mankind must have the portion that belongs to him. God allots to each one his portion; and the portion of the wicked is nothing but wrath, distress, and anguish of soul. Though they may enjoy a few empty and vain pleasures and delights for a few days while they stay in this world, yet that which is allotted to them by the Possessor and Governor of all things to be their portion is only indignation and wrath, tribulation and anguish. This is not the portion that wicked men choose; the portion that they choose is worldly happiness, yet it is the portion that God carves out for them. It is the portion that they in effect choose for themselves; for they choose those things that naturally and necessarily lead to it, and those that they are plainly told, times without number, will issue in it. Proverbs 8:36: "But he that sinneth against Me wrongeth his own soul; all they that hate Me love death." But whether they choose it or not, this will and must be the portion to all eternity of all who live and die wicked men. Indignation and wrath shall pursue them as long as they live in this world, shall drive them out of the world, and shall follow them into another world; and there wrath and misery shall abide upon them throughout eternity.

The method that I shall take in treating this subject will be to describe the wrath and misery of which wicked men shall be the subjects, both here and hereafter, in the successive parts and periods of it, according to the order of time.

I. I shall describe the wrath that often pursues wicked men in this life. Indignation and wrath often begin with them here.

1. God oftentimes in wrath leaves them to themselves. They are left in their sins, left to undo themselves and work out their own ruin. He lets them alone in sin. Hosea 4:17: "Ephraim is joined to his idols; let him alone." He often leaves them to go great lengths in sin, and does not afford them that restraining grace that He does to others. He leaves them to their own blindness so that they remain ignorant of God and Christ, and of the things that belong to their peace. They are sometimes left to hardness of heart, to be stupid and senseless, so that nothing will ever thoroughly awaken them. They are left to their own hearts' lusts, to continue in some wicked practices all their days. Some are left to their covetousness, some to drunkenness, some to uncleanness, some to a proud, contentious, and envious spirit, and some to a spirit of finding fault and quarreling with God. God leaves them to their folly to act exceedingly foolishly, to delay and put off the concerns of their souls from time to time, never to think the present time the best, but always to keep it at a distance, and foolishly to continue flattering themselves with hopes of long life, and to put far away the evil day, and to bless themselves in their

hearts and say, "I shall have peace, though I add drunkenness to thirst." Some are so left that they are miserably hardened and senseless, when others all around them are awakened, are greatly concerned, and inquire what they shall do to be saved.

Sometimes God leaves men to a fatal backsliding for a misimprovement of the strivings of His Spirit. They are left alone to backslide perpetually. Dreadful is the life and condition of those who are thus left of God. We have instances of the misery of such in God's holy Word, particularly of Saul and Judas. Such are, sometimes, very much left to the power of Satan to tempt them, to hurry them on in wicked courses, and exceedingly to aggravate their own guilt and misery.

2. Indignation and wrath are sometimes exercised towards them in this world by their being cursed in all that concerns them. They have this curse of God following them in everything. They are cursed in all their enjoyments. If they are in prosperity, it is cursed to them; if they possess riches, if they have honor, if they enjoy pleasure, there is the curse of God that attends it. Psalm 92:7: "When the wicked spring as the grass, and when all the workers of iniquity do flourish, it is that they may be destroyed for ever."

There is a curse of God that attends their ordinary food—every morsel of bread which they eat and every drop of water which they drink. Psalm 69:22: "Let their table become a snare before them; and that which should have been for their welfare, let it become a trap." They are cursed in all their employments, in whatsoever they put their hands to, when they go into the field to labor or are at work at their respective trades. Deuteronomy 28:16: "Cursed shalt thou be in the city, and cursed shalt thou be in the field." The curse of God remains in the houses where they dwell, and brimstone is scattered in their habitations (Job 18:15). The curse of God attends them in the afflictions which they meet with, whereas the afflictions that good men meet with are fatherly corrections, and are sent in mercy. The afflictions which wicked men meet with are in wrath, and come from God as an enemy, and are the foretaste of their everlasting punishment. The curse of God attends them also in their spiritual enjoyments and opportunities, and it would have been better for them not to have been born in a land of light. Their having the Bible and the sabbath is only to aggravate their guilt and misery. The Word of God, when preached to them, is a savor of death unto death. Better would it be for them if Christ had never come into the world, if there had never been any offer of a Savior. Life itself is a curse to them; they live only to fill up the measure of their sins. What they seek in all the enjoyments, employments, and concerns of life is their own happiness; but they never obtain it. They never obtain any true comfort; all the comforts which they have are worthless and unsatisfying. If they lived a hundred years with never so much of the world in their possession, their life is all filled up with vanity. All that they have is vanity of vanities; they find no true rest for their souls. They do but feed on the east wind and have no real contentment. Whatever outward pleasures they may have, their souls are starving.

They have no true peace of conscience; they have nothing of the favor of God. Whatever they do, they live in vain and to no purpose. They are useless in the creation of God; they do not answer the end of their being. They live without God and have not the presence of God, nor any communion with Him. But, on the contrary, all that they have and all that they do does but contribute to their own misery, and renders their future and everlasting state the more dreadful. The best of wicked men live but miserable and wretched lives. With all their prosperity, their lives are most undesirable; and whatever they have, the wrath of God abides upon them.

3. After a time they must die. Ecclesiastes 9:3: "This is an evil among all things that are done under the sun, that there is one event unto all: yea, also the hearts of the sons of men are full of evil, and madness is in their heart while they live, and after that they go to the dead."

Death is a far different thing, when it befalls wicked men, from what it is when it befalls good men. To the wicked it is an execution of the curse of the law and of the wrath of God. When a wicked man dies, God cuts him off in wrath. He is taken away as a tempest of wrath; he is driven away in his wickedness. Proverbs 14:32: "The wicked is driven away in his wickedness; but the righteous hath hope in his death." Job 18:18: "He shall be driven from light into darkness, and chased out of the world." Job 27:21: "The east wind carrieth him away, and he departeth, and as a storm hurleth him out of his place." Though wicked men, while they live, may live in worldly prosperity, yet they cannot live here always but they must die. The place that knows him shall know him no more; and they who have seen him shall see him no more in the land of the living.

Their bounds are unchangeably set, and when they are come to those bounds they must go, and must leave all their worldly good things. If they have lived in outward glory their glory shall not descend after them; they get nothing while they live that they can carry away. Ecclesiastes 5:15: "As he came forth of his mother's womb, naked shall he return, to go as he came, and shall take nothing of his labor, which he may carry away in his hand." He must leave all his substance unto others. If they are at ease and quietness, death will put an end to their quietness, will spoil all their carnal mirth, and will strip them of all their glory. As they came naked into the world, so naked must they return, and go as they came. If they have laid up much goods for many years, if they have laid in

The Portion of the Wicked

stores, as they hope, for great comfort and pleasure, death will cut them off from all. Luke 12:16–20: "And He spake a parable unto them, saying, The ground of a certain rich man brought forth plentifully; and he thought within himself, saying, What shall I do, because I have no room where to bestow my fruits? And he said, This will I do: I will pull down my barns, and build greater; and there will I bestow all my fruits and my goods. And I will say to my soul, Soul, thou hast much goods laid up for many years; take thine ease, eat, drink, and be merry. But God said unto him, Thou fool! This night thy soul shall be required of thee; then whose shall those things be which thou hast provided?"

If they have many designs and projects in their breasts for promoting their outward prosperity and worldly advantage, when death comes it cuts all off at one blow. Psalm 146:4: "His breath goeth forth, he returneth to his earth; in that very day his thoughts perish." And so whatever diligence they have had in seeking their salvation, death will disappoint all such diligence; it will not wait for them to accomplish their designs and fulfill their schemes. If they have pleased and pampered and adorned their bodies, death will spoil all their pleasures and their glory; it will change their countenances to a pale and ghastly aspect. Instead of their fine apparel and beautiful ornaments, they shall have only a winding sheet; their house must be the dark and silent grave; and that body which they deified shall turn to loathsome rottenness; it shall be eaten of worms and turn to dust.

Some wicked men die in youth; wrath pursues them and soon overtakes them; they are not suffered to live out half their days. Job 36:14: "They die in youth, and their life is among the unclean." Psalm 55:23: "But thou, O God, shall bring them down into the pit of destruction; bloody and deceitful men shall not live out half their days." They are sometimes overtaken in the very midst of their sin and vanity; and death puts a sudden end to all their youthful pleasures. They are often stopped in the midst of a career in sin; and then, if their hearts cleave ever so fast to those things, they must be rent from them. They have no other good but outward good; but then they must eternally forsake it. They must close their eyes forever on all that has been dear and pleasant to them here.

4. Wicked men are oftentimes the subjects of much tribulation and anguish of heart on their deathbeds. Sometimes the pains of body are very extreme and dreadful; and what they endure in those agonies and struggles for life, after they are past speaking, and when body and soul are being rent asunder, none can know. Hezekiah had an awful sense of it; he compared it to a lion's breaking all his bones. Isaiah 38:12–13: "Mine age is departed, and is removed from me as a shepherd's tent: I have cut off as a weaver my life; He will cut me off with pining sickness: from day even to night wilt Thou make an end of me. I reckoned till morning, that, as a lion, so will He break all my bones: from day even to night wilt Thou make an end of me."

But this is but little to what is sometimes undergone by wicked men in their souls when they are on their deathbeds. Death appears sometimes with an exceedingly terrible aspect to them when it comes and stares them in the face. They cannot bear to behold it. It is always so, if wicked men have notice of the approach of death, and have reason and conscience in exercise, and are not either stupid or distracted. When this king of terrors comes to show himself to them, and they are called forth to meet him, Oh, how do they dread the conflict! But meet him they must: "There is no man that hath power over the spirit to retain the spirit, neither hath he power in the day of death; and there is no discharge in that war,

The Portion of the Wicked

neither shall wickedness deliver those that are given to it." Death comes to them with all his dreadful armor, and his sting not taken away; and it is enough to their souls with torment that cannot be expressed.

It is an awful thing for a person to be lying on a sick bed, to be given over by physicians, to have friends stand weeping round the bed as expecting to part with him, and in such circumstances as those to have no hope; to be without an interest in Christ, and to have the guilt of his sins lying on his soul; to be going out of the world without his peace being made with God; to stand before His holy judgment seat in all his sins without anything to plead or answer. To see the only opportunity to prepare for eternity coming immediately to an end, after which there shall be no more time of probation, but his case will be unalterably fixed, and there never will be another offer of a Savior; for the soul to come just to the very edge of the boundless gulf of eternity, and insensibly to launch forth into it without any God or Savior to take care of it; to be brought to the edge of the precipice, and to see himself falling down into the lake of fire and brimstone, and to feel that he has no power to stop himself—who can tell the shrinkings and misgivings of heart in such a case?

How does he endeavor to hang back, but yet he must go on; it is in vain to wish for further opportunity! Oh, how happy does he think those who stand about him, who may yet live, may have their lives continued longer when he must go immediately into an endless eternity! How does he wish it might be with him as with those who have a longer time to prepare for their trial! But it must not be so. Death, sent on purpose to summon him, will give him no release nor respite: he must go before the holy judgment seat of God as he is, to have his everlasting state determined according to his works. To such persons, how differently do things appear from what they did in the time of health, and when they looked at death as at a distance! How differently does sin look to them now, those sins which they used to make light of! How dreadful is it now to look back and consider how they have spent their time! How foolish they have been! How they have gratified and indulged their lusts, and lived in ways of wickedness! How careless they have been, and how they have neglected their opportunities and advantages! How they have refused to hearken to counsel, and have not repented in spite of all the warnings that were given! Proverbs 5:11–13: "And thou mourn at the last, when thy flesh and thy body are consumed, and say, How have I hated instruction, and my heart despised reproof; and have not obeyed the voice of my teachers, nor inclined mine ear to them that instructed me!"

How differently does the world appear to them now! They used to set much by it, and have their hearts taken up with it; but what does it avail them now? How insignificant are all their riches! Proverbs 11:4: "Riches profit not in the day of wrath, but righteousness delivereth from death." What different thoughts have they now of God and His wrath! They used to make light of the wrath of God, but how terrible does it now appear! How does their heart shrink at the thoughts of appearing before such a God! How different are their thoughts of time! Now time appears precious, and oh, what would they not give for a little more time!

Some have in such circumstances been brought to cry out, "Oh, a thousand worlds for an hour, for a moment!" And how differently does eternity now appear! Now it is awful indeed.

Some have been brought on a deathbed to cry out, "Oh, that word 'Eternity! Eternity! Eternity!' " What a dismal gulf does it appear to them when they come to the very brink! They often at such times cry for mercy, and cry in vain. God called and they would not hear. "They set at naught His counsels, and would none of His reproofs. Now also He laughs at their calamity, and mocks when their fear cometh." They beseech others to pray for them; they send for ministers, but all often fails them. They draw nearer and nearer to death, and eternity comes more and more immediately in view. And who can express their horror when they feel themselves clasped in the cold arms of death, when their breath fails more and more, and their eyes begin to be fixed and grow dim! That which is then felt by them cannot be told nor conceived. Some wicked men have much of the horror and despair of hell in their last sickness. Ecclesiastes 5:17: "All his days also he eateth in darkness, and he hath much sorrow and wrath with his sickness."

II. I shall describe the wrath that attends wicked men hereafter.
1. The soul, when it is separated from the body, shall be cast down into hell. There is, without doubt, a particular judgment by which every man is to be tried at death beside the general judgment; for the soul, as soon as it departs from the body, appears before God to be judged. Ecclesiastes 12:7: "Then shall the dust return to the earth as it was; and the spirit shall return unto God who gave it," that is, to be judged and disposed of by Him. Hebrews 9:27: "It is appointed unto men once to die, but after this the judgment." But this particular judgment is probably no such solemn transaction as that which will be at the day of judgment; the soul must appear before God, but not in the manner that men shall appear at the end of the world. The souls of wicked men shall not go to heaven to appear before God; neither shall Christ descend from heaven for the soul to appear before Him; neither is it to be supposed that the soul shall be carried to any place where there is some special symbol of the divine presence in

order to be judged. But as God is everywhere present, so the soul shall be made immediately sensible of His presence. Souls in a separate state shall be sensible of the presence of God and of His operations in another manner than we now are. All separate spirits may be said to be before God: the saints are in His glorious presence, and the wicked in hell are in His dreadful presence; they are said to be tormented in the presence of the Lamb. Revelation 14:10: "The same shall drink of the wine of the wrath of God, which is poured out without mixture into the cup of His indignation; and he shall be tormented with fire and brimstone in the presence of the holy angels, and in the presence of the Lamb." So the soul of a wicked man, at its departure from the body, will be made immediately sensible that it is before an infinitely holy and dreadful God, and his own final Judge. And he will then see how terrible a God He is; he will see how holy a God He is, how infinitely He hates sin. He will be sensible of the greatness of God's anger against sin, and how dreadful is His displeasure. Then will he be sensible of the dreadful majesty and power of God, and how fearful a thing it is to fall into His hands.

Then the soul shall come naked with all its guilt, and in all its filthiness, a vile, loathsome, abominable creature, an enemy to God, a rebel against Him, with the guilt of all its rebellion and disregard of God's commands, and contempt of His authority, and slight of the glorious gospel, before God as its Judge. This will fill the soul with horror and amazement. It is not to be supposed that this judgment will be attended with any voice, or any such outward transactions as the judgment at the end of the world; but God shall manifest Himself in His strict justice inwardly to the immediate view of the soul, and to the sense and apprehension of the conscience. This particular judgment probably will not hinder, but that the soul shall

The Portion of the Wicked

be cast into hell immediately when it goes from the body. As soon as the soul departs from the body, the soul shall know what its state and condition are to be to all eternity. As long as there is life, there is hope. The man, while he lived, though his case was exceedingly dreadful, yet had some hope; when he lay dying, there was a possibility of salvation. But once the union between soul and body is broken, then that moment the case becomes desperate, and there remains no hope, no possibility.

On their deathbeds, perhaps, they had some hope that God would pity them and hear their cries, or that He would hear the prayers of their pious friends for them. They were ready to lay hold on something which they had at some time met with, some religious affection or some change in their external conduct, and to flatter themselves that they were then converted. They were able to indulge some degree of hope from the moral lives that they had lived that God would have respect to them and save them; but as soon as ever the soul departs from the body, from that moment the case will be absolutely determined. There will then be an end forever to all hope, to everything that men hang upon in this life. The soul then shall know certainly that it is to be miserable to all eternity without any remedy. It shall see that God is its enemy; it shall see its Judge clothed in His wrath and vengeance. Then its misery will begin; it will that moment be swallowed up in despair; the great gulf will be fixed between it and happiness; the door of mercy will be forever shut up; the irrevocable sentence will be passed.

Then shall the wicked know what is before them. Before, the soul was in distress for fear how it would be; but now, all its fears shall come upon it. They shall come upon it as a mighty flood, and there will be no escaping. The soul was full of amazement before through fear; but now, who can conceive the amazement that fills it that moment when all hope is cut off, and it knows that there never will be any difference!

When a good man dies, his soul is conducted by holy angels to heaven. Luke 16:22: "And it came to pass that the beggar died, and was carried by the angels into Abraham's bosom; the rich man also died and was buried." So we may well suppose that, when a wicked man dies, his soul is seized by wicked angels; they are round his bed ready to seize the miserable soul as soon as it is parted from the body. And with what fierceness and fury do those cruel spirits fly upon their prey; and the soul shall be left in their hands. There shall be no good angels to guard and defend it. God will take no merciful care of it; there is nothing to help it against those cruel spirits that shall lay hold of it to carry it to hell, there to torment it forever. God will leave it wholly in their hands, and will give it up to their possession, when it comes to die. It shall be carried down into hell, to the abode of devils and damned spirits. If the fear of hell on a deathbed sometimes fills the wicked with amazement, how will they be overwhelmed when they feel its torments, when they shall find them not only as great, but far greater than their fears! They shall find them far beyond what they could conceive of before they felt them; for none know the power of God's anger but those who experience it. Psalm 90:11: "Who knoweth the power of Thine anger? Even according to Thy fear, so is Thy wrath."

Departed spirits of wicked men are doubtless carried to some particular place in the universe which God has prepared to be the receptacle of His wicked, rebellious, and miserable subjects; a place where God's avenging justice shall be glorified; a place built to be the prison where devils and wicked men are reserved till the day of judgment.

2. Here the souls of wicked men shall suffer extreme and

amazing misery in a separate state until the resurrection. This misery is not indeed their full punishment, nor is the happiness of the saints before the day of judgment their full happiness. It is with the souls of wicked men as it is with devils. Though the devils suffer extreme torment now, yet they do not suffer their complete punishment; and therefore it is said that they are cast down to hell and bound in chains. 2 Peter 2:4: "God spared not the angels that sinned, but cast them down to hell, and delivered them into chains of darkness, to be reserved unto judgment." Jude 6: "And the angels which kept not their first estate, but left their own habitation, He hath reserved in everlasting chains under darkness, unto the judgment of the great day." They are reserved in the state they are in; and for what are they reserved, but for a greater degree of punishment? And therefore they are said to tremble for fear. James 2:19: "Thou believest that there is one God; thou doest well: the devils also believe and tremble." Hence when Christ was on earth, the devils were greatly afraid that Christ had come to torment them. Matthew 8:29: "And, behold, they cried out, saying, What have we to do with Thee, Jesus, Thou Son of God? Art Thou come hither to torment us before the time?" Mark 5:7: the unclean spirit "cried with a loud voice, and said, What have I to do with Thee, Jesus, Thou Son of the most high God? I adjure Thee by God, that Thou torment me not."

But yet they are there in extreme and inconceivable misery; they are there deprived of all good; they have no rest nor comfort, and they are subject to the wrath of God. God there executes wrath on them without mercy, and they are swallowed up in wrath. Luke 16:24: "And he cried and said, Father Abraham, have mercy on me, and send Lazarus, that he may dip the tip of his finger in water and cool my tongue; for I am tormented in this flame." Here we are told that, when the rich man died, he lifted up his eyes being in torment, and he told Abraham that he was tormented in a flame. And it seems that the flame was not only *about* him, but *in* him. He therefore asked for a drop of water to cool his tongue. This doubtless is to represent to us that they are full of the wrath of God, as it were, with fire, and they shall there be tormented in the midst of devils and damned spirits; and they shall have inexpressible torment from their own consciences.

God's wrath is the fire that never shall be quenched, and conscience is the worm that never dies. How much do men suffer from horror of conscience sometimes in this world, but how much more in hell! What bitter and tormenting reflections will they have concerning the folly they have been guilty of in their lives in so neglecting their souls when they had such an opportunity for repentance; that they went on so foolishly to treasure up wrath against the day of wrath, to add to the record of their sins from day to day, to make their misery yet greater and greater. How they have kindled the fires of hell for themselves, and spent their lives in gathering the fuel! They will not be able to help revolving such thoughts in their minds; and how tormented will they be!

And those who go to hell never can escape thence; there they remain imprisoned till the day of judgment, and their torments remain continually. Those wicked men who died many years ago, their souls went to hell, and there they are still. Those who went to hell in former ages of the world have been in hell ever since, all the while suffering torment. They have nothing else to spend their time in there but to suffer torment. They are kept in being for no other purpose; and, though they have many companions in hell, yet they are no comfort to them, for there is no friend, no love, no pity, no quietness, no prospect, no hope.

3. The separate souls of the wicked, besides the present

misery that they suffer, shall be in amazing fear of their more full punishment at the day of judgment. Though their punishment in their separate state is exceedingly dreadful and far more than they can bear, though it is as great as to sink and crush them, yet this is not all. They are reserved for a much greater and more dreadful punishment at the day of judgment. Their torment will then be vastly augmented, and will continue in that augmentation to all eternity. Their punishment will be so much greater then that their misery in this separate state is but as an imprisonment before an execution; they, as well as the devils, are bound in chains of darkness to the judgment of the great day. Separate spirits are called "spirits in prison" in 1 Peter 3:19: "By which also He went and preached unto the spirits in prison."

And if the imprisonment is so dreadful, how dreadful indeed will be the execution! When we are under any great pain of body at any time, how do we dread the least addition to it! Its continuance is greatly dreaded, much more its increase. How much more will those separate spirits that suffer the torments of hell dread that augmentation and completing of their torment which there will be at the day of judgment, when what they feel already is vastly more than they can support themselves; when they shall be, as it were, begging for one drop of water to cool their tongues; when they would give ten thousand worlds for the least abatement of their misery! How sinking will it be to think that, instead of that, the day is coming when God shall come forth out of heaven to sentence them to a far more dreadful degree of misery, and to continue them under it forever! What experience they have of the dreadfulness of God's wrath convinces them fully how terrible a thing His wrath is. They will therefore be exceedingly afraid of that full wrath which He will execute at the day of judgment. They will have no hope of escaping it; they will know assuredly that it will come.

    The fear of this makes the devils—those mighty, proud, and stubborn spirits—to tremble. They believe what is threatened, and therefore tremble. If this fear overcomes them, how much more will it overwhelm the souls of wicked men! All hell trembles at the thoughts of the day of judgment.

    4. When the day of judgment comes they shall rise to the resurrection of damnation. When that day comes, all mankind that has died from off the face of the earth shall arise; not only the righteous, but also the wicked. Daniel 12:2: "And many of them that sleep in the dust of the earth shall awake, some to everlasting life, and some to shame and everlasting contempt." Revelation 20:13: "And the sea gave up the dead which were in it, and death and hell delivered up the dead which were in them; and they were judged, every man according to his works." The damned in hell know not the time when the day of judgment will be, but when the time comes it will be made known, and it will be the most dreadful news that ever was told in that world of misery.

    It is always a doleful time in hell. The world of darkness is always full of shrieks and doleful cries; but when the news is heard that the day appointed for the judgment has come, hell will be filled with louder shrieks and more dreadful cries than ever before. When Christ comes in the clouds of heaven to judgment, the news of it will fill both earth and hell with mourning and bitter crying. We read that all the kindreds of the earth shall wail because of Him, and so shall all the inhabitants of hell. And then must the souls of the wicked come up to be united to their bodies and stand before the Judge. They shall not come willingly, but shall be dragged forth as a malefactor is dragged out of his dungeon to execution. They were unwilling, when they died, to leave the earth to go to hell; but now they will be much more unwilling to come out of hell to go to the last judgment. It will be no deliverance to them, it will only be a coming forth to their execution. They will hang back, but must come; the devils and damned spirits must come up together. The last trumpet will then be heard, and this will be the most terrible sound to wicked men and devils that ever was heard.

And not only the wicked who shall then be found dwelling on the earth shall hear it, but also those who are in their graves. John 5:28–29: "Marvel not at this; for the hour is coming in the which all that are in the graves shall hear His voice and shall come forth; they that have done good unto the resurrection of life, and they that have done evil unto the resurrection of damnation." And then must the souls of the wicked enter their bodies again, which will be prepared only to be organs of torment and misery. It will be a dreadful sight to them when they come to their bodies again, those bodies which were formerly used by them as the organs and instruments of sin and wickedness, and whose appetites and lusts they indulged and gratified. The parting of soul and body was dreadful to them when they died, but their meeting again at the resurrection will be more dreadful. They shall receive their bodies loathsome and hideous, agreeably to that shame and everlasting contempt to which they shall arise. As the bodies of the saints shall arise more glorious than when on earth, and shall be like unto Christ's glorious body, so we may well suppose that the bodies of the wicked will arise proportionally more deformed and hideous.

Oftentimes, in this world, a polluted soul is hidden in a fine and comely body, but it will not be so then when things shall appear as they are. The form and aspect of the body shall be answerable to the hellish deformity of the soul. Thus shall they rise out of their graves, and shall lift up their eyes, and see the Son of God in the clouds of heaven, in the glory of His Father, with all His holy angels with Him. Then shall they see their Judge in His awful majesty, which will be the most amazing sight to them that ever they saw, and will still add new horrors. That awful and terrible majesty in which He will appear, and the manifestation of His infinite holiness, will pierce their souls. They shall come forth out of their graves all trembling and astonished; fearfulness shall surprise them.

5. Then must they appear before their Judge to give their account. They will find no mountains or rocks to fall upon them that can cover them and hide them from the wrath of the Lamb. Many of them will see others at that time who were formerly their acquaintances, who shall appear with glorious bodies, and with joyful countenances and songs of praise, and mounting up as with wings to meet the Lord in the air while they are left behind. Many shall see their former neighbors and acquaintances, their companions, their brothers, and their wives taken and they left. They shall be summoned to go appear before the judgment seat; and go they must, however unwilling. They must stand at Christ's left hand in the midst of devils and wicked men. This shall again add still further amazement, and will cause their horror still to be in a further degree than ever. With what horror will that company come together! And then shall they be called to their account; then shall be brought to light the hidden things of darkness; then shall all the wickedness of their hearts be made known; then shall be declared the actual wickedness they have been guilty of; then shall appear their secret sins that they have kept hidden from the eye of the world; then shall be manifested in their true light those sins that they used to plead for, and to excuse and justify. And then shall all their sins be set forth in all their dreadful aggravation; all their filthiness will be brought to light to their everlasting shame and contempt. Then it shall appear how heinous many of those things were

that they in their lifetime made light of; then will it appear how dreadful their guilt is in thus ill treating so glorious and blessed a Savior. And all the world shall see it; many shall rise up in judgment against them and condemn them: their companions whom they tempted to wickedness, and others whom they have hardened in sin by their example shall rise up against many of them; and the heathen who have had no advantages in comparison to them, and many of whom have yet lived better lives than they shall rise up against them; and they shall be called to a special account. The Judge will reckon with them, and they shall be speechless. They shall be struck dumb, their own consciences bearing testimony against them, and shall cry aloud against them, for they shall then see how great and terrible a God He is against whom they have sinned. Then shall they stand at the left hand, while they see others whom they knew on earth sitting at the right hand of Christ in glory, shining forth as the sun, accepted of Christ, and sitting with Him to judge and condemn them.

6. Then the sentence of condemnation shall be pronounced by the Judge upon them. Matthew 25:41: "Depart from Me, ye cursed, into everlasting fire, prepared for the devil and his angels." This sentence will be pronounced with awful majesty; and there shall be great indignation, and dreadful wrath shall then appear in the Judge, and in His voice, with which He shall pronounce the sentence; and what a horror and amazement will these words strike into the hearts of the wicked on whom they shall be pronounced! Every word and syllable shall be like the most amazing thunder to them, and shall pierce their souls like the fiercest lightning. The Judge will bid them depart from Him. He will drive them from His presence, as exceedingly abominable to Him, and He shall give them the epithet "accursed." They shall be an accursed company, and He will not only bid them

depart from His presence, but into everlasting fire, to dwell there as their only fit habitation. And what shows the dreadfulness of the fire is that it is prepared for the devil and his angels. These shall lie forever in the same fire in which the devils, those grand enemies of God, shall be tormented.

When this sentence shall be pronounced, there shall be, in the vast company at the left hand, tremblings, and mourning, and crying, and gnashing of teeth, in a new manner, beyond all that ever was before. If the devils, those proud and lofty spirits, tremble many ages beforehand at the bare thoughts of this sentence, how will they tremble when it comes to be pronounced! And how, alas! will wicked men tremble! Their anguish will be aggravated by hearing that blessed sentence pronounced on those who shall be at the right hand: "Come, ye blessed of My Father, inherit the kingdom prepared for you from the foundation of the world."

7. Then the sentence shall be executed. When the Judge bids them depart, they must go; however loath, yet they must go. Immediately upon the finishing of the judgment and the pronouncing of the sentence will come the end of the world. The frame of this world shall be dissolved. The pronouncing of that sentence will probably be followed with amazing thunders that shall rend the heavens and shake the earth out of its place. 2 Peter 3:10: "But the day of the Lord will come as a thief in the night; in the which the heavens shall pass away with a great noise, and the elements shall melt with fervent heat, the earth also and the works that are therein shall be burnt up." Then shall the sea and the waves roar, the rocks shall be thrown down, the mountains shall be rent asunder, and there shall be one universal wreck of this great world. Then shall the heavens be dissolved and then the earth shall be set on fire. As God in wrath once destroyed the world by a flood of water, so now shall He cause it to be all drowned in a

The Portion of the Wicked

deluge of fire; and the heavens being on fire shall be dissolved, and the elements shall melt with fervent heat (2 Peter 3:10), and that great company of devils and wicked men must then enter into those everlasting burnings to which they are sentenced.

8. In this condition they shall remain throughout the never-ending ages of eternity. Their punishment shall be then complete, and it shall remain in this completion forever. Now shall all that come upon them which they so long trembled for fear of, while their souls were in a separate state. They will dwell in a fire that never shall be quenched, and here they must wear out eternity. Here they must wear out one thousand years after another, and that without end. There is no reckoning up the millions of years or millions of ages. All arithmetic here fails; no rules of multiplication can reach the amount, for there is no end. They shall have nothing to do to pass away their eternity but to conflict with those torments—this will be their work forever and ever. God shall have no other use or employment for them. This is the way that they must answer the end of their being. And they never shall have any rest, nor any atonement, but their torments will hold up to their height, and shall never grow any easier by their being accustomed to them. Time will seem long to them; every moment shall seem long to them, but they shall never have done with the ages of their torment.

Application

1. Hence what need have we to take care that our foundation for eternity is sure! They who build on a false foundation are not secure from this misery. They who build up a refuge of lies will find that their refuge must fail them. The wall that they have daubed with untempered mortar will fall. The more

dreadful the misery is, the more need have we to see that we are safe from it; it will be dreadful indeed to be disappointed in such a case. To please ourselves with dreams and vain imaginations of our being the children of God, of going to heaven, and at last to awake in hell; to see our refuge swept away and our hope eternally gone, to find ourselves swallowed up in flames and to see an endless duration of it before us—how dreadful will this be!

There will be many who will be thus disappointed. Many shall come to the door and shall find it shut who expected to find it open; and shall knock, but Christ will tell them that He knows them not, and He will bid them depart, and it will be in vain for them to tell Christ what affections they have had, how religious they were, and how well they were accounted of on earth. They shall have no other answer but "Depart from Me, I know you not, ye that work iniquity."

Let us all consider this, and give all diligence to see that we build sure, if by any means we may at last be found in Christ. Let us see to it that we are indeed well secured from this dreadful misery. What will it avail us to please ourselves with a notion of being converted and being beloved of God, and what will it avail us to have the good opinion of our neighbors for a few days, if we must at last be cast into hell and appear at the day of judgment at the left hand, and have our eternal portion with unbelievers! A false hope cannot profit us; it is a thousand times worse than none. And who are more miserable than those who think that God has pardoned their sins, and who expect to have a portion with the righteous hereafter, but are all the while going headlong down into this dreadful misery? What case can be more awful than the case of those who are thus led blindfolded to the slaughter, promising themselves a happiness that is never likely to come, but who, on the contrary, are sinking into endless tribulation and anguish!

Let everyone therefore who entertains hope of his own state see to it that he is well built; and let him not rest in past attainment, but reach forth towards those things that are before with all his might.

2. Hence we derive an argument for the awakening of ungodly men. This indignation and wrath, tribulation and anguish, is the portion allotted to you if you continue in your present condition. You are the man spoken of; it is to you that all this misery is assigned by the threatening of God's holy word; it is on you that this wrath of God abides; you are now in a state of condemnation to this misery. John 3:18: "He that believeth not is condemned already, because he hath not believed in the name of the only begotten Son of God." It is not already executed upon you, but you are already condemned to it.

You are not merely exposed to condemnation, but you are under the actual sentence of condemnation. This is the portion that is already allotted to you by the law, and you are under the law and not under grace. This misery is the misery into which you are every day in danger of dropping; you are not safe from it one hour. How soon it may come upon you, you know not; you hang over it by a thread that is continually growing more and more feeble. This dreadful misery in all its successive parts belongs to you, and is your due. Your friends and your neighbors, and all around you, if they knew what your condition was, might well lift up a loud and bitter cry over you whenever they behold you, and say, "Here is an unhappy being condemned to be given up eternally into the hands of devils to be tormented by them; here is a miserable man who is in danger every day of being swallowed up in the bottomless gulf of woe and misery. Here is a wretched undone creature condemned to lie down forever in unquenchable fire, and to dwell in everlasting burnings; and he has no interest in a Savior. He has nothing to defend him, he has nothing wherewith to appease the wrath of an offended God." Here consider two things.

First, you have no reason to question whether those future miseries and torments which are threatened in God's Word are realities. Do not flatter yourself with thinking that it may not be so. Say not, "How do I know that it may not be so?" Say not, "How do I know that there is any such misery to be inflicted in another world? How do I know but all is a fable, and that when I come to die there will be an end of me, and that it will be with me as it is with the beasts?" Do not say, "How do I know but that all those things are only bugbears of man's inventing? How do I know that the Scriptures that threaten those things are the word of God; or, if He has threatened those things, it may be it is only to frighten men to keep them to their duty; it may be He never intends to do as He threatens."

I say that there is no ground for any such suspicion, neither is there any reason for it; for that there should be no future punishment is not only contrary to Scripture, but reason. It is a most unreasonable thing to suppose that there should be no future punishment, to suppose that God, who had made man a rational creature able to know his duty, and sensible that he is deserving punishment when he does it not, should let man alone, and let him live as he will, never punish him for his sins, and never make any difference between the good and the bad; that he should make the world of mankind and then let it alone, and let men live all their days in wickedness, in adultery, murder, robbery, and persecution, and the like, and suffer them to live in prosperity, and never punish them; that he should suffer them to prosper in the world far beyond many good men, and never punish them hereafter. How unreasonable is it to suppose that He who made the world should leave things in such confusion, and never take any care of the government of His creatures, and that He should never judge His reasonable creatures! Reason teaches that there is a God, and reason teaches that, if there is, He must be a wise and just God, and that He must take care to order things wisely and justly among His creatures. Therefore it is unreasonable to suppose that man dies like a beast, and that there is no future punishment. And if there is a future punishment, it is unreasonable to suppose that God has not somewhere or other given men warning of it, and revealed to them what kind of punishment they must expect.

Will a wise Lawgiver keep His subjects in ignorance as to what punishment they must expect for breaking His laws? And if God has revealed it, where is it to be found but in the Scripture? What revelation have we of a future state if it is not there revealed? Where does God tell mankind what kind of rewards and punishments they must expect, if not there? And it is abundantly manifest by innumerable evidences that these threatenings are the threatenings of God, that this awful book is His revelation. And since God has threatened, there is no room to question whether He will fulfill; for He has said it, yea, He has sworn that He will repay the wicked to his face according to threatenings, and that He will glorify Himself in their destruction, and that this heaven and earth shall pass away.

How foolish, then, is the thought that God may only threaten such punishment to frighten men, and that He never intends to execute it! For as surely as God is God, He will do as He has said. He will destroy the mountains of iniquity as He has threatened, and there shall be no escaping. How vain are the thoughts of those who flatter themselves that God will not fulfill His threatenings, and that He only frightens and deceives men in them; as though God could in no other way govern the world than by making use of fallacious tricks and deceits to delude His subjects!

Those who entertain such thoughts, however they may harden themselves by them for the present, will cherish them but a little while; their experience will soon convince them that God is a God of truth, and that His threatenings are no delusions. They will be convinced that He is a God who will by no means clear the guilty, and that His threatenings are substantial and not mere shadows, when it will be too late to escape them. Deuteronomy 29:18–21: "Lest there should be among you man, or woman, or family, or tribe, whose heart turneth away this day from the Lord our God, to go and serve the gods of these nations; lest there should be among you a root that beareth gall and wormwood; and it come to pass, when he heareth the words of this curse, that he bless himself in his heart, saying, I shall have peace, though I walk in the imagination of mine heart, to add drunkenness to thirst: the Lord will not spare him, but then the anger of the Lord and His jealousy shall smoke against that man, and all the curses that are written in this book shall lie upon him, and the Lord shall blot out his name from under heaven. And the Lord shall separate him unto evil out of all the tribes of Israel, according to all the curses of the covenant that are written in this book of the law." Psalm 50:21: "These things hast thou done, and I kept silence; thou thoughtest that I was altogether such an one as thyself: but I will reprove thee, and set them in order before thine eyes."

Second, there is no reason to suspect that ministers possibly set forth this matter beyond what it really is, that possibly it is not so dreadful and terrible as is pretended, and that ministers strain the description of it beyond just bounds. Some may be ready to think so because it seems to them incredible that

The Portion of the Wicked

there should be so dreadful a misery to any creature; but there is no reason for any such thoughts as these, if we consider:

How great a punishment the sins of wicked men deserve. The Scripture teaches us that any one sin deserves eternal death. Romans 6:23: "For the wages of sin is death, but the gift of God is eternal life through Jesus Christ our Lord." And it deserves the eternal curse of God. Deuteronomy 27:26: "Cursed be he that confirmeth not all the words of this law to do them. And all the people shall say, Amen." Galatians 3:10: "For as many as are of the works of the law are under the curse; for it is written, Cursed is every one that continueth not in all things which are written in the book of the law to do them." These things imply that the least sin deserves total and eternal destruction. Eternal death, in the least degree of it, amounts to such a degree of misery as is the perfect destruction of the creature, the loss of all good, and perfect misery; and so being accursed of God implies it. To be cursed of God is to be devoted to perfect and ultimate destruction. The Scripture teaches that wicked men shall be punished to their full desert, that they shall pay all the debt.

There is no reason to think that ministers describe the misery of the wicked beyond what it is because the Scripture teaches us that this is one end of ungodly men: to show the dreadfulness and power of God's wrath. Romans 9:22: "What if God, willing to show His wrath, and to make His power known, endured with much longsuffering the vessels of wrath fitted to destruction?" It is often spoken of as part of the glory of God that He is a terrible and dreadful God (Psalm 68:35: "O God, Thou art terrible out of Thy holy places"), that He is a consuming fire (Psalm 66:3: "How terrible art Thou in Thy works! through the greatness of Thy power shall Thine enemies submit themselves unto Thee"), and that herein one part of the glory of God is represented as consisting in that it is so dreadful a thing to injure and offend God. The wrath of a king is as the roaring of a lion. The wrath of a man is sometimes dreadful, but the future punishment of ungodly men is to show what the wrath of God is; it is to show to the whole universe the glory of God's power. 2 Thessalonians 1:9: "Who shall be punished with everlasting destruction from the presence of the Lord, and from the glory of His power." And therefore the punishment which we have described is not at all incredible, and there is no reason to think that it has been in the least described beyond what it really is.

The Scripture teaches that the wrath of God on wicked men is dreadful beyond all that we can conceive. Psalm 90:11: "Who knoweth the power of Thine anger? Even according to Thy fear, so is Thy wrath." As it is but little that we know of God, as we know and can conceive of but little of His power and His greatness, so it is but a little that we know or can conceive of the dreadfulness of His wrath; and therefore there is no reason to suppose that we set it forth beyond what it is. We have rather reason to suppose that after we have said our utmost and thought our utmost, all that we have said or thought is but a faint shadow of the reality.

We are taught that the reward of the saints is beyond all that can be spoken or conceived of. Ephesians 3:20: "Now unto Him that is able to do exceeding abundantly above all that we can ask or think." 1 Corinthians 2:9: "Eye hath not seen, nor ear heard, neither have entered into the heart of man, the things which God hath prepared for them that love Him." And so we may rationally suppose that the punishment of the wicked will also be inconceivably dreadful.

There is no reason to think that we set forth the misery of hell beyond the reality, because the Scripture teaches us that the wrath of God is according to His fear. Psalm 90:11 asserts that the wrath of

The Portion of the Wicked

God is according to His awful attributes: His greatness and His might, His holiness and power. The majesty of God is exceedingly great and awful, but, according to His awfulness, so is His wrath. This is the meaning of the words, and therefore we must conclude that the wrath of God is indeed terrible beyond all expression and signification. How great and awful indeed is His majesty who has made heaven and earth, and in what majesty will He come to judge the world at the last day! He will come to take vengeance on ungodly men. The sight of this majesty will strike wicked men with apprehensions and fears of destruction.

The description which I have given of the tribulation and wrath of ungodly men is not beyond the truth, for it is the very description which the Scriptures give of it. The Scriptures represent that the wicked shall be cast into a furnace of fire; not only a fire, but a furnace. Matthew 13:42: "And shall cast them into a furnace of fire; there shall be wailing and gnashing of teeth." Revelation 20:15: "And whosoever was not found written in the book of life was cast into the lake of fire." Psalm 21:8–9: "Thine hand shall find out all Thine enemies; Thy right hand shall find out those that hate Thee. Thou shalt make them as a fiery oven in the time of Thine anger; the Lord shall swallow them up in His wrath, and the fire shall devour them."

If, therefore, I have described this misery beyond the truth, then the Scriptures have done the same. It is evident, then, that there is no reason to flatter yourselves with such imaginations. If God is true, you shall find the wrath of God, and your future misery, fully as great; and not only so, but much greater. You will find that we know but little, and have said but little about it, and that all our expressions are faint in comparison to the reality.

3. Hence may be derived an argument to convince wicked men of the justice of God in allotting such a portion to them.

Wicked men, when they hear it declared how awful the misery is of which they are in danger, often have their hearts lifted up against God for it; it seems to them very hard for God to deal so with any of His creatures. They cannot see why God should be so very severe with wicked men for their sin and folly for a little while in this world; and when they consider that He has threatened such punishments, they are ready to entertain blasphemous thoughts against Him. I would therefore endeavor to show you how justly you lie exposed to that indignation and wrath, tribulation and anguish, of which you have heard. Particularly I would show:

First, how just it would be in God forever to leave you to yourself: it would be most just in God to refuse to be with you, or help you.

You have embraced and refused to let go those things which God hates. You have refused to forsake your lusts, and to abandon those ways of sin that are abominable to Him. When God has commanded you to forsake them, how have you refused and still have retained them, and been obstinate in it! Neither is your heart yet to this very day diverted from sin; but it is dear to you. You allow it the best place in your heart; you place it on the throne there. Would it be any wonder, therefore, if God should utterly leave you, seeing you will not leave sin? God has often declared His hatred of iniquity; and is it any wonder that He is not willing to dwell with that which is so odious to Him? Is it not reasonable that God should insist that you should part with your lusts in order to your enjoying His presence? And seeing you have so long refused, how just would it be if God should utterly forsake you? You have retained and harbored God's mortal enemies, sin and Satan. How justly therefore might God stand at a distance! Is God obliged to be present with any who harbor His enemies and refuse to forsake them? Would God be unjust if

The Portion of the Wicked

He should leave you utterly to yourself, so long as you will not forsake your idols? Consider how just it would be in God to let you alone, since you have let God alone. You have not sought God for His presence and help as you ought to have done. You have neglected Him, and would it not therefore be just if He should neglect you? How long have many of you lived in neglecting to seek Him? How long have you restrained prayer before Him? Since therefore you refused so much as to seek the presence and help of God, and did not think them worth praying to Him for, how justly might He forever withhold them, and so leave you wholly to yourself?

You have done what in you lies to drive God away from you, and to cause Him wholly to leave you. When God in times past has not let you alone, but has been unwearied in awakening you, have you not resisted the motions and influences of His Spirit? Have you not refused to be conducted by Him or to yield to Him? Zechariah 7:11: "But they refused to hearken, and pulled away the shoulder, and stopped their ears, that they should not hear." How justly therefore might God refuse to move or strive any more!

When God has been knocking at your door, you have refused to open to Him. How just is it therefore that He would go away and knock at your door no more! When the Spirit of God has been striving with you, have you not been guilty of grieving the Holy Spirit by giving way to a quarreling temper, and by yielding yourself a prey to lust? And have not some of you quenched the Spirit and been guilty of backsliding? And is God obliged, notwithstanding all this, to continue the striving of His Spirit with you, to be resisted and grieved still as long as you please? On the contrary, would it not be just if His Spirit should everlastingly leave you and let you alone?

Second, how just it would be if you should be cursed in all

your concerns in this world. It would be just if God should curse you in everything, and cause everything you enjoy or are concerned in to turn to your destruction.

You live here in all the concerns of life as an enemy to God. You have used all your enjoyments and possessions against God and to His dishonor. Would it not therefore be just if God should curse you in them, and turn them all against you and to your destruction? What temporal blessing has God given you which you have not used in the service of your lusts, in the service of sin and Satan? If you have been in prosperity, you have made use of it to God's dishonor. When you have waxed fat, you have forgotten the God that made you. How just therefore would it be if God's curse should attend all your enjoyments!

Whatsoever employments you have followed, you have not served God in them, but God's enemies. How just therefore would it be if you should be cursed in all your employments! The means of grace that you have enjoyed, you have not made use of as you ought to have done; you have made light of them and have treated them in a careless, disregardful manner. You have been the worse and not the better for them. You have so attended and used sabbaths and spiritual opportunities that you have only made them occasions of manifesting your contempt of God and Christ and divine things by your careless and profane manner of attending them. Would it not therefore be most just that God's curse should attend your means of grace, and the opportunities which you enjoy for the salvation of your soul?

You have improved your time only to heap up provocations and add to your transgressions, in opposition to all the calls and warnings that could be given you. How just therefore would it be if God should turn life itself into a curse to you, and suffer you to live only to fill up the measure of your sins!

You have, contrary to God's counsel, made use of your own enjoyments to the hurt of your soul, and therefore, if God should turn them to the hurt and ruin of your soul, He would but deal with you as you have dealt with yourself. God has earnestly counseled you times without number to use your temporal enjoyments for your spiritual good, but you have refused to hearken to Him. You have foolishly perverted them to treasure up wrath against the day of wrath. You have voluntarily used what God has given you for your spiritual hurt, to increase your guilt and wound your own soul; and therefore, if God's curse should attend them so that they should all turn to the ruin of your soul, you would but be dealt with as you have dealt with yourself.

Third, how just would it be in God to cut off and put an end to your life! You have greatly abused the patience and long-suffering of God, which have already been exercised towards you. God, with wonderful long-suffering, has borne with you when you have gone on in rebellion against Him and refused to turn from your evil ways. He has beheld you going on obstinately in the ways of provocation against Him, and yet He has not let loose His wrath against you to destroy you, but has still waited to be gracious. He has suffered you yet to live on His earth and breathe His air. He has upheld and preserved you, and continued still to feed you and clothe you and maintain you, and still to give you a space to repent; but, instead of being the better for His patience, you have been the worse. Instead of being melted by it, you have been hardened, and it has made you the more presumptuous in sin. Ecclesiastes 8:11: "Because sentence against an evil work is not executed speedily, therefore the heart of the sons of men is fully set in them to do evil."

You have been guilty of despising the riches of His goodness, forbearance, and long-suffering instead of being led to repent by them. You cannot live one day but as God maintains and provides for you; you cannot draw a breath or live a moment unless God upholds you; for in His hand your breath is, and He holds your soul in life, and His visitation preserves your spirit. But what thanks has God had for it? How have you, instead of being turned to God, been only rendered the more fully set and dreadfully hardened in the ways of sin! How just therefore would it be if God's patience should soon be at an end, and He should cease to bear with you any longer!

You have not only abused His past patience, but have also abused His thoughts of future patience. You have flattered yourself that death was not near, that you should live long in the world, and this has made you abundantly the more bold in sin. Since, therefore, such has been the use you have made of your expectation of having your life preserved, how just would it be in God to disappoint that expectation and cut you short of that long life with which you have flattered yourself, and in the thoughts of which you have encouraged yourself in sin against Him! How just would it be if your breath should soon be stopped, and that suddenly, when you think not of it, and you should be driven away in your wickedness!

As long as you live in sin you do but cumber the ground, you are wholly unprofitable and live in vain. He who refuses to live to the glory of God does not answer the end of his creation, and for what should he live? God made men to serve Him; to this end He gave them life, and if they will not devote their lives to this end, how just would it be in God if He should refuse to continue their lives any longer! He has planted you in His vineyard to bear fruit; and if you bring forth no fruit why should He continue you any longer? How just would it be in Him to cut you down!

As long as you live, many of the blessings of God are spent

upon you from day to day. You devour the fruits of the earth and consume much of its fatness and sweetness; and all to no purpose but to keep you alive to sin against God and spend all in wickedness. The whole creation groans, as it were, with you; the sun rises and sets to give you light, the clouds pour down rain upon you, and the earth brings forth her fruits and labors from year to year to supply you; and you, in the meantime, do not answer the end of Him who has created all things. How just therefore would it be if God should soon cut you off, take you away, and deliver the earth from this burden that the creation may no longer groan with you and cast you out as an abominable branch! Luke 13:7: "Then said he unto the dresser of his vineyard, Behold, these three years I come seeking fruit on this fig tree, and find none; cut it down, why cumbereth it the ground?" John 15:2 and 6: "Every branch in Me that beareth not fruit He taketh away; and every branch that beareth fruit He purgeth it, that it may bring forth more fruit. If a man abide not in Me, he is cast forth as a branch, and is withered; and men gather them, and cast them into the fire, and they are burned."

Fourth, how just would it be if you should die in the greatest horror and amazement! How often have you been exhorted to improve your time to lay a foundation of peace and comfort on a deathbed; and yet you have refused to hearken! You have been many and many a time reminded that you must die, that it was very uncertain when, and that you did not know how soon, and have been told how mean and insignificant all your earthly enjoyments would then appear, and how unable to afford you any comfort on a deathbed. You have been often told how dreadful it would be to lie on a deathbed in a Christ-less state, having nothing to comfort you but your worldly enjoyments. You have been often put in mind of the torment and amazement which sinners who have misspent their precious time are subject to when arrested by death. You have been told how infinitely you would then need to have God your friend, and to have the testimony of a good conscience, and a well-grounded hope of future blessedness. And how often have you been exhorted to take care to provide against such a day as this, and to lay up treasure in heaven that you might have something to depend on when you parted from this world, something to hope for when all things here below fail!

But remember how regardless you have been, how dull and negligent from time to time, when you have sat under the hearing of such things; and still you obstinately refuse to prepare for death, and take no care to lay a good foundation against that time. And you have not only been counseled, but you have seen others on their deathbeds in fear and distress, or have heard of them and have not taken warning; yea, some of you have been sick yourselves, and have been afraid that you were on your deathbeds, yet God was merciful to you, and restored you; but you did not take warning to prepare for death. How justly therefore might you be the subject of that horror and amazement of which you have heard when you come to die!

And not only so, but how industriously have you spent your time in treasuring up matter for tribulation and anguish at that time! You have not only been negligent of laying a foundation for peace and comfort then, but have spent your time continually and unweariedly in laying a foundation for distress and horror. How have you gone on from day to day, heaping up more and more guilt; more and more wounding your own conscience, still increasing the amount of folly and wickedness for you to reflect upon! How just therefore would it be that tribulation and anguish should then come upon you!

Fifth, how just it is that you should suffer the wrath of God in another world because you have willfully provoked and stirred up that wrath! If you are not willing to suffer the anger of God, then why did you provoke Him to anger? Why did you act as though you would contrive to make Him angry with you? Why did you willfully disobey God? You know that willful disobedience tends to provoke Him who is disobeyed; it is so in an earthly king, or master, or father. If you have a servant who is willfully disobedient, it provokes your anger. And, again, if you would not suffer God's wrath, why have you so often cast a slight on God? If anyone casts a slight on men, it tends to provoke them: how much more may the Infinite Majesty of heaven be provoked when He is condemned! You have also robbed God of His property: you have refused to give Him that which is His own. It provokes men when they are deprived of their due and are dealt injuriously with; how much more may God be provoked when you rob Him!

You have also slighted the kindness of God to you, and that the greatest love and kindness of which you can conceive. You have been supremely ungrateful and have only abused that kindness. Nothing provokes men more than to have their kindness slighted and abused; how much more may God be provoked when men requite His infinite mercy only with disobedience and ingratitude! If therefore you go on to provoke God and to stir up His wrath, how can you expect any other than to suffer His wrath? If then you should indeed suffer the wrath of an offended God, remember it is what you have procured for yourself; it is a fire of your own kindling.

You would not accept deliverance from God's wrath when it has been offered to you. When God had in mercy sent His only begotten Son into the world, you refused to admit Him. You loved your sins too well to forsake them to come to Christ, and for the sake of your sins you have rejected all the offers of a Savior so that you have chosen death rather than life. After you had procured wrath to yourself, you cleaved fast to it and would not part with it for mercy. "All they that hate Me love death" (Proverbs 8:36).

Sixth, how just would it be that you be delivered up into the hands of the devil and his angels, to be tormented by them hereafter, seeing you have voluntarily given yourself up to serve them here! You have hearkened to them rather than to God. How just therefore would it be if God leaves you to them! You have followed Satan and adhered to his interest in opposition to God, and have subjected yourself to his will in this world rather than to the will of God; how just therefore would it be if God should give you up to his will hereafter!

Seventh, how justly may your bodies be made organs of torment to you hereafter, which you have made organs and instruments of sin in this world! You have given up your bodies as a sacrifice to sin and Satan; how justly therefore may God give them up as a sacrifice to wrath! You have employed your bodies as servants to your vile and hateful lusts. How just therefore would it be for God hereafter to raise your bodies to be organs and instruments of misery, and to fill them as full of torment as they have been filled full of sin!

Eighth, the greatest objection of wicked men against the justice of the future punishment which God has threatened is from the greatness of that punishment, that God should inflict upon the finally impenitent torments so extreme, so amazingly dreadful, to have their bodies cast into a furnace of fire of such immense heat and fierceness, there to lie unconsumed and yet full of sense and feeling, glowing within and without, and the soul full of yet more dreadful horror and torment, and so to remain without any remedy or rest forever and ever and ever. And, therefore, I would mention several things to you to show how justly you lie exposed to so dreadful a punishment:

(1) This punishment, as dreadful as it is, is not more so than the Being is great and glorious against whom you have sinned. It is true this punishment is dreadful beyond all expression or conception, and so is the greatness and gloriousness of God as much beyond all expression or conception; and yet you have continued to sin against Him, yea, you have been bold and presumptuous in your sins, and have multiplied transgressions against Him without end. The wrath of God that you have heard of, dreadful as it is, is not more dreadful than that Majesty which you have despised and trampled on is awful. This punishment is indeed enough to fill one with horror barely to think of it; and so it would fill you with at least equal horror to think of sinning so exceedingly against so great and glorious a God if you conceived of it aright. Jeremiah 2:12–13: "Be astonished, O ye heavens, at this, and be horribly afraid; be ye very desolate, saith the Lord. For My people have committed two evils; they have forsaken Me the fountain of living waters, and hewed them out cisterns, broken cisterns, that can hold no water." God's being so infinitely great and excellent has not influenced you not to sin against Him, but you have done it boldly, and made nothing of it thousands of times; and why should this misery, being so infinitely great and dreadful, hinder God from inflicting it on you? 1 Samuel 2:25: "If one man sin against another, the judge shall judge him: but if a man sin against the Lord, who shall entreat for him?"

(2) Your nature is not more averse to such misery as you have heard of than God's nature is averse to such sin as you have been guilty of. The nature of man is very averse to pain and torment, and especially it is exceedingly averse to such dreadful and eternal torment; but yet that does not hinder that it is just that it should be inflicted, for men do not

hate misery more than God hates sin. God is so holy, and is of so pure a nature, that He has an infinite aversion to sin; but yet you have made light of sin, and your sins have been exceedingly multiplied and enhanced. The consideration of God's hating of it has not at all hindered you from committing it; why, therefore, should the consideration of your hating misery hinder God from bringing it upon you? God represents Himself in His Word as burdened and wearied with the sins of wicked men. Isaiah 1:14: "Your new moons and your appointed feasts My soul hateth; they are a trouble unto Me; I am weary to bear them." Malachi 2:17: "Ye have wearied the Lord with your words. Yet ye say, 'Wherein have we wearied Him?' When ye say, 'Everyone that doeth evil is good in the sight of the Lord, and He delighteth in them;' or, 'Where is the God of judgment?' "

(3) You have not cared how much God's honor suffered, and why should God be careful lest your misery be great? You have been told how much these and those things which you have practiced were to the dishonor of God; yet you did not care for that, but went on still multiplying transgressions. The consideration that the more you sinned the more God was dishonored did not in the least restrain you. If it had not been for fear of God's displeasure, you would not have cared though you had dishonored Him ten thousand times as much as you did. As for any respect you had to God, you did not care what became of God's honor, nor of His happiness either, no, nor of His being. Why then is God obliged to be careful how much you suffer? Why should He be careful of your welfare, or use any caution lest He should lay more on you than you can bear?

(4) As great as this wrath is, it is not greater than that love of God which you have slighted and rejected. God, in infinite mercy to lost sinners, has provided a way for them to es-

cape future misery and obtain eternal life. For that end He has given his only begotten Son, a person infinitely glorious and honorable in Himself, being equal with God, and infinitely near and dear to God. It was ten thousand times more than if God had given all the angels in heaven, or the whole world, for sinners. Him He gave to be incarnate, to suffer death, to be made a curse for us, and to undergo the dreadful wrath of God in our place, and thus to purchase for us eternal glory. This glorious person has been offered to you times without number, and He has stood and knocked at your door, till His hairs were wet with the dews of the night; but all that He has done has not won you; you see no form nor comeliness in Him, no beauty that you should desire Him. When He has thus offered Himself to you as your Savior, you never freely and heartily accepted Him. This love which you have thus abused is as great as that wrath of which you are in danger. If you would have accepted it, you might have had the enjoyment of this love instead of enduring this terrible wrath; so that the misery you have heard of is not greater than the love you have despised and the happiness and glory which you have rejected. How just, then, would it be in God to execute upon you this dreadful wrath, which is not greater than that love which you have despised! Hebrews 2:3: "How shall we escape if we neglect so great a salvation?"

(5) If you complain of this punishment as being too great, then why has it not been great enough to deter you from sin? As great as it is, you have made nothing of it. When God threatened to inflict it on you, you did not mind His threatenings, but were bold to disobey Him and do those very things for which He threatened this punishment. Great as this punishment is, it has not been great enough to keep you from living a willfully wicked life, and going on in ways that you knew were evil. When you have been told that such and such

things certainly exposed you to this punishment, you did not abstain on that account, but went on from day to day in a most presumptuous manner; and God's threatening such a punishment was no effectual check upon you. Why therefore do you now complain of this punishment as too great and quarrel against it, and say that God is unreasonable and cruel to inflict it? In so saying, you are condemned out of your own mouth; for if it is so dreadful a punishment, and more than is just, then why was it not great enough at least to restrain you from willful sinning? Luke 19:21–22: "I feared thee, because thou art an austere man, thou takest up that thou layest not down, and reapest that thou didst not sow. And he said unto him, Out of thine own mouth will I judge thee, thou wicked servant." You complain of this punishment as too great, but yet you have acted as if it was not great enough, and you have made light of it. If the punishment is too great, why have you gone on to make it still greater? You have gone on from day to day to treasure up wrath against the day of wrath, to add to your punishment and increase it exceedingly; and yet now you complain of it as too great, as though God could not justly inflict so great a punishment. How absurd and self-contradictory is the conduct of such a one who complains of God for making His punishment too great, and yet from day to day industriously gathers and heaps up fuel to make the fire the greater!

(6) You have no cause to complain of the punishment being greater than is just; for you have many and many a time provoked God to do His worst. If you should forbid a servant to do a given thing, and threaten that if he did it you would inflict some very dreadful punishment upon him, and he should do it notwithstanding, and you should renew your command and warn him in the most strict manner possible not to do it, and tell him you would surely punish him if he

persisted, and should declare that his punishment should be exceedingly dreadful, and he should wholly disregard you and should disobey you again, and you should continue to repeat your commands and warnings, still setting out the dreadfulness of the punishment, and he should still, without any regard to you, go on again and again to disobey you to your face, and this immediately on your thus forbidding and threatening him—could you take it any otherwise than as daring you to do your worst?

But thus have you done towards God: you have had His commands repeated and His threatenings set before you hundreds of times, and have been most solemnly warned. Yet you have, notwithstanding, gone on in ways which you knew were sinful, and have done the very things which He has forbidden, directly before His face. Job 15:25–26: "For he stretcheth out his hand against God, and strengtheneth himself against the Almighty. He runneth upon him, even on his neck, upon the thick bosses of his bucklers." You have thus bid defiance to the Almighty, even when you saw the sword of His vindictive wrath uplifted that it might fall upon your head. Will it, therefore, be any wonder if He shall make you know how terrible that wrath is in your utter destruction?

The Wicked Useful in Their Destruction Only

"Son of man, What is the vine tree more than any tree? or than a branch which is among the trees of the forest? Shall wood be taken thereof to do any work? or will men take a pin of it to hang any vessel thereon? Behold, it is cast into the fire for fuel; the fire devoureth both the ends of it, and the midst of it is burned. Is it meet for any work?" Ezekiel 15:2–4

The visible church of God is here compared to the vine tree, as is evident by God's own explanation of the allegory in verse 6: "Therefore thus saith the Lord God, As the vine tree among the trees of the forest, which I have given to the fire for fuel, so will I give the inhabitants of Jerusalem." And it may be understood of mankind in general. So Deuteronomy 32:32: "Their vine is the vine of Sodom, and of the fields of Gomorrah. Their grapes are grapes of gall." And especially His professing people, Psalm 80:8: "Thou hast brought a vine out of Egypt"; verse 14: "Look down from heaven, behold, and visit this vine." And Song of Solomon 2:15: "Take us the foxes that spoil the vines; for our vines have tender grapes." Isaiah 5:1–2: "My beloved hath a vineyard, and he planted it with the choicest vine." Jeremiah 2:21: "I had planted thee a noble vine." Hosea 10:1: "Israel is an empty vine." So in chapter 15 of John, visible Christians are compared to the branches of a vine.

Man is very fitly represented by the vine. The weakness

and dependence of the vine on other things which support it well represents to us what a poor, feeble, dependent creature man is, and how, if left to himself, he falls into mischief and cannot help himself. The visible people of God are fitly compared to a vine because of the care and cultivation of the husbandman or vinedresser. The business of husbandmen in the land of Israel was very much about vines; and the care they exercised to fence them, to defend them, to prune them, to prop them up, and to cultivate them well represented that merciful care which God exercises towards His visible people.

In the words now read is represented how wholly useless and profitable, even beyond other trees, a vine is in case of unfruitfulness: "What is a vine tree more than any tree, or than a branch which is among the trees of the forest?" i.e., if it does not bear fruit. Men make much more of a vine than of other trees; they take great care to wall it in, to dig about it, to prune it and the like. It is much more highly esteemed than one of the trees of the forest; they are despised in comparison with it. And if it bears fruit it is indeed much preferable to other trees; for the fruit of it yields a noble liquor. As it is said in Jotham's parable, in Judges 9:13: "And the vine said unto them, Should I leave my wine, which cheereth God and man?" But if it bears no fruit, it is more unprofitable than the trees of the forest; for the wood of them is good for timber, but the wood of the vine is fit for no work. In the text: "Shall wood be taken thereof to do any work? or will men take a pin of it to hang any vessel thereon?" The only thing for which a vine is useful, in case of barrenness, is for fuel: "Behold, it is cast into the fire for fuel." It is wholly consumed; no part of it is worth saving to make any instrument of it, for any work.

DOCTRINE. If men bring forth no fruit to God, they are wholly useless unless in their destruction.

For the proof of this doctrine, I shall show that:

1. There can be but two ways in which man can be useful: either in acting or in being acted upon.
2. Man cannot otherwise be useful actively than by bringing forth fruit to God.
3. If he brings not forth fruit to God, there is no other way in which he can be passively useful but in being destroyed.
4. In that way he may be useful without bearing fruit.

1. There are but two ways in which man can be useful: either in acting or being acted upon. If man is useful, he must be so either actively or passively; there is no medium. What can be more plain than that if a man does nothing himself, and nothing is done with him or upon him by any other, he cannot be in any way at all useful? If man does nothing himself to promote the end of his existence, and no other being does anything with him to promote this end, then nothing will be done to promote this end; and so man must be wholly useless. So there are but two ways in which man can be useful to any purpose: either actively or passively—either in doing something himself or in being the subject of something done to him.

2. Man cannot be useful actively any other way than in bringing forth fruit to God, serving God and living to His glory. This is the only way wherein he can be useful in doing; and that for this reason: the glory of God is the very thing for which man was made and to which all other ends are subordinate. Man is not an independent being, but he derives his being from another, and therefore has his end assigned him by that other: He who gave him his being made him for the end now mentioned. This was the very design and aim of the Author of man; this was the work for which He made him: to serve and glorify his Maker. Other creatures that are inferior

were made for inferior purposes. But man is the highest and nearest to God of any in this lower world; and therefore his business is with God, although other creatures are made for lower ends. There may be observed a kind of gradual ascent, in the order of different creatures, from the meanest clod of earth to man who has a rational and immortal soul. A plant, an herb, or a tree is superior in nature to a stone or clod because it has a vegetable life. The brute creatures are a degree higher still for they have sensitive life. But man, having a rational soul, is the highest of this lower creation and is next to God; therefore his business is with God.

Things without life, as earth and water, are subservient to things above them, as the grass, herbs, and trees. These vegetables are subservient to that order of creatures which is next above them, the brute creation; they are for food to them. Brute creatures, again, are made for the use and service of the order above them; they are made for the service of mankind. But man being the highest of this lower creation, the next step from him is to God. He therefore is made for the service and glory of God. This is the whole work and business of man; it is his highest end, to which all other ends are subordinate.

If it had not been for this end, there never would have been any such creature; there would have been no occasion for it. Other inferior ends may be answered as well without any such creature as man. There would have been no sort of occasion for making so noble a creature, and enduing him with such faculties, only to enjoy earthly good, to eat, and to drink, and to enjoy sensual things. Brute creatures, without reason, are capable of these things as well as man: yea, if no higher end is aimed at than to enjoy sensitive good, reason is rather a hindrance than a help. It does but render man more capable of afflicting himself with care, fears of death, and other future evils, and of vexing himself with many anxieties from which brute creatures are wholly free, and therefore can gratify their senses with less molestation. Besides, reason does but make men more capable of molesting and impeding one another in the gratification of their senses. If man has no other end to seek but to gratify his senses, reason is nothing but an impediment.

Therefore, if man is not made to serve and glorify his Creator, it is wholly to no purpose that such a creature is made. Doubtless, then, the all-wise God, who does all things in infinite wisdom, has made man for this end. And this is agreeable to what He has taught us in many places in the Scriptures. This is the great end for which man was made and for which he was made such a creature, having bodily senses and rational powers. For this purpose is he placed in such circumstances, and the earth is given him for a possession. For this he has dominion given him over the rest of the terrestrial creatures. For this the sun shines and the rain falls on him, the moon and stars are for signs and seasons to him, and the earth yields him her increase. All other ends of man are subordinate to this.

There are indeed inferior ends for which man was made. Men were made for one another, for their friends and neighbors, and for the good of the public. But all these inferior ends are designed to be subordinate to the higher end of glorifying God; and therefore man cannot be actively useful otherwise than by actively bringing forth fruit to God, because that is not actively useful which does not actively answer its end. That which does not answer its end is in vain, for that is the meaning of the proposition that any thing is in vain. So that which does not actively answer its end is, as to its own activity, in vain.

That, as to its own activity, is altogether useless which actively answers only subordinate ends without answering the ultimate end, because the latter is the end of subordinate ones. Subordinate ends are to no purpose, only as they stand related to the highest end. Therefore these inferior ends are good for nothing, though they are obtained, unless they also obtain their end. Inferior ends are not aimed at for their own sake, but only for the sake of that which is ultimate. Therefore he who fails in this is as much to no purpose as if he did not obtain his subordinate end.

I will illustrate this by two or three examples. The subordinate end of the underpinning of a house is to support it, and the subordinate end of the windows is to let in the light. But the ultimate end of the whole is the benefit of the inhabitants. Therefore, if the house is never inhabited the whole is in vain. The underpinning is in vain, though it is ever so strong and supports the building ever so well. The windows also are wholly in vain, though they are ever so large and clear, and though they obtain the subordinate end of letting in the light; they are as much in vain as if they let in no light.

So the subordinate end of the husbandman in plowing and sowing and well manuring his field is that it may bring forth a crop. But his more ultimate end is that food may be provided for him and his family. Therefore, though his inferior end is obtained, and his field brings forth ever so good a crop, yet if after all it is consumed by fire or otherwise destroyed, he plowed and sowed his field as much in vain as if the seed had never sprung up. So if man obtains his subordinate ends ever so full, yet if he altogether fails in his ultimate end he is wholly a useless creature. Thus if men are very useful in temporal things to their families, or greatly promote the temporal interest of the neighborhood or of the public, yet if no glory is brought to God by it they are altogether useless. If men actually bring no glory to God, they are, as to their own activity, altogether useless, however much they may promote the benefit of one another. However much one part of mankind may subserve another, yet, if the end of the whole is not answered, every part is useless.

Thus if the parts of a clock subserve ever so well one another, mutually to assist each other in their motions, one wheel moving another ever so regularly, yet if the motion never reaches the hand or the hammer, it is altogether in vain, as much as if it stood still. So one man was made to be useful to another, and one part of mankind to another, but the use of the whole is to bring glory to God the Maker or else all is in vain.

Altogether a wicked man may, by being serviceable to good men, do what will be an advantage to them to their bringing forth fruit to God; yet that serviceableness is not what he aims at. He does not look so far for an ultimate end. And however this is obtained, no thanks are due to him: he is only the occasion, and not the designing cause of it.

The usefulness of such a man, being not designed, is not to be attributed to him as though it were his fruit. He is not useful as a man, or as a rational creature, because he is not so designedly. He is useful as things without life may be. Things without life may be useful to put the godly under advantages to bring forth fruit, as the timber and stones with which his house is built, the wool and flax with which he is clothed; but the fruit which is brought forth to God's glory cannot be said to be the fruit of these lifeless things, but of the godly man who makes use of them. So it is when wicked men put the godly under advantages to glorify God, as Cyrus, and Artaxerxes, and others have done.

3. If men bring not forth fruit to God, there is no other way in which they can be useful passively but in being destroyed. They are fit for nothing else.

(1) They are not fit to be suffered to continue always in this world. It is not fit that this world should be the constant abode of those who bring forth no fruit to God. It is not fit that the barren tree should be allowed always to stand in the vineyard. The husbandman lets it stand for a while till he digs about it, dungs it, and proves it to be incurable, or till a convenient time to cut it down comes. But it is not fit that they who bring forth no fruit to God should be suffered to live always in a world which is so full of the divine goodness, or that His goodness should be spent upon them forever. This world, though fallen and under a curse, has many streams of divine goodness. But it is not fit that those who bring forth no fruit to God should always be continued in partaking of these streams. There are three different states: one, wherein is nothing but good, which is heaven; another, wherein is a mixture of good and evil, which is the earthly state; and the third, wherein is nothing but evil, which is the state of eternal destruction. Now those who bring forth no fruit to God are not fit for either of the former.

It is not fit that an unprofitable, unfruitful creature who will not glorify his Creator should always live here to consume the fruits of divine bounty, to have the good things of this life spent upon him in vain. While a man lives here the other creatures are subjected to him, The brute creatures serve him with their labor and with their lives. The sun, moon, and stars, the clouds, fields, and trees, all serve him. But why should God always keep His creatures in subjection to that man who will not be subject to Him? Why should the creation be always kept in such bondage as to be subject to wicked men? The creatures indeed are made subject to vanity. God has subjected them to wicked men, and given them for their use. This, however, He would not have done but as it is only for a little while; and the creatures can bear it through the hope of approaching deliverance; otherwise it would have been intolerable. Romans 8:20: "For the creature was made subject to vanity, not willingly, but by reason of Him who hath subjected the same in hope." The creature, as it were, groans by reason of this subjection to wicked men, although it is but for a while (verse 22): "For we know that the whole creation groaneth and travaileth in pain together until now." Therefore, surely, it would be in no way fit that wicked men, who do no good and bring forth no fruit to God, should live here always to have the various creatures subservient to them, as they are now. The earth can scarcely bear wicked men during that short time for which they stay here. It is in no way fit, therefore, that it should be forced to bear them always.

Men who bring forth no fruit to God are cumberers of the ground (Luke 13:7). And it is not meet that they should be suffered to cumber the ground always. God cannot be glorified in this way of disposing of unfruitful persons. If such men should be suffered to live always in such a state as this, it would be so far from being to the glory of God that it would be to the disparagement of His wisdom to continue them in a state so unsuitable for them.

It would also be a disparagement to His justice, for this is a world where "all things come alike to all, and there is one event to the righteous and to the wicked." If there were no other state but this for wicked men, justice could not possibly take place. It would also reflect upon the holiness of God. Forever to uphold this world for a habitation of such persons, and forever to continue the communications of His bounty and goodness to them, would appear as though He were disposed to countenance and encourage wickedness.

(2) If men do not bring forth fruit to God, they are not fit to be disposed of in heaven. Heaven, above all others, is the most improper place for them, Everything pertaining to

that state is unsuitable for them. The company is most unsuitable. The original inhabitants of that world are the angels. But what a disagreeable union would it be to unite wicked men and angels in the same society!

The employments of that world are unsuitable. The employments are serving and glorifying God. How unsuitable then would it be to plant barren trees in that heavenly paradise, trees that would bring forth no fruit to the divine glory!

The enjoyments of heaven are unsuitable. The enjoyments are holy and spiritual, the happiness of beholding the glory of God, praising His name, and the like. But these enjoyments are as unsuitable as can be to the carnal earthly minds of wicked men. They would be no enjoyments to them, but on the contrary would be most disagreeable, and what they cannot relish but entirely nauseate.

The design of heaven is unsuitable to them. The design of God in making heaven was that it might be a place of holy habitation, for the reward of the righteous, and not a habitation for the wicked. It would greatly reflect on the wisdom of God to dispose of wicked men there; for it would be the greatest confusion. But God is not the author of confusion (1 Corinthians 14:33). It would be contrary to the holiness of God to take wicked men so near to Himself, into His glorious presence, to dwell forever in the part of that creation which is, as it were, His own palace, and to sit at His table. We read in Psalm 5:4: "Thou art not a God that hath pleasure in wickedness, neither shall evil dwell with Thee." Therefore it would be impossible that the end of the existence of wicked men should be answered by placing them in heaven.

4. Men who bring forth no fruit to God may yet, in suffering destruction, be useful. Although they are not useful by

anything they do, yet they may be useful in what they may suffer, just as a barren tree, which is in no way useful standing in the vineyard, may be good fuel. God can find use for the most wicked men. He has His use for vessels of wrath as well as for vessels of mercy. 2 Timothy 2:20: "In a great house there are not only vessels of gold and of silver, but also of wood and of earth, and some to honor, and some to dishonor." Proverbs 16:4: "The Lord hath made all things for Himself; yea, even the wicked for the day of evil." I shall briefly take notice of some ends which God accomplishes by it.

(1) Unfruitful persons are of use in their destruction for the glory of God's justice. The vindictive justice of God is a glorious attribute as well as His mercy; and the glory of this attribute appears in the everlasting destruction and ruin of the barren and unfruitful. The glory of divine justice in the perdition of ungodly men appears wonderful and glorious in the eyes of the saints and angels in heaven. Hence we have an account that they sing praises to God and extol His justice at the sight of the awful judgments which He inflicts on wicked men. Revelation 16:5–6: "Thou art righteous, O Lord, which art, and wast, and shalt be, because Thou hast judged thus. For they have shed the blood of saints and prophets, and Thou hast given them blood to drink; for they are worthy." And Revelation 19:1–2: "And after these things I heard a great voice, saying, Alleluia; salvation, and glory, and honor, and power, unto the Lord our God: for true and righteous are His judgments; for He hath judged the great whore, which did corrupt the earth with her fornication, and hath avenged the blood of His servants at their hand."

(2) Unfruitful persons in their destruction are of use for God to glorify His majesty upon them. The awful majesty of God remarkably appears in those dreadful and amazing punishments which He inflicts on those who rise up against

Him. A sense of the majesty of an earthly prince is supported very much by a sense of its being a dreadful thing to affront him. God glorifies His own majesty in the destruction of wicked men; and herein He appears infinitely great in that it appears to be an infinitely dreadful thing to offend Him. How awful does the majesty of God appear in the dreadfulness of His anger! This we may learn to be one end of the damnation of the wicked, from Romans 9:22: "What if God, willing to show His wrath, and to make His power known, endured with much long-suffering the vessels of wrath fitted to destruction?" This is a part of His majesty and glory. God tells Pharaoh that for this cause He raised him up, that He might show His power in him, and that His name might be declared through all the earth in his destruction (Exodus 9:15–16), and again in chapter 14:17: "I will get Me honor upon Pharaoh, and upon all his host, upon his chariots, and upon his horsemen."

(3) The destruction of the unfruitful is of use to give the saints a greater sense of their happiness and of God's grace to them. The wicked will be destroyed and tormented in the view of the saints and other inhabitants of heaven. This we are taught in Revelation 14:10: "The same shall drink of wine of the wrath of God, which is poured out without mixture, into the cup of His indignation; and he shall be tormented with fire and brimstone in the presence of the holy angels, and in the presence of the Lamb." And in Isaiah 66:24: "And they shall go forth, and look upon the carcasses of the men that have transgressed against Me: for their worm shall not die, neither shall their fire be quenched, and they shall be an abhorring unto all flesh." When the saints in heaven shall look upon the damned in hell, it will serve to give them a greater sense of their own happiness. When they shall see how dreadful the anger of God is, it will make them

the more prize His love. They will rejoice the more that they are not the objects of God's anger, but of His favor; that they are not the subjects of His dreadful wrath, but are treated as His children to dwell in the everlasting embraces of His love. The misery of the damned will give them a greater sense of the distinguishing grace and love of God to them that He should from all eternity set His love on them and make so great a difference between them and others who are of the same species, and have deserved no worse of God than they. What a great sense will this give them of the wonderful grace of God to them! And how will it heighten their praises! With how much greater admiration and exultation of soul will they sing of the free and sovereign grace of God to them!

When they shall look upon the damned and see their misery, how will heaven ring with the praises of God's justice towards the wicked and His grace towards the saints! And with how much greater enlargement of heart will they praise Jesus Christ, their Redeemer, that ever He was pleased to set His love upon them, His dying love! and that He should so distinguish them as to shed His blood, and make His soul an offering to redeem them from that misery, and to bring them to such happiness! With what love and ecstasy will they sing that song in Revelation 5:9–10: "Thou art worthy: for Thou wast slain, and hast redeemed us to God by Thy blood out of every tongue, and kindred, and people, and nation; and hast made us unto our God kings and priests." One end which the apostle mentions why God appointed vessels of wrath is the more to make known the wonderfulness of His mercy towards the saints. In Romans 9:22–23 there are two ends mentioned: "What if God, willing to show His wrath, and to make His power known, endured with much long-suffering the vessels of wrath fitted to destruction?" That is one end; another is mentioned immediately after: "And that He might make known the riches of His glory on the vessels of mercy, which He had afore prepared unto glory."

Application

1. Hence we may learn how just and righteous God is in the destruction of those who bring forth no fruit to Him. Seeing there is no other way in which the end of their being can be obtained, certainly it is most just that God should thus dispose of them. Why should He be frustrated of His end through their perverseness? If men will not do the work for which He has made and fitted them—if they, through a spirit of opposition and rebellion, refuse—why should God suffer Himself to be disappointed of His end in making them? It is not becoming His infinite greatness and majesty to suffer Himself to be frustrated by the wickedness and perverseness of sinful worms of the dust. If God should suffer this, it would seem to argue either a want of wisdom to fix upon a good end or a want of power to accomplish it. God made all men that they might be useful; and if they will not be useful in their conduct and actions how just is it that God should make them useful in their sufferings! He made all men for His own glory, and if they, contrary to the revealed will of God, refuse to glorify Him actively and willingly, how just is it that God should glorify Himself upon them!

Men are under no natural necessity of being put to this use of glorifying God in their sufferings. God gives them opportunity of glorifying Him in bringing forth fruit, puts them under advantages for it, and uses many means to bring them to it. But if they will not be useful in this way, it is very just that God should make them useful in the only remaining way in which they can be useful—in their destruction. God is not forward to put them to this use. He tells us that He has "no pleasure in the death of the wicked; but that the wicked turn from his way, and live" (Ezekiel 33:11). He represents the destruction of sinners as a work to which He is backward; yet it is meet that they should be destroyed rather than that they should be suffered to frustrate the end of their being. Who can blame the husbandman for cutting down and burning a barren tree after he has dug about it, dunged it, and used all proper means to make it fruitful? Let those among us consider this who have lived all their lives hitherto unprofitably, and never have brought forth any fruit to God's glory, notwithstanding all the means that have been used with them. Consider how just it would be if God should utterly destroy you, and glorify Himself upon you in that way; and what a wonderful patience it is that God has not done it before now.

2. This subject ought to put you upon examining whether you are not wholly useless creatures. You have now heard that those who bring forth no fruit to God are, as to any good they do, wholly useless. Inquire, therefore, whether you have ever done anything from a gracious respect to God or out of love to Him. Seeking only your worldly interest, or for you to come to public worship on the sabbath, to pray in your families, and other such things, merely in compliance with the general custom, or that you are sober, moral, and religious only to be seen of men, or out of respect to your own credit and honor, is not bringing forth fruit to God. How is that for God which is only for the sake of custom, the esteem of men, or merely from the fear of hell? What thanks are due to you for not loving your own misery, and for being willing to take some pains to escape burning in hell to all eternity? There is not a devil in hell but would do the same. Hosea 10:1: "Israel is an empty vine; he bringeth forth fruit unto himself."

There is no fruit brought forth to God where there is nothing done from love or true respect to Him. God looks at the heart. He does not stand in need of our services, neither is He benefited by anything that we can do. He does not receive anything of us, but only as a suitable testimony of our love and respect to Him. This is the fruit that He seeks. Men themselves will not accept those shows of friendship which they think are hypocritical, and come not from the heart. How much less should God, who searcheth the hearts and trieth the reins of the children of men! John 4:24: "God is a Spirit, and they that worship Him must worship Him in spirit and in truth." Inquire, therefore, whether you ever did the least thing out of love to God. Have you not done all for yourselves? Zechariah 7:5–6: "When ye fasted and mourned in the fifth and seventh month, even those seventy years, did ye at all fast unto Me, even unto Me? And when ye did eat, and when ye did drink, did ye not eat for yourselves, and drink for yourselves?"

3. Another use of this subject may be of conviction and humiliation to those who never have brought forth any fruit to God. If upon examination you find that you have never in all your lives done anything out of a true respect to God, then it has been demonstrated that, as to anything which you do, you are altogether useless creatures. And consider what a shameful thing it is for such rational beings as you are, and placed under such advantages for usefulness, yet to be wholly useless and to live in the world to no purpose! We esteem it a very mean character in any person that he is worthless and insignificant; and to be called so is taken as a great reproach. But consider seriously whether you can clear yourselves of this charge. Set reason to word; can you rationally suppose that you do in any measure answer the end for which God gave you your being, and made you of a nature superior to the beasts?

But that you may be sensible what cause you have to be

ashamed of your unprofitableness, consider the following things:

(1) Consider how much God has bestowed upon you in the endowments of your nature. God has made you rational, intelligent creatures. He has endued you with noble powers, those endowments wherein the natural image of God consists. You are vastly exalted in your nature above other kinds of creatures here below. You are capable of a thousand times as much as any of the brute creatures. He has given you a power of understanding, which is capable of extending itself, of looking back to the beginning of time, of considering what was before the world, and of looking forward beyond the end of time. It is capable of extending beyond the utmost limits of the universe, and is a faculty whereby you are akin to angels, and are capable even of knowing and contemplating the Divine Being and His glorious perfections, manifested in His works and in His Word. You have souls capable of being the habitation of the Holy Spirit of God and His divine grace. You are capable of the noble employments of angels. How lamentable and shameful is it that such a creature should be altogether useless, and live in vain! How lamentable that such a noble and excellent piece of divine workmanship should fail of its end and be to no purpose! Was it ever worthwhile for God to make you such a creature, with such a noble nature, and so much above other kinds of creatures, only to eat and drink and gratify your sensual appetites? How lamentable and shameful to you that such a noble tree should be more useless than any tree of the forest; that man, whom God has thus set in honor, should make himself more worthless than the beasts that perish!

(2) Consider how much God has done for you in the creation of the world. He made the earth and seas and all their fullness for the use of man. Psalm 115:16: "The earth

hath He given to the children of men." He made the vast variety of creatures for man's use and service. Genesis 1:28: "Have dominion over the fish of the sea, and over the fowl of the air, and over every living thing that moveth upon the earth." For the same purpose He made all the plants, and herbs, and trees of the field. Genesis 1:29: "I have given you every herb bearing seed, which is upon the face of all the earth, and every tree, in the which is the fruit of a tree yielding seed; to you it shall be for meat." He made the sun in the heavens, that glorious luminary, that wonderful globe of light, to give light to man and to constitute the difference between day and night. He also made the moon and the vast multitude of stars to be to him signs and seasons. What great provision has God made for man! What a vast variety of good things for food and convenience to put him under advantages to be useful! How lamentable is it, then, that after all these things he should be a useless creature!

(3) Consider how much is done for you in the course of God's common providence! Consider how nature is continually laboring for you. The sun is, as it were, in a ferment for mankind, and spending his rays upon man to put him under advantage to be useful. The winds and clouds are continually laboring for you, and the waters are going in a constant circulation, ascending in the air from the seas, descending in rain, gathering in streams and rivers, returning to the sea, and again ascending and descending for you. The earth is continually laboring to bring forth her fruit for your support. The trees of the field, and many of the poor, brute creatures, are continually laboring and spending their strength for you! How much of the fullness of the earth is spent upon you! How many of God's creatures are devoured by you! How many of the lives of the living creatures of God are destroyed for your sake, for your support and comfort! Now, how lamentable will

it be if, after all, you are altogether useless and live to no purpose! What mere cumberers of the ground will you be (Luke 13:7)! Nature, which thus continually labors for you, will be burdened with you. This seems to be what the apostle means in Romans 8:20–22 where he tells us that the creation is made subject to vanity, and brought into the bondage of corruption, and that the whole creation groans and travails in pain under this bondage.

(4) Consider how much is done for you in the use of the means of grace. How much has God done to provide you with suitable means and advantages for usefulness! How many prophets has He sent into the world in different ages, inspiring them with His Holy Spirit, and enabling them to work many miracles to confirm their word, whereby you now have His written Word to instruct you! How great a thing has God done for you to give you opportunity and advantage to be useful, in that He has sent His own Son into the world! He who is really and truly God united Himself to the human nature and became man, to be a prophet and teacher to you and other sinners. Yea, He laid down His life to make atonement for sin that you might have encouragement to serve God with hopes of acceptance. How many ordinances have been instituted for you! How much of the labor of the ministers of God has been spent upon you! Is not that true concerning you which is said in Isaiah 5 of the vineyard planted in a very fruitful hill, and fenced and cultivated with peculiar care and pains, which yet proved unfruitful? How much has the dresser of the vineyard dug about the barren tree and dunged it, and yet it remains barren!

(5) Consider what a shame it is that you should live in vain when all the other creatures, inferior to you, glorify their Creator according to their nature. You who are so highly exalted in the world are more useless than the brute creation,

yea, than the meanest worms or things without life, as earth and stones, for they all answer their end; none of them fail of it. They are all useful in their places; all render their proper tribute of praise to their Creator while you are mere nuisances in the creation, and burdens to the earth. Any tree of the forest is more useful than the vine if it bears not fruit.

4. Let me, in a further application of this doctrine, exhort you by all means to bring forth fruit to God. Let it be your constant endeavor to be in this way actively useful in the world. Here consider three things:

(1) What an honor it will be to such poor creatures as you are to bring forth fruit to the divine glory. What is such a poor worm as man that he should be enabled to bring forth any fruit to God! It is the greatest honor of his nature that God has given him a capacity of glorifying the great Creator. There is no creature in the visible world that is capable of actively glorifying God but man.

(2) In bringing forth fruit to God you will be so profitable to none as to yourselves. You cannot thereby be profitable to God. Job 22:2: "Can a man be profitable to God?" And though thereby you may be profitable to your fellow creatures, yet the fruit which you bring forth to God will be a greater benefit to yourselves than to anyone living. Although you are under a natural obligation to bring forth fruit to God, yet He will richly reward you for it. In requiring you to bring forth fruit to Him, He does but require you to bring forth fruit to your own happiness. You will taste the sweetness of your own fruit. It will be most profitable for you in this world, and the pleasure will be beyond the labor. Besides this, God has promised to such a life everlasting rewards, unspeakable infinite benefits. So that by it you will infinitely advance your own interest.

(3) If you remain thus unprofitable and are not ac-

tively useful, surely God will obtain His end of you in your destruction. He will say concerning the barren tree, "Cut it down, why cumbereth it the ground?" Christ, in John 15:6, tells us, "If a man abide not in Me, he is cast forth as a branch, and is withered; and men gather them, and cast them into the fire, and they are burned." This is spoken of the barren branches in the vine. How would you do in such a case with a barren tree in an orchard, or with weeds and tares in your fields? Doubtless, if it were in your power, you would utterly destroy them. God will have His end. He will not be frustrated. Though all men and devils unite their endeavors, they cannot frustrate God in anything; and "though hand join in hand, the wicked shall not be unpunished" (Proverbs 11:21). God has sworn by His great name that He will have His glory of men, whether they will actively glorify Him or not. Numbers 14:21–23: "But as truly as I live, all the earth shall be filled with the glory of the Lord. Because all those men which have seen My glory, and My miracles which I did in Egypt and in the wilderness, and have tempted Me now these ten times, and have not hearkened to My voice; surely they shall not see the land which I sware unto their fathers, neither shall any of them that provoked Me, see it." Matthew 3:10: "The axe is laid unto the root of the trees; therefore every tree which bringeth not forth good fruit is hewn down, and cast into the fire." The end of those men who bring forth nothing but briars and thorns, is to be burned, as in Hebrews 6:7–8: "For the earth which drinketh in the rain that cometh oft upon it, and bringeth forth herbs meet for them by whom it is dressed, receiveth blessing from God; but that which beareth thorns and briers is rejected, and is nigh unto cursing; whose end is to be burned." So we read of the tares, Matthew 13:30: "Let both grow together until the harvest; and in the time of harvest I will say to the reapers, Gather ye together first the tares, and bind them in bundles to burn them"; and in verses 40–42: "As therefore the tares are gathered and burned in the fire, so shall it be at the end of the world. The Son of man shall send forth His angels, and they shall gather out of His kingdom all things that offend, and them which do iniquity, and shall cast them into a furnace of fire; there shall be wailing and gnashing of teeth." So it is said of the chaff, Matthew 3:12: "Whose fan is in His hand, and He will thoroughly purge His floor, and gather His wheat into the garner: but He will burn up the chaff with unquenchable fire."

If you continue not to bring forth any fruit to the divine glory, hell will be the only fit place for you. It is a place prepared on purpose to be a receptacle of such persons. In hell nature ceases to labor any more for sinners. There they will have no opportunity to consume the fruits of divine goodness on their lusts; there they can prejudice or encumber nothing upon which God sets any value. There no faithful servants and ministers of God will any longer spend their strength in vain upon them. When the barren tree is in the fire, the servants of the husbandman are freed from any further labor about it. In hell the fruitless will no more have opportunity to clog and discourage the flourishing of religion, and to destroy much good, as they often do in this world; they will no more have opportunity to corrupt others by their ill example; they will no more have it in their power to offend the godly; they may hurt and torment one another, but the godly will be out of their reach. In hell there will be no ordinances, no sabbaths, no sacraments, no sacred things, for them to profane and defile by their careless and hypocritical attendance; but unceasing woe for their abuse.

The Future Punishment of the Wicked Unavoidable and Intolerable

"Can thine heart endure, or can thine hands be strong, in the days that I shall deal with thee? I the Lord have spoken it, and will do it." Ezekiel 22:14

In this former part of this chapter we have a dreadful catalogue of the sins of Jerusalem, as you may see from the first to the thirteenth verse. In the thirteenth, which is the verse preceding the text, God manifests His great displeasure and fearful wrath against them for their iniquities. "Behold, I have smitten Mine hand at thy dishonest gain which thou hast made, and at thy blood which hath been in the midst of thee." The expression of God's smiting His hand signifies the greatness of His anger, and His preparing Himself, as it were, to execute wrath answerable to their heinous crimes. It is an allusion to what we see sometimes in men when they are surprised by seeing or hearing of some horrid offense or most intolerable injury which very much stirs their spirits and animates them with high resentment. On such an occasion they will rise up in wrath and smite their hands together as an expression of the heat of their indignation and full resolution to be avenged on those who have committed the injury. Ezekiel 21:17: "I will also smite Mine hands together, and I will cause My fury to rest: I the Lord have said it." Then in the text the punishment of that people is represented.

1. The nature of their punishment is more generally represented in that God will undertake to deal with them. The prophets could do nothing with them. God had sent them one after another, but those sinners were too strong for them and beat one and killed another. Therefore, now, God Himself undertakes to deal with them.

2. Their punishment is more particularly represented in three things: the intolerableness of it, the remedilessness of it, and the unavoidableness of it.

The intolerableness of it: "Can thine heart endure?"

Its remedilessness, or the impossibility of their doing anything for their own relief: "Can thine hands be strong?"

Its unavoidableness: "I the Lord have spoken it, and will do it."

DOCTRINE: Since God has undertaken to deal with impenitent sinners, they shall neither shun the threatened misery nor deliver themselves out of it, nor can they bear it.

In handling this doctrine I shall show:

1. What is implied in God's undertaking to deal with impenitent sinners.
2. That they therefore cannot avoid punishment.
3. That they cannot in any measure deliver themselves from it, or do anything for their own relief under it.
4. That they cannot bear it.
5. I shall answer an inquiry and then proceed to the use.

1. I shall show what is implied in God's undertaking to deal with impenitent sinners. Others are not able to deal with them. They baffle all the means used with them by those who are appointed to teach and to rule over them.

They will not yield to parents, or to the counsels, warnings, or reproofs of ministers; they prove obstinate and stiffhearted. Therefore God undertakes to deal with them. This implies the following things:

(1) That God will reckon with them and take of them satisfaction to His justice. In this world God puts forth His authority to command them and to require their subjection to Him. In His commands He is very positive, strictly requiring of them the performance of duties, and as positively forbidding things contrary to their duty. But they have no regard to these commands. God continues commanding and they continue rebelling. They make nothing of God's authority. God threatens, but they despise His threatenings. They make nothing of dishonoring God; they care not how much their behavior is to His dishonor. He offers them mercy if they will repent and return, but they despise His mercy as well as His wrath. God calls, but they refuse. Thus they are continually plunging themselves deeper and deeper in debt, and, at the same time, imagine they shall escape the payment of the debt and design entirely to rob God of His due.

But God has undertaken to right Himself. He will reckon with them. He has undertaken to see that the debts due to Him are paid. All their sins are written in His book; not one of them is forgotten, and every one must be paid. If God is wise enough and strong enough, He will have full satisfaction. He will exact the very uttermost farthing. He undertakes it as His part, as what belongs to Him, to see Himself righted wherein He has been wrong. Deuteronomy 32:35: "To Me belongeth vengeance." Also 7:10: "He will not be slack to him that hateth Him; He will repay him to his face."

(2) He has undertaken to vindicate the honor of

His majesty. His majesty they despise. They hear that He is a great God, but they despise His greatness; they look upon Him as worthy of contempt and treat Him accordingly. They hear of Him by the name of a great king, but His authority they regard not, and sometimes trample upon it for years together.

But God has not left the honor of His majesty wholly to their care. Though they now trample it in the dust, yet that is no sign that it will be finally lost. If God had left it wholly to their hands, it would indeed be lost. But God does not leave His honor and His glory with His enemies; it is too precious in His eyes to be so neglected. He has reserved the care of it to Himself. He will see to it that His own injured majesty is vindicated. If the honor of God upon which sinners trample finally lies in the dust it will be because He is not strong enough to vindicate Himself. He has sworn in Numbers 14:21: "As truly as I live, all the earth shall be filled with the glory of the Lord."

Sinners despise His Son and trample Him under their feet; but He will see if He cannot make the glory of His Son appear with respect to them that all the earth may know how evil a thing it is to despise the Son of God. God intends that all men and angels, all heaven and all earth, shall see whether He is sufficient to magnify Himself upon sinners who now despise Him. He intends that the issue of things with respect to them shall be open that all men may see it.

(3) He has undertaken to subdue impenitent sinners. Their hearts, while in this world, are very unsubdued. They lift up their heads and conduct themselves very proudly and contemptuously, and often sin with a high hand. They set their mouths against the heavens, and their tongues walk through the earth. They practically say, as did

Pharaoh, "Who is the Lord? I know not the Lord, neither will I obey His voice" (Exodus 5:2). They say to God, "Depart from us, for we desire not the knowledge of Thy ways" (Job 21:14).

Some, who cover their sin with their specious show, who put on a face of religion, and a demure countenance and behavior, yet have this spirit secretly reigning in their breasts. Notwithstanding all their fair show and good, external carriage, they despise God in their hearts and have the weapons of war about them, though they carry their swords under their skirts. They have most proud, stubborn, and rebellious hearts, which are ready to rise in opposition to contend with Him and to find fault with His dispensations. Their hearts are full of pride, enmity, stubbornness, and blasphemy which work in them in many ways while they sit under the preaching of the Word and while the Spirit of God is striving with them. And they always continue to oppose and resist God as long as they live in the world. They never lay down the weapons of their rebellion.

But God has undertaken to deal with them and to subdue them, and those proud and stubborn hearts which will not yield to the power of God's Word shall be broken by the power of His hand. If they will not be willing subjects to the golden scepter, and will not yield to the attractiveness of His love, they shall be subject to the force of the iron rod whether they will or not.

Those who proudly set up their own righteousness and their own wills, God has undertaken to bring down; and without doubt it will be done. He has undertaken to make those who are now regardless to regard Him. They shall know that He is Jehovah. Now they will not own that He is the Lord, but they shall know it. Isaiah 26:11: "Lord, when Thy hand is lifted up, they will not see; but they shall see."

Now wicked men not only hate God, but they slight Him; they are not afraid of Him. But He will subdue their contempt. When He shall come to take them in hand, they will hate Him still; but they will not slight Him. They will not make light of His power as they now do. They will see and feel too much of the infinity of His power to slight it. They are now wont to slight His wrath, but then they will slight it no more. They will find by sufficient experience that His wrath is not to be slighted. They will learn this to their cost and they will never forget it.

(4) God has undertaken to rectify their judgments. Now they will not be convinced of those things God tells them in His Word. Ministers take much pains to convince them, but all is vain. Therefore God will undertake to convince them, and He will do it effectually. Now they will not be convinced of the truth of divine things. They have indeed convincing arguments set before them; they hear and see enough to convince them, yet so prone are they to unbelief and atheism that divine things never seem to them to be real. But God will hereafter make them seem real.

Now they are always doubting the truth of the Scriptures, questioning whether they are the Word of God and whether the threatenings of Scripture are true. But God has undertaken to convince them that those threatenings are true, and He will make them know that they are true so that they will never doubt any more forever. They will be convinced by dear experience. Now they are always questioning whether there is any such place as hell. They hear much about it, but it always seems to them like a dream. But God will make it seem otherwise than a dream. Now they are often told of the vanity of the world, but we may as well preach to the beasts to persuade them of the vanity of earthly things. But God will undertake to convince them of this. He will hereafter give them a thorough conviction of it so that they shall have a strong sense of the vanity of all these things.

Now ministers often tell sinners of the great importance of an interest in Christ, and that it is the one thing needful. They are also told of the folly of delaying the care of their souls, and how much it concerns them to improve their opportunity. But the instructions of ministers do not convince them; therefore God will undertake to convince them.

Impenitent sinners, while in this world, hear how dreadful hell is. But they will not believe that it is as dreadful as ministers represent. They cannot think that they shall, to all eternity, suffer such exquisite and horrible torments. But they shall be taught and convinced to purpose that the representations ministers give of those torments, agreeable to the Word of God, are indeed as dreadful as they declare. Since God has undertaken to deal with sinners, and to rectify their judgments in these matters, He will do it thoroughly, for His work is perfect. When He undertakes to do things, He does not do them by halves; therefore, before He shall have done with sinners He will convince them effectually so that they shall never be in danger of relapsing into their former errors. He will convince them of their folly and stupidity in entertaining such notions as they now entertain.

Thus God has undertaken to deal with obstinate unbelievers. They carry things on in great confusion; but we need not be dismayed at it. Let us wait and we shall see that God will rectify things. Sinners will not always continue to rebel and despise with impunity. The honor of God will in due time be vindicated, and they shall be subdued and convicted and shall give an account. There is no sin, not so much as an idle word that they shall speak, but they must give an account of it (Matthew 12:36). And their sins must be fully balanced and recompensed, and satisfaction obtained. Because judgment against their evil works is not speedily executed, their hearts are fully set in them to do evil. Yet God is a righteous Judge. He will see that judgment is executed in due time.

2. I come now to show that therefore impenitent sinners shall not avoid their due punishment. God has undertaken to inflict it. He has engaged to do it. He takes it as what properly belongs to Him and we may expect it of Him. If He has sworn by His life that He will do it, and if He has sufficient power, if He is the living God, doubtless we shall see it done. And that God has declared that He will punish impenitent sinners is manifest from many Scriptures. Deuteronomy 32:41: "I will render vengeance to Mine enemies, and will reward them that hate Me." Deuteronomy 7:10: "He will not be slack to him that hateth Him: He will repay him to his face." Exodus 34:7: God "will by no means clear the guilty." Nahum 1:3: "The Lord is slow to anger, and great in power, and will not at all acquit the wicked."

God says in the text, "I the Lord have spoken it, and will do it," which leaves no room to doubt the actual fulfillment of the threatenings in its utmost extent. Some have flattered themselves that, although God has threatened very dreadful things to wicked men for their sins, yet in His heart He never intends to fulfill His threatenings, but only to terrify them and make them afraid while they live. But would the infinitely holy God, who is not a man that He should lie, and who speaks no vain words, utter Himself in this manner ("I the Lord have spoken it, and will do it. I have not only threatened, but I will also fulfill my threatenings") when at the same time these words do not agree with His heart, but He secretly knew that, though He had spoken, yet He did not intend to do it? Who is he who dares to entertain such horrid blasphemy in his heart?

No, let no impenitent sinner flatter himself so vainly and foolishly. If it were indeed only a man, a being of like impotence and mutability as themselves, who had undertaken to deal with them, they might perhaps with some reason flatter themselves that they should find some means to avoid the threatened punishment. But since an omniscient, omnipotent, immutable God has undertaken this, vain are all such hopes.

There is no hope that possibly they may steal away to heaven though they die unconverted. There is no hope that they can deceive God by a false show of repentance and faith, and so be taken to heaven through mistake; for the eyes of God are as a flame of fire: they perfectly see through every man; the inmost closet of the heart is all open to Him.

There is no hope of escaping the threatened punishment by sinking into nothing at death like brute creatures. Indeed, many wicked men upon their deathbeds wish for this. If it were so, death would be nothing to them in comparison to what it is now. But all such wishes are vain.

There is no hope of their escaping without notice when they leave the body. There is no hope that God, by reason of the multiplicity of affairs which He has to mind, will happen to overlook them and not take notice of them when they come to die; that their souls will slip away privately and hide themselves in some secret corner and so escape divine vengeance.

There is no hope that they shall be missed in a crowd at the day of judgment, and that they can have opportunity to hide themselves in some cave or den of the mountains, or in any secret hole of the earth; and that, while doing so, they will not be minded by reason of the many things which will be the objects of attention on that day. Neither is there any hope that they will be able to crowd themselves in among the multitude of the saints at the right hand of the Judge, and so go to heaven undiscovered. Nor is there any hope that God will alter His mind, or that He will repent of what He has said, for He is not a man that He should repent. Has He said, and shall He not do it? Has He spoken, and shall He not make it good? When did God ever undertake to do anything and fail?

3. I come now to show that as impenitent sinners cannot shun the threatened punishment, so neither can they do anything to deliver themselves from it or to relieve themselves under it. This is implied in those words of the text, "Can thine hands be strong?" It is with our hands that we make and accomplish things for ourselves. But the wicked in hell will have no strength of hand to accomplish anything at all for themselves or to bring to pass any deliverance or any degree of relief.

(1) They will not be able in that conflict to overcome their enemy and so to deliver themselves. God, who will then undertake to deal with them, and will gird Himself with might to execute wrath, will be their enemy, and will act the part of an enemy with a witness, and they will have no strength to oppose Him. Those who live negligent of their souls under the light of the gospel act as if they supposed that they should be able hereafter to make their part good with God. 1 Corinthians 10:22: "Do we provoke the Lord to jealousy? are we stronger than He?" But they will have no power, no might to resist that omnipo-

tence which will be engaged against them.

(2) They will have no strength in their hands to do anything to appease God or in the least to abate the fierceness of His wrath. They will not be able to offer any satisfaction; they will not be able to procure God's pity. Though they cry, God will not hear them. They will find no price to offer to God in order to purchase favor or to pay any part of their debt.

(3) They will not be able to find any to befriend them and intercede with God for them. They had the offer of a mediator often made them in this world, but they will have no such offers in hell; all there will be their enemies. They will have no friend in heaven; none of the saints or angels will befriend them; or, if they should, it would be to no purpose. There will be no creature that will have any power to deliver them, nor will any ever pity them.

(4) Nor will they ever be able to make their escape. They will find no means to break prison and flee. In hell they will be reserved in chains of darkness forever and ever. Malefactors have often found means to escape the hand of civil justice. But none ever escaped out of the prison of hell, which is God's prison. It is a strong prison; it is beyond any finite power or the united strength of all wicked men and devils to unlock or break open the door of that prison. Christ has the key of hell. "He shall shut and none shall open" (Isaiah 22:22).

(5) Nor will they ever be able to find anything to relieve them in hell. They will never find any resting place there, any secret corner which will be cooler than the rest, where they may have a little respite, a small abatement of the extremity of their torment. They never will be able to find any cooling stream or fountain in any part of that world of torment; no, nor so much as a drop of water to

cool their tongues. They will find no company to give them any comfort or to do them the least good. They will find no place where they can remain and rest and take breath for one minute, for they will be tormented with fire and brimstone, and will have no rest day or night forever and ever.

Thus impenitent sinners will be able neither to shun the punishment threatened nor to deliver themselves from it, nor to find any relief under it.

4. Having shown that impenitent sinners will hereafter be able neither to avoid the punishment threatened nor to deliver themselves from it, nor to find any relief under it, I come now to show that neither will they be able to bear it. Neither will their hands be strong to deliver them from it, nor will their hearts be able to endure it. It is common with men, when they meet with calamities in this world, in the first place to endeavor to shun them. But, if they find that they cannot shun them, then, after they have come, they endeavor to deliver themselves from them as soon as they can, or at least to deliver themselves in some degree. But if they find that they can by no means deliver themselves, and see that they must bear them, then they fortify their spirits and take up a resolution so that they will support themselves under them as well as they can.

But it will be utterly in vain for impenitent sinners to think to do thus with respect to the torments of hell. They will not be able to endure them, or at all to support themselves under them; the torment will be immensely beyond their strength. What will it signify for a worm which is about to be pressed under the weight of some great rock, to be let fall with its whole weight upon it, to collect its strength to set itself up to bear the weight of the rock and to preserve itself from being crushed? Much more vain will it be for a poor damned soul to endeavor to support itself under the weight of the wrath of Almighty God. What is the strength of man, who is but a worm, to support himself against the power of Jehovah, and against the fierceness of His wrath? What is man's strength, when set to bear up against the exertions of infinite power? Matthew 21:44: "Whosoever shall fall on this stone shall be broken; but on whomsoever it shall fall, it will grind him to powder."

When sinners hear of hell torments, they sometimes think to themselves: "Well, if it shall come to that, that I must go to hell, I will bear it as well as I can." As if by clothing themselves with resolution and firmness of mind they would be able to support themselves in some measure, when, alas! they will have no resolution, no courage at all. However they have prepared themselves and collected their strength, yet as soon as they shall begin to feel that wrath their hearts will melt and be as water. However they may seem to harden their hearts in order to prepare themselves to bear it, yet the first moment they feel it their hearts will become like wax before the furnace. Their courage and resolution will be all gone in an instant; it will vanish away like a shadow in the twinkling of an eye. The stoutest and most sturdy will have no more courage than the feeblest infant; let a man be an infant or a giant, it will be all one. They will not be able to keep alive any courage, any strength, any comfort, any hope at all.

5. I come now, as was proposed, to answer an inquiry which may be naturally raised concerning these things. Some may be ready to ask:

QUESTION. If this is the case, if impenitent sinners can neither shun future punishment nor deliver them-

selves from it nor bear it, what will then become of them?
ANSWER. They will wholly sink down into eternal death. There will be that sinking of heart of which we now cannot conceive. We see how it is with the body when in extreme pain. The nature of the body will support itself for a considerable time under very great pain so as to keep from wholly sinking. There will be great struggles, lamentable groans and pantings, and, it may be, convulsions. These are the strugglings of nature to support itself under the extremity of the pain. There is, as it were, a great loathness in nature to yield to it; it cannot bear wholly to sink.

But yet sometimes pain of body is so very exquisite that the nature of the body cannot support itself under it; however loath it may be to sink, yet it cannot bear the pain. There are a few struggles and throes and pantings, and, it may be, a shriek or two, and then nature yields to the violence of the torments, sinks down, and the body dies. This is the death of the body. So it will be with the soul in hell: it will have no strength or power to deliver itself, and its torment and horror will be so great, so mighty, so vastly disproportioned to its strength that having no strength in the least to support itself, although it is infinitely contrary to the nature and inclination of the soul utterly to sink, yet it will utterly and totally sink without the least degree of remaining comfort, strength, courage, or hope. Although it will never be annihilated, its being and perception will never be abolished; yet such will be the infinite depth of gloominess into which it will sink that it will be in a state of death—eternal death.

The nature of man desires happiness. It is the nature of the soul to crave and thirst after well-being. And if it is under misery, it eagerly pants after relief; and the greater the misery is, the more eagerly it struggles for help. But if all relief is withheld, all strength overborne, all support utterly gone, then it sinks into the darkness of death.

We can conceive but little of the matter, but to help your conception imagine yourself to be cast into a fiery oven or a great furnace where your pain would be as much greater than that occasioned by accidentally touching a coal of fire as the heat is greater. Imagine also that your body were to lie there for a quarter of an hour, full of fire, and all the while full of quick sense: what horror would you feel at the entrance of such a furnace! And how long would that quarter of an hour seem to you! And after you had endured it for one minute, how overbearing would it be to you to think that you had to endure it the other fourteen!

But what would be the effect on your soul if you knew you must lie there enduring that torment to the full for twenty-four hours! And how much greater would be the effect if you knew you must endure it for a whole year; and how much vastly greater still if you knew you must endure it for a thousand years! Oh, then, how would your hearts sink if you knew that you must bear it forever and ever! that there would be no end! that after millions of ages, your torment would be no nearer to an end and that you never, never should be delivered!

But your torment in hell will be immensely greater than this illustration represents. How then will the heart of a poor creature sink under it! How utterly inexpressible and inconceivable must the sinking of the soul be in such a case!

This is the death threatened in the law. This is dying in the highest sense of the word. This is to die sensibly, to die and know it, to be sensible of the gloom of death. This is to be undone; this is worthy of the name of destruction. This sinking of the soul under an infinite weight, which it cannot bear, is the gloom of hell. We read in Scripture of the blackness of darkness; this is it, this is the very thing. We read in Scripture of sinners being lost and of their losing their souls. This is the thing intended; this is to lose the soul. Those who are subjects of this are utterly lost.

Application

This subject may be applied in a use of awakening to impenitent sinners. What has been said under this doctrine is for you, O impenitent sinner, O poor wretch, who are in the same miserable state in which you came into the world, except that you are loaded with vastly greater guilt by your actual sins. These dreadful things which you have heard are for you who are yet unconverted, and still remain an alien and stranger, without Christ and without God in the world. They are for you who to this day remain an enemy to God and a child of the devil, even in this remarkable season when others, both here and elsewhere, far and near, are flocking to Christ, for you who hear the fame of these things, but know nothing of the power of godliness in your own heart.

Whoever you are, whether young or old, little or great, if you are in a Christ-less, unconverted state, this is the wrath, this is the death to which you are condemned. This is the wrath that abides on you; this is the hell over which you hang, and into which you are ready to drop every day and every night.

If you shall remain blind and hard and dead in sin a little longer, this destruction will come upon you. God has spoken and He will do it. It is in vain for you to flatter yourself with hopes that you shall avoid it, or to say in your heart, "Perhaps it will not be; perhaps things have been represented worse than they are." If you will not be convinced by the word preached to you by men in the name of God, God Himself will undertake to convince you (Ezekiel 14:4, 7–8).

Does it seem to you not real that you shall suffer such a dreadful destruction because it seems to you that you do not deserve it? and because you do not see anything so horrid in yourself as to answer such a dreadful punishment? Why is it that your wickedness does not seem bad enough to deserve this punishment? The reason is because you love your wickedness; your wickedness seems good to you; it appears lovely to you; you do not see any such hatefulness in it as to answer such misery.

But know, you stupid, blind, hardened wretch, that God does not see as you see with your polluted eyes. Your sins in His sight are infinitely abominable. You know that you have a thousand and a thousand times made light of the majesty of God. And why should not that majesty, which you have thus despised, be manifested in the greatness of your punishment? You have often heard what a great and dreadful God Jehovah is, but you have made so light of it that you have not been afraid of Him. You have not been afraid to sin against Him, nor to go on day after day by your sins to provoke Him to wrath, nor to cast His commands under foot and trample on them. Now why may not God, in the greatness of your destruction, justly vindicate and manifest the greatness of that majesty which you have despised?

You have despised the mighty power of God; you have not been afraid of it. Now why is it not fit that God should show the greatness of His power in your ruin? What king is there who will not show his authority in the punishment of those subjects who despise it, and who will not vindicate his royal majesty in executing vengeance on those who rise in rebellion? And are you such a fool as to think that the great King of heaven and earth, before whom all other kings are so many grasshoppers, will not vindicate His kingly majesty on such contemptuous rebels as you are? You are very much mistaken if you think so. If you disregard God's majesty, be it known to you that God does not disregard His own majesty. He takes care of its honor and will vindicate it.

Think it not strange that God should deal so severely with you, or that the wrath which you shall suffer should be so great. For as great as it is, it is no greater than that love of God which you have despised. The love of God, and His grace, condescension, and pity to sinners in sending His Son into the world to die for them, are every whit as great and wonderful as this inexpressible wrath. This mercy has been held forth to you and described in its wonderful greatness hundreds of times, and as often has it been offered to you. But you would not accept Christ; you would not have this great love of God; you despised God's dying love; you trampled the benefits of it underfoot. Now why should you not have wrath as great as that love and mercy which you despised and rejected? Does it seem incredible to you that God should so harden His heart against a poor sinner so as to destroy him and to bear him down with infinite power and merciless wrath? And is this a greater thing than it is for you to harden your heart, as you have done, against infinite mercy and against the dying love of God?

Does it seem incredible to you that God should be so utterly regardless of the sinner's welfare as to sink him into an infinite abyss of misery? Is this shocking to you? And is it not at all shocking to you that you should be so utterly regardless as you have been of the honor and glory of the infinite God?

It arises from your stupidity, and because you have a heart of stone, that you are so senseless of your own wickedness as to think that you have not deserved such a punishment, and it is to you incredible that it will be inflicted upon you. But if, when all is said and done, you are not convinced, wait but a little while and you will be convinced. God will undertake to do the work which ministers cannot do. Though judgment against your evil works is not yet executed, and God now lets you alone, yet He will soon come upon you with His great power. And then you shall know what God is and what you are.

Flatter not yourself that if these things shall prove true and the worst shall come you will set yourself to bear it as well as you can. What will it signify to set yourself to bear and to collect your strength to support yourself when you shall fall into the hands of that omnipotent King, Jehovah? He who made you can make His sword approach unto you. His sword is not the sword of man, nor is His wrath the wrath of man. If it were, possibly stoutness might be maintained under it. But it is the fierceness of the wrath of the great God who is able to baffle and dissipate all your strength in a moment. He can fill your poor soul with an ocean of wrath, a deluge of fire and brimstone; or He can make it ten thousand times fuller of torment than ever an oven was full of fire, and, at the same time, can fill it with despair of ever seeing any end to its torment or any rest from its misery. And then where will be your strength? What will become of your courage? What will signify your attempts to bear?

What are you in the hands of the great God who made heaven and earth by speaking a word? What are you when dealt with by that strength which manages all this vast universe, holds the globe of the earth, directs all the motions of the heavenly bodies from age to age, and, when the fixed time shall come, will shake all to pieces? There are other wicked beings a thousand times stronger than you. There are strong and proud spirits of a gigantic stoutness and hardness. But how little are they in the hands of the great God! They are less than weak infants; they are nothing and less than nothing in the hands of an angry God, as will appear at the day of judgment. Their hearts will be broken; they will sink; they will have no strength nor courage left; they will be as weak as water; their souls will sink down into an infinite gloom, an abyss of death and despair. Then what will become of you, a poor worm, when you shall fall into the hands of that God, when He shall come to show His wrath and make His power known on you?

If the strength of all the wicked men on earth and of all the devils in hell were united in one, and you were possessed of it all; and if the courage, greatness, and stoutness of their hearts were united in your single heart, you would be nothing in the hands of Jehovah. If it were all collected, and you should set yourself to bear as well as you could, all would sink under His great wrath in an instant and would be utterly abolished. Your hands would drop down at once and your heart would melt as wax. The great mountains, the firm rocks cannot stand before the power of God. He can tear the earth in pieces in a moment, yea, He can shatter the whole universe and dash it to pieces at one blow. How, then, will your hands be strong or your heart endure?

You cannot stand before a lion of the forest; an angry

wild beast, if stirred up, will easily tear such a one as you are in pieces. Yea, not only so, but you are crushed before the moth. A little thing, a little worm or spider, or some such insect, is able to kill you. What, then, can you do in the hands of God? It is vain to set the briars and thorns in battle array against glowing flames; the points of thorns, though sharp, do nothing to withstand the fire.

Some of you have seen buildings on fire. Imagine, therefore, with yourselves what a poor hand you would make at fighting with the flames if you were in the midst of so great and fierce a fire. You have often seen a spider or some other disgusting insect, when thrown into the midst of a fierce fire, and have observed how immediately it yields to the force of the flames. There is no long struggle, no fighting against the fire, no strength exerted to oppose the heat or to fly from it; and the fire takes possession of it and at once it becomes full of fire. Here is a little image of what you will be in hell unless you repent and fly to Christ. To encourage yourselves that you will set yourselves to bear hell torments as well as you can is just as if a worm that is about to be thrown into a glowing furnace should swell and fortify itself and prepare itself to fight the flames.

What can you do with lightnings? What does it signify to fight with them? What an absurd figure would a poor, weak man make who, in a thunderstorm, should expect a flash of lightning on his head or his breast and should go forth, sword in hand, to oppose it, when a flash would, in an instant, drink up all his spirits and his life and melt his sword!

Consider these things, all you enemies of God and rejecters of Christ, whether you are old men and women, Christ-less heads of families, or young people and wicked children. Be assured that if you do not hearken and repent,

The Future Punishment of the Wicked

God intends to show His wrath and make His power known upon you. He intends to magnify Himself exceedingly in sinking you down in hell. He intends to show His great majesty at the day of judgment in your misery before a vast assembly; before a greater assembly many thousandfold than ever yet appeared on earth; before a vast assembly of saints and a vast assembly of wicked men, a vast assembly of holy angels, and before all the crew of devils. God will, before all these, get Himself honor in your destruction; you shall be tormented in the presence of them all. Then all will see that God is a great God indeed; then all will see how dreadful a thing it is to sin against such a God and to reject such a Savior, such love and grace as you have rejected and despised. All will be filled with awe at the great sight, and all the saints and angels will look upon you and adore that majesty, that mighty power, and that holiness or justice of God which shall appear in your ineffable destruction and misery.

It is probable that some who hear me are at this very moment unawakened, and are in a great degree careless about their souls. I fear there are some among us who are most fearfully hardened; their hearts are harder than the very rocks. It is easier to make impressions upon an adamant than upon their hearts. I suppose some of you have heard all that I have said with ease and quietness; it appears to you as great-sounding words, but does not reach your hearts. You have heard such things many times; you have been much too used to the roaring of heaven's cannon to be frightened at it. It will therefore probably be in vain for me to say anything further to you. I will only put you in mind that ere long God will deal with you. I cannot deal with you; you despise what I say. I have no power to make you sensible of your danger and misery, and of the dreadfulness of the wrath of God. The attempts of men in this way have often proved vain.

However, God has undertaken to deal with such men as you are. It is His manner commonly, first, to let men try their utmost strength, particularly to let ministers try that thus He may show ministers their own weakness and impotence; and when they have done what they can and all fails, then God takes the matter into His own hands. So it seems by your obstinacy as if God intended to undertake to deal with you. He will undertake to subdue you. He will see if He cannot cure you of your senselessness and lack of regard for His threatenings. And you will be convinced; you will be subdued effectually; your strength will utterly be broken, your courage and hope will sink. God will surely break those who will not bow.

Having girded Himself with His power and wrath, He has heretofore undertaken to deal with many hard, stubborn, senseless, obstinate hearts; and He never failed. He always did His work thoroughly.

It will not be long before you will be wonderfully changed. You who now hear of hell and the wrath of the great God, and who sit here so easy and quiet and go away so carelessly, by and by you will shake and tremble, and cry out and shriek and gnash your teeth, and will be thoroughly convinced of the vast weight and importance of these things which you now despise.

Wrath to the Uttermost

"To fill up their sins always; for the wrath is come upon them to the uttermost." 1 Thessalonians 2:16

In verse 14, the apostle commends the Christian Thessalonians that they became the followers of the churches of God in Judea, both in faith and in sufferings; in faith in that they received the Word not as the word of man, but as it is in truth the Word of God; in sufferings in that they had suffered like things of their own countrymen as they had of the Jews. Upon this the apostle sets forth the persecuting, cruel, and perverse wickedness of that people "who both killed the Lord Jesus and their own prophets, and have," says he, "persecuted us; and they please not God, and are contrary to all men, forbidding us to speak to the Gentiles that they might be saved." Then come the words of the text: "To fill up their sins always; for the wrath is come upon them to the uttermost."

In these words we may observe two things:

1. To what effect was the heinous wickedness and obstinacy of the Jews: "to fill up their sins." God has set bounds to every man's wickedness. He suffers men to live, and to go on in their sins, till they have filled up their measure, and then He cuts them off. To this effect was the wickedness and obstinacy of the Jews: they were exceedingly wicked, and thereby filled up the measure of their sins at a great pace. And the reason why they were permitted to be so obstinate under the preaching and miracles of Christ, and of the apostles, and under all the means used with them was that they might fill up the measure of their

sins. This is agreeable to what Christ said in Matthew 23:31-32: "Wherefore be ye witnesses unto yourselves, that ye are the children of them which killed the prophets. Fill ye up then the measure of your fathers."

2. The punishment of their wickedness: "The wrath is come upon them to the uttermost." There is a connection between the measure of men's sin and the measure of their punishment. When they have filled up the measure of their sin, then is filled up the measure of God's wrath.

The degree of their punishment is the uttermost degree. This may respect both a national and personal punishment. If we take it as a national punishment, a little after the time when the epistle was written, wrath came upon the nation of the Jews to the uttermost in their terrible destruction by the Romans when, as Christ said, was "great tribulation, such as never was since the beginning of the world to that time" (Matthew 24:21). That nation had before suffered many of the fruits of divine wrath for their sins, but this was beyond all; this was their highest degree of punishment as a nation. If we take it as a personal punishment, then it respects their punishment in hell. God often punishes men very dreadfully in this world; but in hell "wrath comes on them to the uttermost."

By this expression is also denoted the certainty of this punishment. For though the punishment was then future, yet it is spoken of as present: "The wrath *is* come upon them to the uttermost." It was as certain as if it had already taken place. God, who knows all things, speaks of things that are not as though they were; for things present and things future are equally certain with Him.

It also denotes the near approach of it. The wrath *is* come; i.e., it is just at hand. It is at the door, as it proved to be with respect to that nation: their terrible destruction by the Romans was soon after the apostle wrote this doctrine.

DOCTRINE. When those who continue in sin shall have filled up the measure of their sin, then wrath will come upon them to the uttermost.

PROPOSITION 1. There is a certain measure that God has set to the sin of every wicked man. God says, concerning the sin of man, as He says to the raging waves of the sea, "Hitherto shalt thou come, and no further." The measure of some is much greater than of others. Some reprobates commit but a little sin in comparison with others, and so are to endure proportionably a smaller punishment. There are many vessels of wrath, but some are smaller and others greater vessels. Some will contain comparatively but little wrath, others a great measure of it. Sometimes, when we see wicked men go to dreadful lengths and become very heinously wicked, we are ready to wonder that God lets them alone. He sees them go on in such audacious wickedness and keeps silent, nor does anything to interrupt them; but they go smoothly on and meet with no hurt. But sometimes the reason God lets them alone is because they have not filled up the measure of their sins. When they live in dreadful wickedness, they are but filling up the measure which God has limited for them.

This is sometimes the reason why God suffers very wicked men to live so long: because their iniquity is not yet full. Genesis 15:16: "The iniquity of the Amorites is not yet full." For this reason also God sometimes suffers them to live in prosperity. Their prosperity is a snare to them, and an occasion of their sinning a great deal more. Wherefore God suffers them to have such a snare, because He suffers them to fill up a larger measure. So, for this cause, He sometimes suffers them to live under great light and great means and advantages and at the same time to neglect and misimprove all. Every one shall live till he has filled up his measure.

PROPOSITION 2. While men continue in sin, they are filling the measure set for them. This is the work in which they spend their whole lives. They begin in their childhood, and, if they live to grow old in sin, they still go on with this work. It is the work with which every day is filled up. They may alter their business in other respects; they may sometimes be about one thing and sometimes about another; but they never change from this work of filling up the measure of their sins. Whatever they put their hands to, they are still employed in this work. This is the first thing that they set themselves about when they awake in the morning and the last thing they do at night. They are all the while treasuring up wrath against the day of wrath, and against the revelation of the righteous judgment of God.

It is a gross mistake of some natural men who think that when they read and pray they do not add to their sins; but, on the contrary, they think they diminish their guilt by these exercises. They think that instead of adding to their sins they do something to satisfy for past offenses. But instead of that they only add to the measure by their best prayers, and by those services with which they themselves are most pleased.

PROPOSITION 3. When once the measure of their sins is filled up, the wrath will come upon them to the uttermost. God will then wait no longer upon them. Wicked men think that God is altogether such a one as themselves because, when they commit such wickedness, He keeps silent. "Because sentence against an evil work is not executed speedily, therefore the heart of the sons of men is fully set in them to do evil" (Ecclesiastes 18:11). But when once they shall have filled up the measure of their sins, judgment will be executed. God will not bear with them any longer. Now is the day of grace and the day of patience, which they spend in filling up their sins; but when their sins shall be full, then will come the day of wrath, the day of the fierce anger of God.

God often executes His wrath on ungodly men in a lesser degree in this world. He sometimes brings afflictions upon them, and that in wrath. Sometimes He expresses His wrath in very sore judgments; sometimes He appears in a terrible manner, not only outwardly, but also in the inward expressions of it on their consciences. Some, before they died, have had the wrath of God inflicted on their souls in degrees that have been intolerable. But these things are only forerunners of their punishment, only slight foretastes of wrath. God never stirs up all His wrath against wicked men while in this world, but once wicked men shall have filled up the measure of their sins, then wrath will come upon them to the uttermost, and that in the following respects:

1. Wrath will come upon them without any restraint or moderation in the degree of it. God always lays, as it were, a restraint upon Himself. He does not stir up His wrath. He stays His rough wind in the day of His east wind. He lets not His arm light down on wicked men with its full weight. But when sinners shall have filled up the measure of their sins, there will be no caution, no restraint. His rough wind will not be stayed or moderated. The wrath of God will be poured out like fire. He will come forth not only in anger, but in the fierceness of His anger. He will execute wrath with power so as to show what His wrath is and make His power known. There will be nothing to alleviate His wrath. His heavy wrath will lie on them without anything to

lighten the burden or to keep off, in any measure, the full weight of it from pressing the soul. His eye will not spare, neither will He regard the sinner's cries and lamentations, however loud and bitter. Then shall wicked men know that God is the Lord. They shall know how great that misery is which they have despised, and how dreadful that threatened wrath is which they have so little regarded. Then shall come on wicked men that punishment which they deserve. God will exact of them the uttermost farthing. Their iniquities are marked before Him; they are all written in His book; and in the future world He will reckon with them, and they must pay all the debt. Their sins are laid up in store with God; they are sealed up among His treasures, and them He will recompense, even recompense into their bosoms. The consummate degree of punishment will not be executed till the day of judgment. But the wicked are sealed over to this consummate punishment immediately after death. They are cast into hell and there bound in chains of darkness to the judgment of the great day; and they know that the highest degree of punishment is coming upon them. Final wrath will be executed without any mixture. All mercy, all enjoyments will be taken away. God sometimes expresses His wrath in this world, but here good things and evil are mixed together. In the future there will be only evil things.

2. Wrath will then be executed without any merciful circumstances. The judgments which God executes on ungodly men in this world are attended with many merciful circumstances. There is much patience and long-suffering, together with judgment. Judgments are joined with continuance of opportunity to seek mercy. But in hell there will be no more exercises of divine patience. The judgments which God exercises on ungodly men in this world

are warnings to them to avoid greater punishments; but the wrath which will come upon them when they shall have filled up the measure of their sin will not be of the nature of warnings. Indeed, they will be effectually awakened and made thoroughly sensible by what they shall suffer; yet their being awakened and made sensible will do them no good. Many a wicked man has suffered very awful things from God in this world which have been a means of saving good; but that wrath which sinners shall suffer after death will be in no way for their good. God will have no merciful design in it; neither will it be possible that they should get any good by that or by anything else.

3. Wrath will be so executed as to perfect the work to which wrath tends, i.e., utterly to undo the subject of it. Wrath is so often executed in this life as greatly to distress persons and bring them into great calamity, yet not so as to complete the ruin of those who suffer it. But in another world it will be so executed as to finish their destruction and render them utterly and perfectly undone. It will take away all comfort, all hope, and all support. The soul will be, as it were, utterly crushed; the wrath will be wholly intolerable. It must sink, and will utterly sink, and will have no more strength to keep itself from sinking than a worm would have to keep itself from being crushed under the weight of a mountain. The wrath will be so great, so mighty and powerful, as wholly to abolish all manner of welfare. Matthew 21:44: "But on whomsoever it shall fall, it will grind him to powder."

4. When persons shall have filled up the measure of their sin, that wrath will come upon them which is eternal. Though men may suffer very terrible and awful judgments in this world, yet those judgments have an end. They may be long continued, yet they commonly admit of relief.

Temporal distresses and sorrows have intermission and respite, and commonly by degrees abate and wear off; but the wrath that shall be executed when the measure of sin shall have been filled up will have no end. Thus it will be to the uttermost as to its duration; it will be of so long continuance that it will be impossible it should be longer. Nothing can be longer than eternity.

5. When persons shall have filled up the measure of their sin, then wrath will come upon them to the uttermost of what is threatened. Sin is an infinite evil, and the punishment which God has threatened against it is very dreadful. The threatenings of God against the workers of iniquity are very awful, but these threatenings are never fully accomplished in this world. However dreadful things some men may suffer in this life, yet God never fully executes His threatenings for so much as one sin till they have filled up the whole measure. The threatenings of the law are never answered by anything that man suffers here. The most awful judgment in this life does not answer God's threatenings either in degree, in circumstances, or in duration. If the greatest sufferings that ever are endured in this life should be eternal, it would not answer the threatening. Indeed, temporal judgments belong to the threatenings of the law, but these are not answered by them. They are but foretastes of the punishment. "The wages of sin is death." No expressions of wrath that are suffered before men have filled up the measure of their sin are its full wages. But then, God will reckon with them, and will recompense into their bosoms the full deserved sum.

Application

The use I would make of this doctrine is of warning to natural men to rest no longer in sin and to make haste to flee from it. The things which have been said under this doctrine may well be awakening, awful considerations to you. It is awful to consider whose wrath it is that abides upon you, and of what wrath you are in danger. It is impossible to express the misery of a natural condition. It is like being in Sodom, with a dreadful storm of fire and brimstone hanging over it, just ready to break forth and to be poured down upon it. The clouds of divine vengeance are full and just ready to burst. Here let those who yet continue in sin in this town consider particularly:

1. *Under what great means and advantages you continue in sin.* God is now favoring us with very great and extraordinary means and advantages in that we have such extraordinary tokens of the presence of God among us. His Spirit is so remarkably poured out, and multitudes of all ages and all sorts are converted and brought home to Christ. God appears among us in the most extraordinary manner, perhaps, that ever He did in New England. The children of Israel saw many mighty works when He brought them out of Egypt, but we, at this day, see works more mighty, and of a more glorious nature.

We who live under such a light have had loud calls, but now above all. Now is a day of salvation. The fountain has been set open among us in an extraordinary manner, and has stood open for a considerable time, yet you continue in sin and the calls that you have hitherto had have not brought you to be washed in it. What extraordinary advantages have you lately enjoyed to stir you up! How has everything in the town of late been of that tendency! Those things which used to be the greatest hindrances have been removed. You have not the ill examples of immoral persons to be a temptation to you. There is not now that vain, worldly talk and ill company to divert you and to be a hindrance to you which there used to be. Now you have multitudes of good examples set before you. There are many now all around you who, instead of diverting and hindering you, are earnestly desirous of your salvation, and willing to do all that they can to move you to flee to Christ. They have a thirsting desire for it. The chief talk in the town has of late been about the things of religion, and has been such as has tended to promote, and not to hinder, your soul's good. Everything all around you has tended to stir you up, and will you yet continue in sin?

Some of you have continued in sin till you were far advanced in life. You were warned when you were children, and some of you had awakenings then; however, the time went away. You became men and women, and then you were stirred up again; you had the strivings of God's Spirit; and some of you have fixed the times when you would make thorough work of seeking salvation. Some of you, perhaps, determined to do it when you should be married and settled in the world, others when you should have finished such a business, and when your circumstances should be so and so altered. Now these times have come and are past, yet you continue in sin.

Many of you have had remarkable warnings of providence. Some of you have been warned by the deaths of near relations. You have stood by and seen others die and go into eternity, yet this has not been effectual. Some of you have been near death yourselves, have been brought nigh the grave in sore sickness, and were full of promises as to how you would behave yourselves if it should please God to spare your lives. Some of you have narrowly escaped death by dangerous accidents, but God was pleased to spare you, to give you a further space to repent—yet you continue in sin.

Some of you have seen times of remarkable outpourings of the Spirit of God in this town in times past, but it has had no good effect on you. You had the strivings of the Spirit of God too as well as others. God did not so pass by your door, but He came and knocked—yet you stood it out. Now God has come again in a more remarkable manner than ever before, and has been pouring out His Spirit for some months in its most gracious influence—yet you remain in sin until now. In the beginning of this awakening, you were warned to flee from wrath and to forsake your sins. You were told what a wide door there was open, what an accepted time it was, and were urged to press into the kingdom of God. And many *did* press in: they forsook their sins and believed in Christ. But you, when you had seen it, repented not that you might believe Him.

Then you were warned again, and still others have been pressing and thronging into the kingdom of God. Many have fled for refuge and have laid hold on Christ—yet you continue in sin and unbelief. You have seen multitudes of all sorts, of all ages, young and old, flocking to Christ, many of them about your age and circumstances. But you are still in the same miserable condition in which you used to be. You have seen persons daily flocking to Christ like doves to their windows. God has not only poured out His Spirit on this town, but also on other towns around us; and they are flocking in there as well as here. This blessing spreads further and further. Many, far and near, seem to be setting their faces Zionward. Yet you who live here, where this work first began, continue behind still. You have no lot or portion in this matter.

2. *How dreadful the wrath of God is when it is executed to the uttermost.* To make you in some measure sensible of that, I desire you to consider whose wrath it is. The wrath of a king is the roaring of a lion, but this is the wrath of Jehovah, the Lord God Omnipotent. Let us consider, what can we rationally think of it? How dreadful must be the wrath of such a Being when it comes upon a person to the uttermost without any pity, moderation, or merciful circumstances! What must be the uttermost of His wrath who made heaven and earth by the word of His power; who spoke and it was done, who commanded and it stood fast! What must His wrath be who commands the sun and it rises not, and seals up the stars! What must His wrath be who rebukes the sea and makes it dry, who removes the mountains out of their places and overturns them in His anger! What must His wrath be whose majesty is so awful that no man could live in the sight of it! What must the wrath of such a Being be when it comes to the uttermost, when He makes His majesty appear and shine bright in the misery of wicked men! And what is a worm of the dust before the fury and under the weight of this wrath which the stoutest devils cannot bear, but utterly sink and are crushed under it!

Consider how dreadful the wrath of God is sometimes in this world, only in a little taste or view of it. Sometimes, when God only enlightens conscience to have some sense of His wrath, it causes the stout-hearted to cry out. Nature is ready to sink under it, when indeed it is but a little glimpse of divine wrath that is seen. This has been observed in many cases. But if a slight taste and apprehension of wrath is so dreadful and intolerable, what must it be when it comes upon persons to the uttermost! When a few drops or little sprinkling of wrath is so distressing and overbearing to the soul, how must it be when God opens the floodgates and lets the mighty deluge of His wrath come pouring down upon men's guilty heads, and brings in all His waves and billows upon their souls! How little of God's wrath will sink them! Psalm 2:12: "When His wrath is kindled but a little, blessed are all they that put their trust in Him."

3. Consider that you know not what wrath God may be about to execute upon wicked men in this world. Wrath may, in some sense, be coming upon them in the present life to the uttermost, for all we know. When it is said of the Jews, "The wrath is come upon them to the uttermost," respect is had not only to the execution of divine wrath on that people in hell, but that terrible destruction of Judea and Jerusalem which was then near approaching by the Romans. We know not but the wrath is now coming in some peculiarly awful manner on the wicked world. God seems, by the things which He is doing among us, to be coming forth for some great thing. The work which has been lately wrought among us is no ordinary thing. He does not work in His usual way, but in a way very extraordinary; and it is probable that it is a forerunner of some very great revolution. We must not pretend to say what is in the womb of Providence, or what is in the book of God's secret decrees, yet we may and ought to discern the signs of these times.

Though God is now about to do glorious things for the church and people, yet it is probable that they will be accompanied with dreadful things for His enemies. It is the manner of God, when He brings about any glorious revolution for His people, at the same time to execute very awful judgments on His enemies. Deuteronomy 32:43: "Rejoice, O ye nations, with His people: for He will avenge the blood of His servants, and will render vengeance to His adversaries." Isaiah 3:10–11: "Say ye to the righteous that it shall be well with him: for they shall eat the fruit of their doings. Woe unto the wicked, it shall be ill with him: for the rewards of his hands shall be given him." Isaiah 65:13–14: "Therefore thus saith the Lord God, Behold, My servants shall eat, but ye shall be hungry: behold, My servants shall drink, but ye shall be thirsty: behold, My servants shall rejoice, but ye shall be ashamed: behold, My servants shall sing for joy of heart, but ye shall cry for sorrow of heart, and shall howl for vexation of spirit."

We find in Scripture that where glorious times are prophesied to God's people, there are at the same time awful judgments foretold to His enemies. What God is now about to do, we know not; but this we may know: there will be no safety to any but those who are in the ark. Therefore it behoves all to haste and flee for their lives, to get into a safe condition, to get into Christ. Then they need not fear, though the earth be removed and the mountains carried into the midst of the sea; though the waters thereof roar and be troubled; though the mountains shake with the swelling thereof; for God will be their refuge and strength. They need not be afraid of evil tidings. Their hearts may be fixed, trusting in the Lord.

Concerning the Endless Punishment of Those Who Die Impenitent

1. The word "everlasting" is used in the very sentence of the Judge at the last day, whom we cannot suppose to use rhetorical tropes and figures. The wicked that are finally impenitent are represented as wholly cast away, lost, and made no account of, which is quite inconsistent with their punishment being medicinal, for their good and purification, and to fit them for final and eternal happiness. Eternal punishment is not eternal annihilation. Surely they will not be raised to life at the last day only to be annihilated.

"The words used to signify the duration of the punishment of the wicked do, in their etymology, truly signify a proper eternity; and if they are sometimes used in a less strict sense, when the nature of the thing requires it, yet that can never pass as any reason why they are not to be understood absolutely when the subject is capable of it. These terms are the most expressive of an endless duration of any that can be used or imagined. And they always signify so far positively endless as to be express against any other period or conclusion than what arises from the nature of the thing. They are never used in Scripture in any other limited sense than to exclude all positive abolition, annihilation, or conclusion, other than what the natural intent or constitution of the subject spoken of must necessarily admit. The word *aiwnios*, which is the word generally used by the sacred writers, is, we know, derived from the adverb *aei*, which signifies forever, and cannot without force be used in any lower sense. And, particularly, this is the word by which the eternal immutable attributes of Deity are several times expressed" (Dodwell's Sermon in answer to Whiston, pp. 15, 16).

2. If the torments of hell are purifying pains that purge the damned from their sins, it must be by bringing them to repentance, convincing them of the evil of sin, inducing them to forsake it and with a sincere heart to turn from sin to God, and heartily to choose virtue and holiness. There is no other way for sinners to be purged as moral agents; and if hellfire is the means of any other purification it cannot be a moral purification.

If the wicked in hell are the subjects of torments, in order to their purification, and so being fitted for, and finally brought to, eternal happiness, then they are the subjects of a dispensation that is truly a dispensation of love, and of divine and infinite goodness and benevolence towards them. And if the design of the pains of hell is that of kind and benevolent chastisement to bring sinners to repentance and compliance with the divine will, then we cannot suppose that they will be continued after the sinner has repented and is actually brought to yield and comply. For that would be to continue them for no purpose—to go on using means and endeavors to obtain the end when the end is accomplished and the thing aimed at is fully obtained already.

Moreover, if the damned, after many ages of suffering extreme torment in hell, are to be delivered, and made perfectly and eternally happy, then they must be in a state of probation during this long season of their confinement to such extreme misery. If they are not in a state of probation, or on any trial how they will behave themselves under these severe and terrible inflictions of wrath, but are to be delivered and made eternally happy at the end of a certain period, then what restraints are they under from giving an unbounded looseness and license to their wickedness in expression of enmity against God in cursing and blaspheming and whatever their hearts are inclined to? And if they are in such a state as this wherein they are thus left to unrestrained wickedness, and every curb to their most wicked inclination is taken off, being nevertheless sure of deliverance and everlasting happiness, how far is this state fit to be a state of purgation of rational creatures and moral agents from sin, being a state wherein they are so far from means of repentance, reformation, and entirely reclaiming and purging them from sin that all manner of means are rather removed; and so much is every restraint taken off that they are given up wholly to sin which, instead of purifying them, will tend, above all things that can be conceived, to harden them in sin and desperately establish the habits of it?

3. A state of purgation of moral agents, that is, a state to bring sinners to repentance and reformation and not a state of trial, is a gross absurdity.

OBJECTION. If any should say, "Though we should maintain that the pains of hell are purifying pains to bring sinners to repentance in order to their deliverance and eternal happiness, yet there will be no necessity of supposing either that they may sin with impunity, and so without restraint, or that they are properly in a state of probation; for they have no probation whether they shall finally have eternal happiness, because it is absolutely determined by the benevolent Creator, concerning His intelligent creatures, that they shall finally be brought to a state of happiness; but yet their circumstances may be such as may tend greatly to restrain their wickedness, because the time of their torment shall be longer or shorter, according as they behave themselves under their chastisements more or less perversely; or that their torment shall be raised to a greater height, and additions shall be made in proportion to the wickedness they commit in their purgatory flames."

ANSWER. Even on this supposition they are in a state of probation for a more speedy possession of eternal life and happiness, and deliverance from further misery and punishment; this makes their state as much a state of probation as their state in the present life. For here it is supposed by these men that sinners are not in a state of trial, whether ever they shall obtain eternal happiness or not; because that is absolutely determined, and the determination known or knowable concerning all without any trial. But it is only a state of trial whether they shall obtain eternal life so soon as at the end of their lives or at the day of judgment. Neither have they any trial during this life whether they shall escape all affliction and chastisement for sin or not, but whether they shall be relieved from a state of suffering so soon, and shall escape those severer and longer chastisements that, with respect to many, are to come afterwards.

And on the supposition of the objection, there must be the proper circumstances of a state of probation in hell as well as on earth. There they must likewise be continued in that state of free agency that renders them properly the subjects of judgment and retribution; for on the supposition of the objection they shall be punished for their wickedness in hell by an addition to their misery proportioned to their sin; and they shall be the subjects of God's merciful strivings, endeavors, and means to bring them to repentance as well as there. And there must be a divine judgment after the trial, to determine their retribution as much as after this life. And the same or like things must be determined by the supreme Judge as will be determined at the day of judgment. At that great day, on the supposition of such as I oppose, what will be determined concerning the impenitent? Not what their eternal state shall be, but only whether they shall have eternal happiness immediately; whether they have repented and are qualified for immediate admission to heavenly glory, or whether the bestowment of it shall be delayed and farther chastisements made use of, and so it must be again after their castigatory purifying pains.

At the end of all, there must be a judgment whether now they truly repent, and so have performed the condition of deliverance, and immediate admission to the state of the blessed, or whether there shall be a further season of misery which brings it in all respects to be a proper judgment, as much as at the general resurrection. And the preceding time of the use of means and God's striving with them to bring them to repentance is as much a proper time of trial in order to judgment as the time of this life.

4. But if the damned are in a state of trial, let it be considered how unreasonable this is. If they are in a state of trial, then they must be in a state of liberty and moral agency, as those men will doubtless own. So they, according to their notion of liberty, must be under no necessity of continuing in their rebellion and wickedness, but may cast away their abominations and turn to God and their duty in a thorough subjection to His will very speedily. And then, seeing the end of their probationary state and the severe means God uses with them to bring them to repentance is obtained, how unreasonable will it be to suppose that God, after this, would continue them still under hell torments for a long succession of ages? But if God should speedily deliver them on their speedy repentance, how are the threatenings and predictions of their everlasting punishment fulfilled in any sense, according to the sense even of those who deny the absolute eternity of the misery of hell, and hold that the words "everlasting" and

"forever," when applied to the misery of the damned, are not to be taken in the strictest sense? They yet allow they signify a very long time, a great many ages.

5. If the devils and damned spirits are in a state of probation, have liberty of will, are under the last and most extreme means to bring them to repentance, and, consequently, the greatest means, having the strongest tendency of all to be effectual, I say, if thus, then is it possible that the greatest part, if not all, of them may be reclaimed by those extreme means, and may be brought to thorough repentance before the day of judgment? Yea, it is possible, it might be very soon. And, if so, how could it certainly be predicted, concerning the devil, that he would do such and such great things in opposition to Christ and His Church from age to age? and that at last he should be judged and punished, and have God's wrath more terribly executed upon him? Revelation 20:10: "And the devil that deceived them was cast into the lake of fire and brimstone, where the beast and false prophet are, and shall be tormented day and night, for ever and ever." And how is it said in Scripture that when he fell he was cast down from heaven and reserved under chains of darkness unto judgment? The expression seems naturally to signify strong and irrefrageable bonds which admit of no comfort or hope of escape.

And besides, being reserved in chains unto judgment is not consistent with the appointment of another time of trial and opportunity to escape the judgment and condemnation. Jude 6: they are "reserved in everlasting chains under darkness unto the judgment of the great day." And if any of the separate souls of the wicked that are in the case that the soul of the rich man was in (when he died and lifted up his eyes in hell being in torments) should repent and be delivered before the day of judgment, and so should appear at the right hand among the righteous at that day, then how could that be verified which is said in 2 Corinthians 5:10: "For we must all stand before the judgment seat of Christ, that every one may receive the things done in his body, whether good or bad"? And we have reason to think that the time of standing before the judgment seat of Christ which the apostle has a special respect to is the day of judgment, if we compare this with other Scripture, such as that of the same apostle, Acts 17:31: "He hath appointed a day in which He will judge the world in righteousness by that man whom He hath ordained." And many other places.

6. And how does their being in a state of trial, many of them for so many ages after death before the day of judgment, during all which time they have opportunity to repent, consist with those words of Christ in Mark 8:38: "Whosoever therefore shall be ashamed of Me and My words in this adulterous and sinful generation, of him also shall the Son of man be ashamed, when He cometh in the glory of His Father, with the holy angels"? How is their continuing in a state of trial from the time of that generation, and from the end of their lives to the day of judgment, consistent with its being declared to them from God beforehand that they shall certainly be condemned at the day of judgment? or with Christ's certifying to them beforehand that whatever trial they shall have, whatever opportunity God should give them for repentance and pardon for so many ages, all would be in vain; which in effect is passing the sentence?

We may argue in like manner from those words in Matthew 10:14–15: "And whosoever shall not receive you, nor hear your words, verily I say unto you, It shall be more tolerable for the land of Sodom and Gomorrah in the day of judgment than for that city." Also Matthew 11:21–24: "Woe unto thee, Chorazin, woe unto thee, Bethsaida; I say unto you, It shall be more tolerable for Tyre and Sidon in the day of judgment than for you. And thou, Capernaum, which art exalted to heaven, shalt be brought down to hell. I say unto you, It shall be more tolerable for the land of Sodom, in the day of judgment, than for thee."

It is declared what the state of those obstinate unbelievers should be at the day of judgment for their wickedness here in the body, with an asseveration, "I say unto you." And sentence indeed is passed beforehand upon them by their Judge concerning the punishment that shall be executed upon them at the day of judgment. The declaration is made in the form of a solemn denunciation or sentence: "Woe unto thee, Chorazin, woe unto thee, Bethsaida." And is it reasonable to suppose that the very Judge that is to judge them at the end of the world would peremptorily declare that they should not escape punishment at the day of judgment, yea, solemnly denounce sentence upon them, dooming them to the distinguished punishment they should then suffer for their obstinacy in their lifetime, and yet appoint another time of trial of a great many hundred years between their death and the day of judgment wherein they should have opportunity to escape that punishment?

7. It is here also to be observed that the wicked inhabitants of Sodom and Gomorrah should be condemned to misery at the day of judgment, though they had already been in their purifying flames and in a state of probation. The apostle (Romans 2:16) repeatedly tells us when these things shall be that men shall thus receive their retribution: "In the day when God shall judge the secrets of men according to my gospel," which shows that this life is the only state of trial, and that all men shall be judged at the end of the world according to their behavior in this life, and not according to their behavior in another state of trial between this life and that day.

So it is apparent by 2 Thessalonians 1:5–9: "Which is a manifest token of the righteous judgment of God, seeing it is a righteous thing with God to recompense tribulation to them that trouble you, when the Lord Jesus shall be revealed from heaven with his mighty angels, in flaming fire, taking vengeance on them that know not God, and obey not the gospel of Jesus Christ; who shall be punished with everlasting destruction." Here it is manifest that all who are obstinate unbelievers, rejecters of the gospel, shall at the day of judgment be punished with everlasting destruction. So that no room is left for a state of trial and a space to repent before that time for ages in hell. So it is apparent from Matthew 25 that none will be found at the right hand but they who have done such good works as can be done only in this world, which would not be declared beforehand if there was an opportunity given for millions of others to obtain that privilege.

8. It may be proven that the day of man's trial, and the time of God's striving in the use of means to bring him to repentance, and waiting for his repentance under the use of means, will not be continued after this life from those words in Genesis 6:3: "My Spirit shall not always strive with man, for that he also is flesh; yet his days shall be 120 years." It is as much as to say that it is not fit that this day of trial and opportunity should last always to obstinate, perverse sinners. "It is fit [that] some bounds should be set to My striving and waiting on such as abuse the day of My patience; and that merciful means and gracious calls should not be continued without limits to those who trample all means and mercies underfoot, and turn a deaf ear to all calls and invitations, and treat them with constant contempt. Therefore I will fix a certain limit. I will set their bounds to 120 years, when, if they repent not, I will put an end to all their lives, and with their lives shall be an end of my striving and waiting."

This, which in Genesis is called God's Spirit striving, is by the apostle Peter expressed by the waiting of the long-suffering of God in 1 Peter 3:20. But, according to the doctrine we are opposing, instead of God's striving and using means to bring those wicked men to repentance, and waiting in the use of striving and endeavors 120 years, or to the end of their lives and no longer, He has gone on still since that for above 4000 years, striving with them in the use of more powerful means to bring them to repentance, and waiting on them, and will continue to do so for so long a time afterwards that the time is often called everlasting, and represented as enduring forever and ever.

9. Those words of Christ, "I must work the works of Him that sent Me, while it is day; the night cometh when no man can work" (John 9:4), prove that there is no other day of trial after this life. Christ, having undertaken for us, and taken on Himself our nature, appearing in the form of a servant and standing as our Surety and representative, had a great work appointed Him of God to do in this life for eternity. He could not obtain eternal life and happiness for Himself in any other way than by doing that work in this life which was the time of His probation for eternity as well as ours. And therefore His words imply as much as if He had said, "I must do that work which God has appointed Me to do for eternity, that great service which must be done, as I would be eternally happy, now while the day of life lasts, which is the only day appointed for the trial of man's faithfulness in the service of God in order to his being accepted to eternal rewards. Death is coming, which will be the setting of the sun, and the end of this day; after which no work will remain, nothing to be done that will be of any significance in order to the obtaining of the recompense of eternal felicity."

10. And doubtless to the same purpose is Ecclesiastes 9:10:

"Whatsoever thy hand findeth to do, do it with thy might; for there is no work [or "no man can work"], nor device, nor knowledge, nor wisdom in the grave, whither thou goest." As much as to say, "After this life, nothing can be done, nothing invented or devised in order to your happiness; no wisdom or art will serve you to any such purpose if you neglect the time of the present life."

It is unreasonable to suppose the wise man means only that we should in this life do all that we can in temporal concerns and to promote our temporal interest, and that nothing can be done towards this after this life—not only as this would be an observation of very little importance, it being as flat and impertinent as if he had said, "Whatever your hand finds to do this year, do it with your might; for nothing that you do or devise the next year will signify anything to promote your interest and happiness this year"; but also because the wise man himself, in the conclusion of this book, informs us that his drift through the whole book is to induce us to do a spiritual work: to fear God and keep His commandments, in order not to gain happiness in this life (which he tells us throughout the book is never to be expected), but in order to gain a future happiness and retribution in consequence of a judgment to come. Chapter 12:13–14: "Let us hear the conclusion of the whole matter: Fear God, and keep His commandments; for this is the whole duty (i.e., the whole business, the whole concern) of man. For God will bring every work into judgment, whether it be good, or whether it be evil."

11. If the wicked in hell are in a state of trial, under severe chastisement, as means in order to their repentance and obtaining the benefit of God's favor in eternal rewards, then they are in a state of such freedom as makes them moral agents and the proper subjects of judgment and retribution. Then those terrible chastisements are made use of as the most

powerful means of all, more efficacious than all the means used in this life which prove ineffectual, and which, proving insufficient to overcome sinners' obstinacy and prevail with their hard hearts, God is compelled to relinquish them all, and have recourse to those torments as the last means, the most effectual and powerful. If the torments of hell are to last for ages of ages, then it must be because sinners in hell all this while are obstinate; and though they are free agents, as to this matter, yet they willfully and perversely refuse even under such great means to repent, forsake their sins, and turn to God. It must be further supposed that all this while they have the offers of immediate mercy and deliverance made to them, if they will comply.

Now, if this is the case, and they shall go on in such wickedness, and continue in such extreme obstinacy and pertinaciousness for so many ages (as is supposed by its being thought their torments shall be so long continued), how desperately will their guilt be increased! How many thousand times more guilty will they be at the end of the term than at the beginning! And therefore they will be much the more proper objects of divine severity, deserving God's wrath, and still a thousand times more severe and longer continued chastisements than in the past. Therefore it is not reasonable to suppose that all the damned should be delivered from misery, received to God's favor, and made the subjects of eternal salvation and glory at that time when they are many thousand times more unworthy of it, more deserving of continuance in misery than when they were first cast into hell. It is not likely that the infinitely wise God should so order the matter. And if their misery should be augmented and still lengthened out much longer to atone for their newly contracted guilt, they must be supposed to continue impenitent till that second additional time of torment is ended, at the end of which their guilt will still be risen higher and vastly increased beyond what it was before. And at this rate where can there be any place for an end of their misery?

12. It further appears from what was observed above that the sinner who continues obstinate in wickedness, under such powerful means to reclaim him for so long a time, will be so far from being more and more purged, or brought nearer to repentance, that he will be farther from it. Wickedness in his heart will be vastly established and increased. For it may be laid down as an axiom that the longer men continue willfully in wickedness, the more is the habit of sin established, and the more and more will the heart be hardened in it. Again, it may be laid down as another axiom that the greater and more powerful the means are that are used to bring men to reform and repent, which they resist and are obstinate under, the more desperately are men hardened in sin, and the more the principle of it in the heart is confirmed. It may be laid down as a third axiom that long continuance in perverse and obstinate rebellion against any particular kind of means tends to render those particular means vain, ineffectual, and hopeless.

After the damned in hell have stood it out with such prodigious perverseness and stoutness for ages of ages in their rebellion and enmity against God, refusing to bow to His will under such constant, severe, mighty chastisements, attended all the while with offers of mercy, what a desperate degree of hardness of heart and fixed strength of habitual wickedness will they have contracted at last, and inconceivably farther will they be from a penitent, humble, and pure heart than when first cast into hell! And if the torments should be lengthened out still longer, and also their impenitence (as by the supposition one will not end before the other does), still the farther will the heart be from being purified. And so, at this rate, the torments will never at all answer their end and must be lengthened out to all eternity.

13. Matthew 5:25-26: "Agree with thine adversary quickly, while thou art in the way with him; lest at any time the adversary deliver thee to the judge, and the judge deliver thee to the officer, and thou be cast into prison. Verily I say unto thee, Thou shalt not come out thence, till thou hast paid the uttermost farthing." These words imply that sinners are in the way with their adversary, having opportunity to be reconciled to him but for a short season, inasmuch as it is intimated that they must agree with him quickly or they shall cease to be in the way with him, or to have opportunity to obtain his favor any more. But if they shall be continued in a state of probation after death to the end of the world, and after that for ages, how far, how very far, are these words of Christ from representing the matter as it is?

14. That some even in this world are utterly forsaken of God and given up to their own hearts' lusts proves that these men never will be purified from their sins. That God should, in the future world, use great means to purify them and fit them for eternal happiness and glory, in the enjoyment of Himself, is not consistent with the supposition that, after the use of great means and endeavors with them in this world, He gives them up to sin because of their incorrigibleness and perverse, obstinate continuance in rebellion under the use of those great means, and so leaves them to be desperately hardened in sin and go on and increase their guilt and multiply transgressions to their utter ruin. This is agreeable to manifold representations of Scripture. This is not agreeable to the scheme of such as suppose that God is all the while, before and after death, prosecuting the design of purifying and preparing them for eternal glory. Consider Psalm 92:7: "When the wicked spring as grass, and when all the workers of iniquity do flourish, it is that they shall be destroyed for ever."

These places show that God has no merciful design with those whom He gives up to sin.

15. The apostle, in Hebrews 6:4–6, says, "It is impossible for those who were once enlightened, and have tasted of the heavenly gift . . . if they fall away, to renew them again unto repentance, seeing they crucify to themselves the Son of God afresh, and put Him to an open shame." The apostle speaks of their renovation to repentance as never likely to happen for this reason: that they have proven irreclaimable under such great means to bring them to repentance, and have thereby so desperately hardened their hearts, and contracted such great guilt by sinning against such great light and trampling on such great privileges. But if so, how much more unlikely still will it be that they should ever be renewed to repentance after they have gone still more and more to harden their hearts by an obstinate, willful continuance in sin, many thousand years longer, under much greater means, and have therefore done immensely more to establish the habit of sin and increase the hardness of their hearts; and after their guilt is so vastly increased instead of being diminished! If it is impossible to bring them to repentance, after they have rebelled against such light and knowledge of Christ and the things of another world as they had in this life, how much more impossible is it when, added to this, they have had that infinitely greater and clearer knowledge and view of those things to be manifested at the day of judgment! Then they shall see Christ in the glory of His Father with all His holy angels; they shall see His great majesty, and know the truth of His promises and threatenings by sight and experience, and shall see all those ineffable manifestations of the glory of Christ: of His power, omniscience, strict inflexible justice, infinite holiness and purity, truth and faithfulness, and His infinite mercy to penitents. They shall then see the dreadful

consequences of rebellion and wickedness, and the infinitely happy and glorious consequences of the contrary; and, even at this time (on the supposition) they have the offers of mercy and deliverance from that dreadful misery, and the enjoyment of the favor of the great Judge, and participation in all the happiness and glory of the righteous which they shall see at His right hand, if then they will throw down the weapons of their rebellion and repent and comply with His will.

But if they still, from the greatness of their enmity and perverseness, obstinately and willfully refuse, yea, and continue still thus refusing even after they have actually felt the terrible wrath of God, and are cast into the lake of fire; yea, after they have continued there many ages, all the while under offers of mercy on repentance, I say, if it is impossible to renew them to repentance after their rebelling against and trampling on the light and knowledge and means used with them in this world, so that it is not to be expected, because of the degree of hardness and guilt contracted by it, how much less is it to be expected at the day of judgment, after all this obstinacy manifested, and guilt contracted? If such guilt is contracted, by despising such means and advantages as the apostle has respect to in this life, that it may be compared to guilt that would be contracted by crucifying Christ afresh, how much more when, added to this, they shall so openly have despised Christ, when appearing to them in all the terrors, glories, and love that shall be manifested at the day of judgment in their immediate and most clear view, and all is offered to them if they will but yield subjection to Him, and their enmity shall have appeared so desperate as rather to choose that dreadful lake of fire; and shall have continued in their choice even after they have felt the severity of that torment without rest day or night for many ages?

16. That all shall not be finally purified and saved is mani-

fest from Matthew 12:31–32: "Wherefore I say unto you, All manner of sin and blasphemy shall be forgiven unto men; but the blasphemy against the Holy Ghost shall not be forgiven unto men. And whosoever speaketh a word against the Son of man, it shall be forgiven him; but whosoever speaketh against the Holy Ghost, it shall not be forgiven him, neither in this world, neither in the world to come." Also Mark 3:28–29: "Verily I say unto you, All sins shall be forgiven unto the sons of men, and all blasphemies wherewith soever they shall blaspheme; but he that shall blaspheme against the Holy Ghost hath never forgiveness, but is in danger of eternal damnation." 1 John 5:16: "If any man see his brother sin a sin which is not unto death, he shall ask, and He shall give him life for them that sin not unto death. There is a sin unto death; I do not say he shall pray for it."

From each of these places it is manifest that he who is guilty of blasphemy against the Holy Ghost shall surely be damned, without any deliverance from his punishment or end to it. The various expressions that are used serve much to certify and fix the import of others. In Matthew 12:31 it is said, "The blasphemy against the Holy Ghost shall not be forgiven unto men." The negative is general, and equally respects all times. If this sin should be forgiven at a remote time, it would be as contrary to such a negative as if it were forgiven immediately. But to convince us that Christ has respect to all times, even the remotest, and that He means to deny that he shall be forgiven at any time whatsoever, in Mark it is said, "He shall never be forgiven," or "hath never forgiveness." And, lest this "never" should be interpreted to mean "never as long as he lives," or "never in this world," it is said in Matthew 12:32: "It shall not be forgiven him, neither in this world, nor in the world to come." And lest it should be said that, although he never is forgiven, yet that does not hinder but that there may be an end to his punishment, because he may suffer all he deserves in suffering a temporal punishment, or punishment of a limited, long duration, and he that is acquitted in paying all his debt—is not said to be forgiven his debt: another expression is used in Mark which shows that he shall ever suffer damnation, and never have deliverance from his misery, whether by forgiveness or without it: "hath never forgiveness, but is in danger of eternal damnation." And the forementioned expressions, "He shall never be forgiven," "He hath never forgiveness," and "shall not be forgiven in this world, nor the world to come" show the meaning of the word "eternal" here to be such as absolutely excludes any period, any time of favor, wherein condemnation and punishment shall have ceased.

And what the apostle John says of those who commit the unpardonable sin confirms the whole, and proves that he who has committed this sin remains under no dispensation of mercy, and that no favor is ever to be hoped for from God. And therefore it is not our duty to pray for such favor. "There is a sin unto death, I do not say he shall pray for it"; or, "I give you no direction to pray for them who sin this sin unto death."

17. Thus it is evident that all wicked men will not have an end to their damnation; but when it is said they are in danger of eternal or everlasting damnation, the word "eternal" is to be understood in the strictest sense. The same terms are used concerning all impenitent sinners, that they shall be sentenced to eternal punishment and shall go into everlasting punishment; that their worm dieth not and their fire is not quenched, and they shall be tormented forever and ever. Such terms are used after this world comes to an end; and also when they who have committed the unpardonable sin, and others, shall be sentenced all together to an everlasting

fire, in the same terms. It is unreasonable to suppose that the punishment of some will be everlasting in an infinitely different sense from others jointly sentenced, and that the duration of the punishment of one shall be perfectly as nothing compared with the duration of the punishment of the other, infinitely less than a second to a million ages. It is unreasonable to suppose such a difference also on this account: that there cannot be such a difference in the demerit of those who commit the unpardonable sin and the demerit of the sins of all other wicked men, some of whom are exceedingly and, almost, inconceivably wicked. There cannot be a truly infinite difference in their guilt, as there must be a properly infinite difference between the dreadfulness of those torments that have an end, however long continued and however great, and the torments of a truly and strictly everlasting fire.

18. If the damned in hell shall all finally be saved, they shall be saved without Christ. It is manifest that Christ's saving work will be at an end at the day of judgment, for, as Christ has a twofold office—that of the Savior of the world and the Judge of the world—so the business of the latter office properly succeeds the former. It is not fit, in the nature of things, that He should come into the world and appear openly in the character of universal Judge to decide men's state—in consequence of the trial there has been for making their state better by salvation—till that trial is over and all its effects completed, when no more is to be hoped as to altering their state for the better by His salvation. Therefore Christ, at His first coming, appeared in order to save men from condemnation and a sentence of eternal misery, and not to judge them, as He tells us in John 12:47: "If any man hear My words and believe not, I judge him not: for I came, not to judge the world, but to save the world" (see also John 3:17 and 8:15).

But the great business He will come upon at His second

coming, as is abundantly declared, is to judge the world. And it is also exceedingly plain that Christ's saving work will be at an end at the day of judgment because we read in 2 Corinthians 15 that at the end of the world He will deliver up His kingdom. He will resign His commission, which proves that the work of salvation, which is the design of it, will be at an end when all His enemies, all who rejected Him, who would not have Him to rule over them, and so have failed of His salvation, shall be made His footstool, shall be condemned and destroyed. Instead of their being the heirs of salvation, He shall come "in flaming fire to take vengeance on them that know not God, and obey not the gospel of Jesus Christ, who shall be punished with everlasting destruction . . . when He shall come to be glorified in His saints, and admired in all them that believe" (2 Thessalonians 1:8–10).

19. If the damned, after they have suffered awhile, are to be delivered and to have eternal life, then the present dispensation of grace and life to the fallen children of men that was introduced by Christ and His apostles is not the last; but another is to be introduced after this has proved unprofitable and ineffectual. But that a new dispensation of grace should thus be introduced, because that which was brought in by Christ and His apostles proves weak and unprofitable through men's corruption, and there appears to be need of one which shall be more effectual, is not agreeable to the Scripture. For this dispensation is spoken of as the last and most perfect, wherein perfection was reached (Hebrews 7:19): "For the law made nothing perfect, but the bringing in of a better hope did." And chapter 11:40: "God having provided some better thing for us, that they without us should not be made perfect." The ancient dispensation is spoken of as that which God found fault with, in proving ineffectual through the corruption of men; and so He introduced a new administration that

should not be liable to exception, and therefore should not wax old or be ever liable to vanish away and give place to another (Hebrews 8:6–13). So he speaks of the things of that ancient dispensation as things which were liable to be shaken and removed, but of the things of the new dispensation then introduced as those that could not be shaken, but should remain forever (Hebrews 12:25–29 and 2 Corinthians 3:11). The dispensation of the New Testament is often spoken of in the prophecies of the Old Testament as an everlasting dispensation (Jeremiah 31:31–32; 32:40; Isaiah 61:8; Ezekiel 37:26).

20. To suppose that, after all the means of grace that are used in this world, Moses and the prophets, Christ and the gospel, the warnings of God's Word, and the exhibitions of glorious gospel grace have been despised and obstinately withstood, so as to make the case desperate as to their success, God has other means in reserve to be used afterwards to make men holy that will be more powerful and shall be effectual, is not agreeable to Scripture. Particularly, Luke 16:27–31: "Then he said, I pray thee therefore, father, that thou wouldst send him to my father's house, for I have five brethren; that he may testify to them, lest they also come into this place of torment. Abraham saith unto him, They have Moses and the prophets, let them hear them. And he said, Nay, father Abraham, but if one went unto them from the dead, they will repent. And he said unto him, If they hear not Moses and the prophets, neither will they be persuaded though one rose from the dead." And this is especially manifest from Revelation 22:10–12: "And he saith unto me, Seal not the sayings of the prophecy of this book, for the time is at hand. He that is unjust, let him be unjust still; and he that is filthy, let him be filthy still. . . . And behold I come quickly, and My reward is with Me, to give every man according as his works shall be."

I think the meaning must be either that the time is quickly

coming when every man's state will be fixed, inasmuch as Christ is quickly coming to judgment, to fix every man's state unalterably, according as his work shall be; and after that there will be no alteration now, any means or endeavors, in order to it; but he that is unjust, let him be unjust still; and he that is filthy, let him be filthy still. And if this is the meaning, it makes it evident that Christ will not immediately proceed to the use of the most powerful and effectual means of all to change the state of the unjust and filthy, to purify them and make them holy and fit them for eternal glory with infallible success. Or the meaning must be this, which seems to be much the most probable: Christ, having given this last revelation to His Church to be added to the book of Scripture, with which the canon was to be shut up and sealed by the instrumentality of the apostle John, who lived the longest of the apostles, and wrote this book after all the rest were dead, orders John (verse 10) to publish this book, wherein such great future judgments are revealed as coming on the wicked, and such an affecting declaration of the future glory of the saints, to enforce the rest of God's Word and means of grace. Then he intimates that no more revelations are to be expected, no more instructions and warnings are to be added to the Word of God as the steady means of grace any further to confirm and enforce the rest. And the next revelation that is to be expected, and that Christ will make of Himself to the world, is to be His immediate appearance in judgment to fix unalterably every man's state according to his works, according to the improvement he shall have made of those past revelations, instructions, and warnings; and therefore those who will not be purified by those means are not to expect that better or other means will ever be used with them. But "he that is unjust must remain so still; and he that is filthy must be filthy still; and he that is righteous shall be righteous still; and he that is holy shall be holy still." Thus Christ takes leave of His Church till His last coming, warning them to improve the means of grace they have, and informing them that they are never to have any other. That is, "They have Moses and the prophets; and, in the writings of the New Testament, they have more glorious, powerful, and efficacious revelations of Me. Those writings I now finish and seal. Let them hear these and make a good improvement of them, for these are the last means I shall ever use to change man's state." This is inconsistent with His reserving His greatest and most powerful means with a determined, certain success to be used after the day of judgment.

21. Those who suppose the damned are made to suffer the torments of hell for their purification suppose that God is herein prosecuting His grand design of benevolence to His creatures, yea, benevolence to the sufferers, and that He does not use these severe means but from necessity for their good because all gentle remedies prove ineffectual. Now it is unreasonable to suppose that God is under any necessity of inflicting such extreme torments upon them for so long a time in order to their being brought to repentance, and that:

(1) If we consider the nature of things. Torments inflicted have no tendency to bring a wicked man to repentance directly and properly, if by repentance we mean an alteration of the disposition, appetites, and taste of the mind. We know by experience that pain inflicted for gratifying an appetite may make men afraid to gratify the appetite, but they do not change the inclination or destroy the appetite. They may make men willing to comply with external exercises for which they have a distaste, and to which their heart, in its relish and inclinations, is averse, yet not from love to the things complied with, but from hatred of pain and love of ease. So the man complies in some sense, but his heart does not comply.

He is only driven, and is, as it were, forced; and an increase of pain alters not the nature of things. It may make a man more earnestly to desire freedom from pain, but still there is no more to be expected from it than is in the tendency of pain, which is not to give a new nature, a new heart, or a new natural relish and disposition. It is not granted that even long-continued pains and practice will gradually raise a habitual love to virtue. The pains of the damned, being great and long continued, may more and more convince them of the folly of their negligence and fearlessness in sin; it may make them willing to take some pains, but will not show them the beauty of holiness or the odiousness of sin, so as to cause them to hate sin on its own account.

Can anyone who considers human nature, especially of those who deny an innate, desperate wickedness of heart (as the men that we have this controversy with generally do), doubt in the least whether, if a man should be in a furnace of fire for one day only, alive and full of quick sense, and should retain a full and lively remembrance of his misery, it would not be sufficient to make him wholly comply with all the pains and outward self-denial requisite in order to a universal, external obedience to the precepts of the Word of God, rather than have those torments renewed and continued for ages, and, indeed, rather than endure one more such day? What pains would not such a man be willing to suffer? What labors could be too much? What would he not be willing to part with in foregoing worldly wealth or pleasures? Would not the most covetous man who had felt such a rod as this, be willing to part with all his treasures of silver and gold? the most ambitious man be willing to live in a cottage or wilderness? the most voluptuous man to part with his pleasures? Would he need first to endure many ages of such torment before he would be willing thus far to comply? It is against all principles of human nature to suppose it.

If he retains the remembrance of the torment in a lively idea of it, it must unspeakably outweigh the most lively, affecting and attractive ideas of the good things of the world. The supposition, therefore, of his not being brought to compliance by less torment is as unreasonable as to suppose that a mote of dust would sink the scale, being put in a balance with a talent of lead or with ten thousand talents. If the Most High is compassionate towards these poor wretches, and has nothing but a kind and gracious design of infinite mercy and bounty towards them, why does He take such dreadful measures with them? Will no other do? Cannot infinite wisdom find out some gentler method to bring to pass the same design? If it is said that no other can accomplish the effect consistently with the freedom of will, I answer, what means can be devised, having a greater tendency to drive men, and compel them to comply with the thing required (if there is any such thing), without acting freely, and as persons left to their own free choice, than such a rod not only held over, but used upon them in such an amazing manner by an omnipotent hand?

(2) It is apparent, from what has often come to pass, that God is in no necessity of making use of such dreadful and long-continued torments in order to bring sinners to repentance. It is most unreasonable to suppose that no sinners who ever were converted in this world were, before their conversion, as wicked and as hard-hearted as some of those who have died impenitent: as Saul the persecutor, afterwards the apostle Paul, and some of the converts in the second chapter of Acts who had had a hand in Christ's crucifixion, and innumerable instances of persecutors and others who have been brought to repentance since those days. Such were converted by gentler means than those pains of hell in what the

Scripture calls "everlasting burnings," and that without any infringement of liberty necessary to their being moral agents. It would be unreasonable to suppose that all those eighteen on whom the tower of Siloam fell were good men. But Christ would not have His hearers imagine that they were worse than themselves; and yet He intimates that there was a possibility of their escaping future misery by repentance.

(3) So far as pain and affliction are made use of to bring men to repentance, it is apparent God can make infinitely less severe chastisement effectual, together with such influences and assistances of His Spirit as are not inconsistent with the person's moral agency in their forsaking sin and turning to God. And if it should be said that none of them had the habits of sin so confirmed as all such as die in sin, I would answer that this is very unreasonably supposed; and if it should be allowed, yet it cannot be pretended that the difference of guilt and hard-heartedness is proportional at all to the severity of the chastisement used for purgation. If no more than ten degrees of pain or one year's chastisement be requisite for the overcoming of five degrees of strength of the habit of sin, one would think that less than 100,000 degrees or 100,000 years' chastisement should be sufficient to overcome ten degrees of strength of the same habit.

22. If the torments of hell are purifying pains, and are used by a God of universal benevolence towards His creatures as necessary means for the purgation of the wicked from sin, and their being fitted for, and finally brought to, eternal happiness in the enjoyment of the love of God, then it will follow that the damned in hell are still the objects of God's mercy and kindness, and that in the torments they suffer they are the subjects of a dispensation of grace and benevolence. All is for their good; all is the best kindness that can be done them, the most benevolent treatment they are capable of in their

Concerning Endless Punishment

state of mind, and, in all, God is but chastising them as a wise and loving Father with a grieved and compassionate heart, gives necessary chastisement to sons whom He loves, and whose good He seeks to the utmost.

In all He does He is only prosecuting a design of infinite kindness and favor. And, indeed, some of the chief of those who are in the scheme of purifying pains expressly maintain that, instead of being the fruits of vindictive justice, they are the effects of God's benevolence, not only to the system of intelligent creatures in general, but to the sufferers themselves. Now, how far are these things from being agreeable to the representation which is made of things in the Holy Scriptures?

The Scriptures represent the damned as thrown away of God, as things that are good for nothing, and of which God makes no account (Matthew 13:48), as dross, and not gold and silver or any valuable metal. Psalm 119:119: "Thou puttest away all the wicked of the earth as dross" (see Ezekiel 22:18; Jeremiah 6:28–30), as salt that has lost its savor, as good for nothing but to be cast out and trodden under foot of men; as stubble that is left, and as the chaff thrown out to be scattered by the wind, and go whither that shall happen to carry it, instead of being gathered and laid up as that which is of any value (Psalm 1:4; Job 21:18 and 35:5); as that which shall be thrown away as wholly worthless; as chaff, stubble, and tares, all which are thrown away as not worthy of any care to save them, yea, are thrown into the fire to be burnt up as mere nuisances, as fit for nothing but to be destroyed, and therefore are cast into the fire to be destroyed and done with (Matthew 3:12 and 12:30; Job 21:18); as barren trees, trees that are good for nothing, and not only so, but cumberers of the ground; and as such they shall be cut down and cast into the fire (Matthew 3:10 and 7:19; Luke 13:7); as barren branches in a vine that are cut off and cast away as good for nothing, and gathered and burned (John 15:6); as thrown out and purged away as the filth of the world.

Thus, it is said in Job 20:7 that "the wicked shall perish for ever, as his own dung." They are spoken of as those who shall be spewed out of God's mouth; as thrown into the lake of fire; as the great sink of all the filth of the creation. Revelation 21:8: "But the fearful, and unbelieving, and the abominable, and murderers, and whoremongers, and sorcerers, and idolaters, and all liars, shall have their share in the lake that burns with fire and brimstone." They are as briars and thorns that are not only wholly worthless in a field, but hurtful and pernicious, and are nigh unto cursing, whose end is to be burned (Hebrews 6:8). In other words, the husbandman throws them into the fire, and so has done with them forever. He does not still take care of them in order to make them fruitful and flourishing plants in his garden of delights. The wicked, it is said, shall be driven from light into darkness and chased out of the world (Job 18:18).

Instead of being treated by God with benevolence, chastening them with the compassion and kindness of a father for their great and everlasting good, they at that day, when God shall gather His children together to make them experience the blessed fruits of the love of a heavenly Father, shall be shut out as dogs (Revelation 21:7–8 and 22:14–15). They are represented as vessels of dishonor, vessels of wrath, fit for nothing else but to contain wrath and misery. They are spoken of as those who perish and lose their souls, as those who are lost (2 Corinthians 4:4); those who lose themselves and are cast away; those who are destroyed and consumed. These representations do not agree with such as are under a dispensation of kindness and the means of a physician in order to their eternal life, health, and happiness, though the means are severe. When God, of old, by His prophets, denounced His terrible judgments against Jerusalem and the people of Israel, against Moab, Tyre, Egypt, and Assyria, these judgments, though long continued, were not designed to be perpetual. There were mixed with those awful denunciations or added to them, promises or intimations of future mercy.

But when the Scripture speaks of God's dealings with ungodly men in another world, there are nothing but declarations and denunciations of wrath and misery, and no intimations of mercy—no gentle terms used, no significations of divine pity, no exhortations to humiliation under God's awful hand, or calls to seek His face and favor and turn and repent. The account that the Scripture gives of the treatment that wicked men shall meet with after this life is very inconsistent with the notion of their being from necessity subjected to harsh means of cure and severe chastisement with a benevolent, gracious design of their everlasting good—particularly the manner in which Christ will treat them at the day of judgment. He will bid the wicked depart from Him as cursed.

23. We have no account of any invitations to accept mercy, any counsels to repent, that they may speedily be delivered from this misery. But it is represented that then they shall be made His footstool. He shall triumph over them. He will trample upon them as men are wont to tread grapes in a winepress when they trample with all their might to the very end that they may effectually crush them in pieces. He will tread them in His anger, trample them in His fury, and, as He says, their blood shall be sprinkled on His garments, and He will stain all His raiment (Isaiah 63:1–6; Revelation 14:19–20 and 19:15, in which last place it is said, "He treadeth the winepress of the fierceness and wrath of Almighty God"). These things do not savor of chastening with compassion and benevolence, and as still prosecuting a design of love toward

them that He may in the end actually be their Savior and the means of their eternal glory.

There is nothing in the account of the day of judgment that looks as though saints had any love or pity for the wicked, on account of the terrible long-continued torments which they must suffer. Nor indeed will the accounts that are given admit of supposing any such thing. We have an account of their judging them and being with Christ in condemning them, concurring in the sentence, wherein He bids them be gone from Him as cursed with devils into eternal fire; but there is no account of their praying for them, nor of their exhorting them to consider and repent.

They shall not be grieved, but rather rejoice at the glorious manifestations of God's justice, holiness, and majesty in their dreadful perdition, and shall triumph with Christ (Revelation 18:20, and 19:1–7). They shall be made Christ's footstool, and so they shall be the footstool of the saints. Psalm 68:23: "That thy foot may be dipped in the blood of thine enemies, and the tongue of thy dogs in the same." If the damned were the objects of divine benevolence, and designed by God for the enjoyment of His eternal love, doubtless it would be required of all God's children to love them, pity them, pray for them, and seek their good; as here in this world it is required of them to love their enemies, to be kind to the evil and unjust, and to pity and pray for the vilest of men, who were their own persecutors, because they are the subjects of God's mercy, in many respects, and are fit objects of infinite divine mercy and love. If Christ, the Head of all the Church, pities the damned and seeks their good, doubtless His members ought to do so too. If the saints in heaven ought to pity the damned, as well as the saints on earth are obligated to pity the wicked who dwell here, doubtless their pity ought to be in some proportion to the greatness of the calamities of the objects of it, and the greatness of the number of those they see in misery. But if they had pity and sympathizing grief in such measure as this for so many ages, what an alloy would it be to their happiness! God is represented as whetting His glittering sword, bending His bow and making ready His arrows on the string against wicked men, and lifting His hand to heaven and swearing that He will render vengeance to His enemies, and reward those who hate Him and make His arrows drunk with their blood, and that His sword shall devour their flesh (Deuteronomy 32:40-42 and Psalm 7:11-13). Certainly this is the language and conduct of an enemy, not of a friend or of a compassionate, chastising father.

24. The degree of misery and torment that shall be inflicted is an evidence that God is not acting the part of benevolence and compassion, and only chastening from a kind and gracious principle and design. It is evident that it is God's manner, when He thus afflicts men for their good and chastens them with compassion, to stay His rough wind in the day of His east wind; to correct in measure; to consider the frame of those who are corrected; to remember their weakness and consider how little they can bear. He turns away His anger and does not stir up all His wrath (Psalm 78:37-39; Isaiah 27:8; Jeremiah 30:11 and 46:28). And it is His manner, in the midst even of the severest afflictions, to order some mitigating circumstances and to mix some mercy.

But the misery of the damned is represented as unmixed. "The wine of the wrath of God is poured out without mixture into the cup of His indignation that they may be tormented with fire and brimstone in the presence of the holy angels, and in the presence of the Lamb; and the smoke of their torment shall ascend up for ever and ever, and they have no rest day nor night" (Revelation 14:10-11). They are tormented in a flame that burns within them as well as round about them, and they shall be denied so much as a drop of water to cool their tongues. And God's wrath shall be inflicted in such a manner as to show His wrath and make His strength known on the vessels of wrath, and which shall be punished with everlasting destruction, answerable to that glory of Christ's power in which He shall appear at the day of judgment when He shall come in the glory of His Father with power and great glory, "in flaming fire, taking vengeance on them that know not God, and obey not the gospel."

Can any imagine that in all this God is only correcting from love, and that the subjects of these inflictions are some of those happy ones whom God corrects in order to teach them out of His law, whom He makes sore and binds up (Job 5:17–18; Psalm 94:12)? There is nothing in Scripture that looks as if the damned were under the use of means to bring them to repentance. It is apparent that God's manner is, when He afflicts men, to bring to repentance by affliction, to join instructions, admonitions, and arguments to persuade.

But if we judge by Scripture representations of the state of the damned, they are left destitute of all these things. There are no prophets, ministers, or good men to admonish them to reason, and expostulate with them or set them good examples. There is a perfect separation made between all the righteous and the wicked by a great gulf, so that there can be no passing from one to the other. They are left wholly to the company of devils, and others like them. When the rich man in hell cried to his father Abraham, begging a drop of water, he denied his request and added no exhortation to repentance. Wisdom is abundantly represented in the book of Proverbs as counseling, warning, calling, inviting, and expostulating with such as are under means for the obtaining of wisdom, and as waiting upon them in the use of means that they may turn at her reproof. But as for such as are obstinate under these means of grace and calls of wisdom till the time of their punishment comes, it is represented that their fear shall come as desolation and destruction as a whirlwind; that distress and anguish shall come upon them, and that then it will be in vain for them to seek wisdom; that if they seek her early they shall not find her, and if they call upon her, she will not hear; but instead of this, she will laugh at their calamity, and mock when their fear comes. This certainly does not consist with the idea that the God of wisdom is still striving with them, and using means in a benevolent and compassionate manner to bring them to seek and embrace wisdom, still offering wisdom with all her unspeakable benefits if they will hearken to her voice and comply with her counsel. Is wisdom then actually using the most powerful and effectual means to bring them to this happiness, even such as shall surely be successful, though they have obstinately refused all others, and when wisdom called they heretofore refused, and when she stretched forth her hand they did not regard? Is she still most effectually acting the part of a friend, to deliver them from their distress and anguish instead of laughing at their calamity (Proverbs 1:26)? This declaration of wisdom, if it ever is fulfilled at all, will surely be fulfilled most completely and perfectly at the time appointed for obstinate sinners to receive their most perfect and complete punishment.

If all mankind, even such as live and die in their wickedness, are and ever will be the objects of Christ's goodwill and mercy, and those whose eternal happiness He desires and seeks, then surely He would pray for all. But Christ declares that there are some that He prays not for. John 17:9: "I pray for them: I pray not for the world, but for them which Thou hast given Me; for they are Thine." Compare it with verse 14: "The world hath hated them, because they are not of the world, even as I am not of the world." Verse 25: "The world hath not known Thee, but I have known Thee; and these have known that Thou hast sent Me." And verse 20: "Neither pray I for these alone, but for them also which shall believe on Me through their word." By this it appears that Christ prayed for all who should ever be true believers. But He prayed not for those who should not be brought by the word of the apostles, and such means of grace as are used in this world, to believe in Him, and should continue, notwithstanding, not to know God, and in enmity against true holiness or Christianity. These were such as Christ prayed not for.

25. If sin and misery and the second death are to continue and prevail for so long a time after the day of judgment, with respect to great multitudes whom Christ will finally save and deliver from those things, having perfectly conquered and abolished them, then how can the Scriptures truly represent that all enemies shall be put under His feet at the end of the world, and that the last enemy that shall be destroyed is death, and that then, having perfectly subdued all His enemies, He shall resign up the kingdom to the Father, and He himself be subject to the Father (1 Corinthians 15:20-28)? The time of Christ's victory over death will be at the general resurrection and day of judgment, as is evident by verse 54 with the foregoing context. The chief enemies that Christ came to destroy, with regard to such as should be saved and be of His Church, were sin and misery, or death consisting in sin, and death consisting in suffering the second death, unspeakably the greatest enemy that came by sin, infinitely more terrible than temporal death. But if the notion I am opposing is true, these greatest and worst enemies, instead of being subdued, shall have their principal reign afterwards for many ages at least—sin in the sad effect and consequence of it, men's misery. And God shall have His strongest conflict with those enemies afterward, that is, shall strive against them in

Concerning Endless Punishment

the use of the most powerful means.

26. There is a great evidence that the devil is not the subject of any dispensation of divine mercy and kindness, and that God is prosecuting no design of infinite goodness towards him, and that his pains are not purifying pains. It is manifest that, instead of any influence of his torments to bring him nearer to repentance, he has been from the beginning of his damnation constantly, with all his might, exerting himself in prosecuting his wickedness, his violent, most haughty, and malignant opposition to God and man; fighting especially with peculiar virulence against Christ and His Church. He opposes with all his might everything that is good, seeking the destruction and misery of all mankind with boundless and insatiable cruelty; on which account he is called Satan, the adversary, Abaddon, and Apollyon, the destroyer. He is represented as a roaring lion, seeking whom he may devour; a viper, the old serpent, the great red dragon, red on account of his bloody, cruel nature. He is said to be a murderer from the beginning. He has murdered all mankind, murdered their souls as well as their bodies. He was the murderer of Jesus Christ by instigating Judas and His crucifiers. He has most cruelly shed the blood of an innumerable multitude of the children of God. He is emphatically called the evil one, that wicked one. He is "the spirit that worketh in the children of disobedience" (Ephesians 2:2). It is said that "he that committeth sin is of the devil; for the devil sinneth from the beginning" (1 John 3:8). And all wicked men are spoken of as his children.

He has set up himself as god of this world, in opposition to the true God, and has erected a vast kingdom over the nations. He is constantly carrying on a war with the utmost earnestness, subtlety, malice, and venom against Jesus Christ and all His holy and gracious designs; as maintaining a kingdom of darkness, wickedness, and misery in opposition to Christ's kingdom of light, holiness, and peace. And thus will He continue to do till the end of the world, as appears by Scripture prophecies.

27. And God's dealings with him are infinitely far from being those of a friend, kindly seeking his infinite good, and designing nothing else in the end but to make him eternally happy in love and favor and blessed union with Him. God is represented everywhere as acting the part of an enemy to him, who seeks and designs nothing in the final event but his destruction. The grand work of God's providence which He is prosecuting from the beginning to the end of the world, the work of redemption, is against him, to bruise or break in pieces his head, to cast him like lightning from heaven, from that height of power and dominion to which he has exalted himself, to tread him under foot and to cause His people to trample and bruise or crush him under foot and gloriously to triumph over him. Christ, when He conquered him, made a show of him openly, triumphing over him. And it is evident that as it will be with the devil in this respect, so it will be with the wicked. This is reasonable to suppose from what the Scripture represents of the relation wicked men stand in to the devil as his children, servants, subjects, instruments, and his property and possession. They are all ranked together with him in one kingdom, in one interest and one company. And many of them are the great ministers of his kingdom, and to whom he has committed authority; such as the beast and false prophet that we read of in the Revelation. Now, how reasonable and natural is it to suppose that those who are thus united should have their portion and lot together! As Christ's disciples, subjects, followers, soldiers, children, instruments, and faithful ministers shall have their part with Him in His eternal glory, so we may reasonably believe that the devil's

disciples, followers, subjects, soldiers in his army, his children, instruments, and ministers of his kingdom should have their part with him, and not that such an infinite difference should be made between them that the punishment of the one should be eternal and that of the other but temporal, and therefore infinitely less, infinitely disproportionate—so that the proportion between the punishment of the latter and that of the former is as nothing, infinitely less than a unit to a million of millions. This is unreasonable to be supposed in itself, as the difference of guilt and wickedness cannot be so great, but must be infinitely far from it; especially considering the aggravations of the wickedness of a great part of damned men as committed against Christ, and gospel grace and love, which exceedingly great aggravation the sin of the devils never had.

28. As the devil's ministers, servants, and instruments, of the angelic nature, those that are called the devil's angels, shall have their part with him, for the like reason we may well suppose his servants, and instruments of the human nature, will share with him. And not only is this reasonable in itself, but the Scripture plainly teaches us that it shall be so. Revelation 19:20: "The beast and the false prophet were both cast alive into the lake of fire burning with brimstone." So it is said in 20:10: "The devil that deceived them was cast into the lake of fire and brimstone, where the beast and false prophet are, and shall be tormented day and night for ever and ever." This expresses both the kind of misery and the duration. Just in the same manner it is said concerning the followers of the beast in Revelation 14:9–11: "Saying with a loud voice, If any man worship the beast, the same shall be tormented with fire and brimstone, and the smoke of their torment ascendeth up for ever and ever, and they have no rest day or night."

In Revelation 21:8, speaking of wicked men in general, it is said that "they shall have their part in the lake which burneth with fire and brimstone." So we find in Christ's description of the day of judgment that the wicked are sentenced to everlasting fire prepared for the devil and his angels. By this it appears most plainly that they share with the devil in suffering misery of the same kind, and also share with him in suffering misery of the same everlasting continuance.

And, indeed, not only would the punishment infinitely differ as to quantity and duration, if the punishment of the devils was to be eternal and of wicked men only temporal; but, if this were known, it would, as it were, infinitely differ in kind: the one suffering God's hatred and mere vengeance—inflictions that have no pity or kindness in them—the other, the fruit of His mercy and love, and infinitely kind intention; the one attended with absolute despair, and a black and dismal sinking prospect of misery, absolutely endless, the other with the light of hope, and a supporting prospect not only of an end to their misery, but of an eternal unspeakable happiness to follow.

According to the notion which I am opposing, the judgment that shall take place at the end of the world will be so far from being the last judgment, or any proper judgment to settle all things in their final state, that it will, with respect to the wicked, be no more than the judgment of a physician whether more sharp and powerful remedies must not be applied in order to the relief of sinners, and the cure of their disease, which, if not cured, will make them eternally miserable!

29. It is evident that the future misery of the wicked in hell is not come to an end, and to be succeeded by eternal happiness, and that their misery is not subservient to their happiness, because the Scripture plainly signifies, concerning those who die in their sins, that they have all the good and comfort in this life that ever is designed for them. Luke 6:24: "Woe

unto you that are rich, for ye have received your consolation." Luke 16:25: "Son, remember that thou in thy lifetime receivedst thy good things." Psalm 17:13–14: "Deliver my soul from the wicked, from the men of the world, which have their portion in this life, and whose belly Thou fillest with Thy hid treasure."

30. According to the opinion I am now opposing, God will surely at last deliver all the damned from their misery and make them happy. So God will see to it that the purifying torments shall certainly at last have their effect: to turn them from sin. Now, how can this consist with God's treating them as moral agents, and their acting from the freedom of their own wills in the affair of their turning from sin, and becoming morally pure and virtuous according to the notions of freedom and moral agency which now prevail, and are strenuously maintained by some of the chief assertors of this opinion concerning hell torments? This notion of freedom implies contingence, and is wholly inconsistent with the necessity of the event. If after all the torments used to bring sinners to repentance, the consequence aimed at, their turning from sin to virtue, is not necessary, but it shall still remain a contingent event whether there ever will be any such consequence of those severe, long-continued chastisements or not, then how can it be determined that this will surely be the consequence? How can it be a thing infallible that such a consequence of means used will follow when, at the same time, it is not a consequence in any way necessarily connected with the means used, it being only a thing contingent whether it will follow or not? If God has determined absolutely to make them all pure and happy, and yet their purity and happiness depend on the freedom of their will, then here is an absolute, divine decree, consistent with the freedom of men's will, which is a doctrine utterly rejected by the generality of that sort of men who deny

the eternity of hell torments.

If it is said that God has not absolutely determined the duration or measure of their torments, but intends to continue them till they repent, or to try lesser torments first, and, if these do not answer, to increase them till they are effectual, determining that He will raise or continue them till the effect shall finally and infallibly follow, that is the same thing as to necessitate the effect. And here is necessity in such a case, as much as when a blacksmith puts a piece of metal into a furnace with a resolution to melt it, and, if continuing it there a little while will not dissolve it, that he will keep it there till it dissolves; and if, by reason of its peculiar hardness, an ordinary degree of heat of the furnace will not be effectual, that he will increase the vehemence of the heat, till the effect shall certainly follow.

31. If any should maintain this scheme of temporary future punishments: that the torments in hell are not purifying pains, and that the damned are not in a state of trial with regard to any expected admission to eternal happiness, and that therefore they are not the proper objects of divine benevolence; that the dispensation they are under is not truly a dispensation of mercy, but that their torments are properly penal pains wherein God displays His vindictive justice; that they shall suffer misery to such a degree, and for so long a time as their obstinate wickedness in this world deserves; and that indeed they shall be miserable a very long time, so long that it is often figuratively spoken of in Scripture as being everlasting, and that then they shall be annihilated. On this I would observe that there is nothing gotten by such a scheme, no relief from the arguments taken from Scripture for the proper eternity of future punishment. For if it is owned that Scripture expressions denote a punishment that is properly eternal, but that it is in no other sense properly so than as the annihila-

tion, or state of nonexistence, to which the wicked shall return will be eternal; and that this eternal annihilation is that death which is so often threatened for sin, perishing forever, everlasting destruction, being lost, utterly consumed, and that the fire of hell is called eternal fire in the same sense that the external fire which consumed the cities of Sodom and Gomorrah is called eternal fire (Jude 7), because it utterly consumed those cities so that they might never be built more; and that this fire is called that which cannot be quenched, or at least not until it has destroyed them that are cast into it—if this is all that these expressions denote, then they do not at all signify the length of the torments or long continuance of their misery; so that the supposition of the length of their torments is brought in without any necessity. The Scripture says nothing of it, having no respect to it, when it speaks of their everlasting punishments; and it answers the Scripture expressions as well to suppose that they shall be annihilated immediately without any long pains, provided the annihilation is everlasting.

32. If any should suppose that the torments of the damned in hell are properly penal, and in execution of penal justice, but yet that they are neither eternal, nor shall end in annihilation, but shall be continued till justice is satisfied, and they have truly suffered as much as they deserve, whereby their punishment shall be so long as to be called everlasting, but that then they shall be delivered, and finally be the subjects of everlasting happiness; and that therefore they shall not in the meantime be in a state of trial, nor will they be waited upon in order to repentance, nor will their torments be used as means to bring them to it; for the term and measure of their punishment shall be fixed, from which they shall not be delivered on repentance, or any terms or conditions whatsoever, until justice is satisfied.

I would observe in answer to this that if it is so, the damned, while under their suffering, are either answerable for the wickedness that is acted by them while in that state or may properly be the subjects of a judicial proceeding for it or not. If the former is supposed, then it will follow that they must have another state of suffering and punishment after the ages of their suffering for the sins of this life are ended. And it cannot be supposed that this second period of suffering will be shorter than the first, for the first is only for the sins committed during a short life, often represented in Scripture for its shortness, to be a dream, a tale that is told, a blast of wind, a vapor, a span, a moment. But the time of punishment is always represented as exceedingly long, called everlasting; represented as enduring forever and ever, as having no end.

If the sins of a moment must be followed with such punishment, then, doubtless, the sins of those endless ages must be followed with another second period of suffering, much longer. For it must be supposed that the damned continue sinning all the time of their punishment; for none can rationally imagine that God would hold them under such extreme torments, terrible manifestations and executions of His wrath, after they have thoroughly repented and turned from sin, and have become pure and holy, and conformed to God, and so have left off sinning. And if they continue in sin during this state of punishment, with assurance that God still has a great benevolence for them, even so as to intend finally to make them everlastingly happy in the enjoyment of His love, then their sin must be attended with great aggravation. They will have the evil and ill desert of sin set before them in the most affecting manner in their dreadful sufferings for it, attended besides with evidence that God is infinitely benevolent towards them, and intends to bestow infinite blessing upon them.

But if this first long period of punishment must be followed with a second as long or longer, for the same reason the second must be followed by a third as long, or longer than that; and so the third must be followed by a fourth, and so *ad infinitum*; and, at this rate, there never can be an end of their misery. So this scheme overthrows itself.

33. And if the damned are not answerable for the wickedness they commit during their state of punishment, then we must suppose that, during the whole of their long and, as it were, eternal state of punishment, they are given up of God to the most unrestrained wickedness, having this to consider: that however far they go in the allowed exercises and manifestations of their malice and rage against God and Christ, saints and angels and their fellow damned spirits, they have nothing to fear from it; it will be never the worse. And surely, continuing in such unrestrained wickedness for such duration must most desperately confirm the habit of sin, must increase the root and fountain of it in the heart.

Now, how unreasonable is it to suppose that God would thus deal with such as were objects of His infinite kindness, and the appointed subjects of the unspeakable and endless fruits of His love, in a state of perfect holiness and purity and conformity to and union with Himself; thus to give them up beforehand to unrestrained malignity against Himself, and every kind of hellish wickedness, as it were, infinitely to increase the fountain of sin in the heart, and the strength of the principle and habit! Now, how incongruous is it to suppose, with regard to those for whom God has great benevolence, and designs eternal favor, that He would lay them under a necessity of extreme, unbounded hatred of Him, blasphemy and rage against Him, for so many ages—such necessity as should exclude all liberty of their own in the case! If God intends not only punishment, but purification, by these torments, on this supposition, instead of their being purified they must be set at an infinitely greater distance from purification. And if God intends them for a second time of probation in order to their being brought to repentance and the love of God after their punishment is finished, then how can it be certain beforehand that they shall finally be happy, as is supposed? How can it be certain that they will not fail in their second trial, or in their third, if there is a third?

Yea, how much more likely is it that they will fail of truly turning in heart from sin to the love of God, in their second trial, if there is any proper trial in the case, after their hearts have been so much more brought under the power of a strong habit of sin and enmity to God! If the habit proved so strong in this life that the most powerful means and mighty inducements of the gospel would not prevail, so that God was, as it were, under a necessity of cutting them down and dealing thus severely with them, how much less likely will it be that they will be prevailed upon to love God and the ways of virtue after their hearts are set at so much greater distance from those things! Yea, unless we suppose a divine interposition of almighty, efficacious power, to change the heart in the time of this second trial, we may be sure that, under these circumstances, the heart will not turn to love God.

34. And besides, if they are laid under such a necessity of hating and blaspheming God for so many ages, in the manner that has been spoken of, how extremely incongruous is such an imagination, that God would lay those He intended for the eternal bounty and blessedness of dear children under such circumstance that they must necessarily hate Him, and with devilish fury curse and blaspheme Him for innumerable ages, and yet never have cause, even when they are delivered and made happy in God's love, to condemn themselves for it, though they see the infinite hatefulness and unreasonable-

ness of it, because God laid them under such a necessity that they could use no liberty of their own in the case! I leave it for all to judge whether God's thus ordering things, with regard to such as, from great benevolence, He intended for eternal happiness in a most blessed union with Himself, be credible.

35. The same disposition and habit of mind and manner of viewing things is indeed the main ground of the cavils of many of the modern freethinkers, and fashionable writers, against the extremity and eternity of hell torments, which, if relied upon, would cause them to be dissatisfied with almost anything that is very uncomfortable in a future punishment, so much as the enduring of the pain that is occasioned by the thrusting of a thorn under the nail of the finger for a whole year together, day and night, without any rest or the least intermission or abatement. There are innumerable calamities that come to pass in this world through the permission and ordination of Divine Providence, against which (were it not that they are what we see with our eyes, and are universally known and incontestable facts) this cavilling, unbelieving spirit would strongly object; and which, if they were only proposed in theory as matters of faith, would be opposed as exceedingly inconsistent with the moral perfections of God. And the opinions of such as asserted them would be cried out against, as in numberless ways contrary to God's wisdom, His justice, goodness, mercy; such as the innumerable calamities that have happened to poor, innocent children, through the merciless cruelty of barbarous enemies, their being gradually roasted to death, shrieking and crying for their fathers and mothers; the extreme pains they sometimes are tormented with, by terrible diseases which they suffer; the calamities that have many times been brought on whole cities, while besieged, and when taken by merciless soldiers, destroying all, men, women, and children, without any pity; the extreme

miseries which have been suffered by millions of innocent persons, of all ages, sexes, and conditions, in times of persecution, when there has been no refuge to be found on earth; yea, those things that come to pass universally, of which all mankind are the subjects, in temporal death, which is so dreadful to nature.

The Eternity of Hell Torments

"These shall go away into everlasting punishment."
Matthew 25:46

In this chapter we have the most particular description of the day of judgment of any in the whole Bible. Christ here declares that when He shall hereafter sit on the throne of His glory, the righteous and the wicked shall be set before Him and separated one from the other, as a shepherd divides his sheep from the goats. Then we have an account how both will be judged according to their works, how the good works of the one and the evil works of the other will be rehearsed, and how the sentence shall be pronounced accordingly. We are told what the sentence will be on each, and then we have an account of the execution of the sentence on both. In the words of the text is the account of the execution of the sentence on the wicked or the ungodly, concerning which it is to my purpose to observe two things:

1. The duration of the punishment on which they are here said to enter: it is called everlasting punishment.

2. The time of their entrance on this everlasting punishment: after the day of judgment when all these things that are of a temporary continuance shall have come to an end, and even those of them that are most lasting—the frame of the world itself, the earth which is said to abide forever, the ancient mountains and everlasting hills, the sun, moon, and stars. When the heavens shall have waxed old like a garment, and as a vesture shall be changed, then shall be the time when the wicked shall enter on their punishment.

DOCTRINE. The misery of the wicked in hell will be absolutely eternal.

There are two opinions which I mean to oppose in this doctrine. One is that the eternal death with which wicked men are threatened in Scripture signifies no more than eternal annihilation: God will punish their wickedness by eternally abolishing their being.

The other opinion which I mean to oppose is that though the punishment of the wicked shall consist in sensible misery, yet it shall not be absolutely eternal, but only of a very long continuance.

Therefore to establish the doctrine in opposition to these different opinions, I shall undertake to show that:

I. It is not contrary to the divine perfections to inflict on wicked men a punishment that is absolutely eternal.

II. The eternal death which God threatens is not annihilation, but an abiding, sensible punishment or misery.

III. This misery will not only continue for a very long time, but will be absolutely without end.

IV. Various good ends will be obtained by the eternal punishment of the wicked.

I. I aim to show that it is not contrary to the divine perfections to inflict on wicked men a punishment that is absolutely eternal.

This is the sum of the objections usually made against this doctrine, that it is inconsistent with the justice and especially with the mercy of God. And some say, "If it is strictly just, yet how can we suppose that a merciful God can bear eternally to torment His creatures?"

1. I shall briefly show that it is not inconsistent with the justice of God to inflict an eternal punishment. To evidence this, I shall use only one argument: sin is heinous enough to

deserve such a punishment, and such a punishment is no more than proportionate to the evil or demerit of sin. If the evil of sin is infinite, as the punishment is, then it is manifest that the punishment is no more than proportionate to the sin punished, and is no more than sin deserves. And if the obligation to love, honor, and obey God is infinite, then sin, which is the violation of this obligation, is a violation of infinite obligation, and so is an infinite evil. Again, if God is infinitely worthy of love, honor, and obedience, then our obligation to love, honor, and obey Him is infinitely great. So that God being infinitely glorious, or infinitely worthy of our love, honor, and obedience, our obligation to love, honor, and obey Him, and so to avoid all sin, is infinitely great. Again, our obligation to love, honor, and obey God being infinitely great, sin is the violation of infinite obligation, and so is an infinite evil. Once more, sin, being an infinite evil, deserves an infinite punishment; an infinite punishment is no more than it deserves. Therefore such punishment is just, which was the thing to be proved. There is no evading the force of this reasoning but by denying that God, the sovereign of the universe, is infinitely glorious, which I presume none of my hearers will venture to do.

2. I am to show that it is not inconsistent with the mercy of God to inflict an eternal punishment on wicked men. It is an unreasonable and unscriptural notion of the mercy of God that He is merciful in such a sense that He cannot bear that penal justice should be executed. This is to conceive of the mercy of God as a passion to which His nature is so subject that God is liable to be moved, affected, and overcome by seeing a creature in misery so that He cannot bear to see justice executed. This is a most unworthy and absurd notion of the mercy of God, and would, if true, argue great weakness. It would be a great defect—and not a perfection—in the

sovereign and supreme Judge of the world to be merciful in such a sense that He could not bear to have penal justice executed. It is a very unscriptural notion of the mercy of God. The Scriptures everywhere represent the mercy of God as free and sovereign, and not that the exercises of it are necessary, so that God cannot bear that justice should take place. The Scriptures abundantly speak of it as the glory of the divine attribute of mercy, that it is free and sovereign in its exercises; and not that God cannot but deliver sinners from misery. This is a mean and most unworthy idea of the divine mercy.

It is most absurd also, as it is contrary to plain fact. For if there is any meaning in the objection, this is supposed in it, that all misery of the creature, whether just or unjust, is in itself contrary to the nature of God. For if His mercy is of such a nature that a very great degree of misery, though just, is contrary to His nature, then it is only to add to the mercy, and then a lesser degree of misery is contrary to His nature; again to add further to it, and a still lesser degree of misery is contrary to His nature. And so, the mercy of God being infinite, all misery must be contrary to His nature, which we see to be contrary to fact; for we see that God in His providence indeed inflicts very great calamities on mankind even in this life.

However strong such kind of objections against the eternal misery of the wicked may seem to the carnal, senseless hearts of men, as though it were against God's justice and mercy, yet their seeming strength arises from a want of sense of the infinite evil, odiousness, and provocation there is in sin. Hence it seems to us not suitable that any poor creature should be the subject of such misery because we have no sense of anything abominable and provoking in any creature answerable to it. If we had, then this infinite calamity would not seem unsuitable. For one thing would but appear answerable and proportionate to another, and so the mind would rest in it as fit and

The Eternity of Hell Torments

suitable, and no more than what is proper to be ordered by the just, holy, and good Governor of the world.

That this is so, we may be convinced by this consideration: that when we hear or read of some horrid instances of cruelty, it may be, to some poor, innocent child, or some holy martyr, and their cruel persecutors, having no regard to their shrieks and cries, only sported themselves with their misery, and would not vouchsafe even to put an end to their lives, we have a sense of the evil of them, and they make a deep impression on our minds. Hence it seems just, in every way fit and suitable, that God should inflict a very terrible punishment on persons who have perpetrated such wickedness. It seems in no way disagreeable to any perfection of the Judge of the world; we can think of it without being at all shocked. The reason is that we have a sense of the evil of their conduct, and a sense of the proportion there is between the evil or demerit and the punishment.

Just so, if we saw a proportion between the evil of sin and eternal punishment, if we saw something in wicked men that should appear as hateful to us as eternal misery appears dreadful, something that should as much stir up indignation and detestation as eternal misery does terror, all objections against this doctrine would vanish at once. Though now it seems incredible; though when we hear of it and are so often told of it we know not how to realize it; though when we hear of such a degree and duration of torments as are held forth in this doctrine, and think what eternity is, it is ready to seem impossible that such torments should be inflicted on poor feeble creatures by a Creator of infinite mercy; yet this arises principally from these two causes: (1) it is so contrary to the depraved inclinations of mankind that they hate to believe it and cannot bear it should be true; (2) they see not the suitableness of eternal punishment to the evil of sin; they see not that it is no more than proportionate to the demerit of sin.

Having thus shown that the eternal punishment of the wicked is not inconsistent with the divine perfections, I shall now proceed to show that it is so far from being inconsistent with the divine perfections that those perfections evidently require it. They require that sin should have so great a punishment either in the person who has committed it or in a surety; and therefore, with respect to those who believe not in a surety, and have no interest in Him, the divine perfections require that this punishment should be inflicted on them.

This appears as it is not only not unsuitable that sin should be thus punished, but it is positively suitable, decent, and proper. If this is made to appear, that it is positively suitable that sin should be thus punished, then it will follow that the perfections of God require it; for certainly the perfections of God require what is proper to be done. The perfection and excellency of God require that to take place which is perfect, excellent, and proper in its own nature. But that sin should be punished eternally is such a thing; which appears by the following considerations:

It is suitable that God should infinitely hate sin and be an infinite enemy to it. Sin, as I have before shown, is an infinite evil, and therefore is infinitely odious and detestable. It is proper that God should hate every evil, and hate it according to its odious and detestable nature. And, sin being infinitely evil and odious, it is proper that God should hate it infinitely.

If infinite hatred of sin is suitable to the divine character, then the expressions of such hatred are also suitable to His character, because that which is suitable to be is suitable to be expressed; that which is lovely in itself is lovely when it appears. If it is suitable that God should be an infinite enemy to sin, or that He should hate it infinitely, then it is suitable that He should act as such an enemy. If it is suitable that He should hate and have enmity against sin, then it is suitable for Him to express that hatred and enmity in that to which hatred and enmity by its own nature tends. But, certainly, hatred in its own nature tends to opposition, to set itself against that which is hated, and to procure its evil and not its good—and that in proportion to the hatred. Great hatred naturally tends to the great evil, and infinite hatred to the infinite evil, of its object.

Whence it follows that if it is suitable that there should be infinite hatred of sin in God, as I have shown it is, it is suitable that He should execute an infinite punishment on it. And so the perfections of God require that He should punish sin with an infinite or, which is the same thing, with an eternal punishment.

Thus we see not only the great objection against this doctrine answered, but the truth of the doctrine established by reason. I now proceed further to establish it by considering the remaining particulars under the doctrine.

II. That eternal death or punishment which God threatens to the wicked is not annihilation, but an abiding, sensible punishment or misery. The truth of this proposition will appear by the following particulars:

1. The Scripture everywhere represents the punishment of the wicked as implying very extreme pains and sufferings; but a state of annihilation is no state of suffering at all. Persons annihilated have no sense or feeling of pain or pleasure, and much less do they feel that punishment which carries in it an extreme pain or suffering. They no more suffer to eternity than they did suffer from eternity.

2. It is agreeable both to Scripture and reason to suppose that the wicked will be punished in such a manner that they shall be sensible of the punishment they are under; that they

should be sensible that now God has executed and fulfilled what He threatened, what they disregarded and would not believe. They should know themselves that justice takes place upon them, that God vindicates that majesty which they despised, that God is not so despicable a being as they thought Him to be. They should be sensible for what they are punished while they are under the threatened punishment. It is reasonable that they should be sensible of their own guilt, and should remember their former opportunities and obligations, and should see their own folly and God's justice. If the punishment threatened is eternal annihilation, they will never know that it is inflicted; they will never know that God is just in their punishment or that they have their deserts. And how is this agreeable to the Scriptures, in which God threatens that He will repay the wicked to his face (Deuteronomy 7:10)? Add to that Job 21:19–20: "God rewardeth him, and he shall know it; his eyes shall see his destruction, and he shall drink of the wrath of the Almighty." Add to that Ezekiel 22:21–22: "Yea, I will gather you, and blow upon you in the fire of My wrath, and ye shall be melted in the midst thereof. As silver is melted in the midst of the furnace, so shall ye be melted in the midst thereof; and ye shall know that I the Lord have poured out My fury upon you." And how is it agreeable to that expression so often annexed to the threatenings of God's wrath against wicked men, "And ye shall know that I am the Lord"?

3. The Scriptures teach that the wicked will suffer different degrees of torment according to the different aggravations of their sins. Matthew 5:22: "Whosoever is angry with his brother without a cause shall be in danger of the judgment: and whosoever shall say to his brother, Raca, shall be in danger of the council: but whosoever shall say, Thou fool, shall be in danger of hell fire." Here Christ teaches us that the torments

of wicked men will be different in different persons, according to the different degrees of their guilt. It shall be more tolerable for Sodom and Gomorrah, for Tyre and Sidon, than for the cities where most of Christ's mighty works were wrought. Again, our Lord assures us that he who knows his Lord's will and prepares himself not, nor does according to His will, shall be beaten with many stripes. But he who knows not, and commits things worthy of stripes, shall be beaten with few stripes. These several passages of Scripture infallibly prove that there will be different degrees of punishment in hell, which is utterly inconsistent with the supposition that the punishment consists in annihilation, in which there can be no degrees.

4. The Scriptures are very express and abundant in this matter: The eternal punishment of the wicked will consist in sensible misery and torment, and not in annihilation. What is said of Judas is worthy to be observed here: "It had been good for that man if he had not been born" (Matthew 26:24). This seems plainly to teach us that the punishment of the wicked is such that their existence, upon the whole, is worse than non-existence. But if their punishment consists merely in annihilation, this is not true. The wicked in their punishment are said to weep, wail, and gnash their teeth—which implies not only real existence, but life, knowledge, and activity, and that they are in a very sensible and exquisite manner affected with their punishment (Isaiah 33:14). Sinners in the state of their punishment are represented to dwell with everlasting burnings. But if they are only turned into nothing, where is the foundation for this representation? It is absurd to say that sinners will dwell with annihilation; for there is no dwelling in the case. It is also absurd to call annihilation a burning, which implies a state of existence, sensibility, and extreme pain; in annihilation there is neither.

It is said that they shall be cast into a lake of fire and brimstone. How can this expression with any propriety be understood to mean a state of annihilation? Yea, they are expressly said to have no rest day nor night, but to be tormented with fire and brimstone forever and ever (Revelation 20:10). But annihilation is a state of rest, a state in which not the least torment can possibly be suffered. The rich man in hell lifted up his eyes being in torment, and saw Abraham afar off, and Lazarus in his bosom, and entered into a particular conversation with Abraham—all which proves that he was not annihilated.

The spirits of ungodly men before the resurrection are not in a state of annihilation, but in a state of misery; they are spirits in prison, as the apostle said of those who were drowned in the flood (1 Peter 3:19). And this appears very plainly from the instance of the rich man before mentioned, if we consider him as representing the wicked in their separate state between death and the resurrection. But if the wicked even then are in a state of torment, much more will they be when they shall come to suffer that which is the proper punishment of their sins.

Annihilation is not so great a calamity but that some men have undoubtedly chosen it, rather than a state of suffering even in this life. This was the case of Job, a good man. But if a good man in this world may suffer that which is worse than annihilation, doubtless the proper punishment of the wicked, in which God means to manifest His peculiar abhorrence of their wickedness, will be a calamity vastly greater still, and therefore cannot be annihilation. That must be a very mean and contemptible testimony of God's wrath towards those who have rebelled against His crown and dignity—broken His laws, and despised both His vengeance and His grace—which is not so great a calamity as some of His true children have suffered in life.

The eternal punishment of the wicked is said to be the second death, as in Revelation 20:14 and 21:8. It is doubtless called the second death in reference to the death of the body; and as the death of the body is ordinarily attended with great pain and distress, so the like, or something vastly greater, is implied in calling the eternal punishment of the wicked the second death. And there would be no propriety in calling it so if it consisted merely in annihilation. And this second death wicked men will suffer, for it cannot be called the second death with respect to any other than men. It cannot be called so with respect to devils, as they die no temporal death, which is the first death. In Revelation 2:11 it is said, "He that overcometh shall not be hurt of the second death," implying that all who do not overcome their lusts, but live in sin, shall suffer the second death.

Again, wicked men will suffer the same kind of death with the devils, as in Matthew 25:41: "Depart, ye cursed, into everlasting fire, prepared for the devil and his angels." Now the punishment of the devil is not annihilation, but torment; he therefore trembles for fear of it, not for fear of being annihilated—he would be glad of that. What he is afraid of is torment, as appears by Luke 8:28 where he cries out and beseeches Christ that He would not torment him before the time. And it is said in Revelation 20:10: "The devil that deceived them was cast into the lake of fire and brimstone, where the beast and the false prophet are, and shall be tormented day and night, for ever and ever."

It is strange how men will go directly against so plain and full revelations of Scripture as to suppose, notwithstanding all these things, that the eternal punishment threatened against the wicked signifies no more than annihilation.

III. As the future punishment of the wicked consists in sensible misery, so it shall not only continue for a very long time, but shall be absolutely without end.

Of those who have held that the torments of hell are not absolutely eternal, there have been two sorts. Some suppose that in the threatenings of everlasting punishment the terms used do not necessarily import a proper eternity, but only a very long duration. Others suppose that if they import a proper eternity, yet we cannot necessarily conclude thence that God will fulfill his threatenings.

Therefore I shall, first, show that the threatenings of eternal punishment very plainly and fully import a proper, absolute eternity, and not merely a long duration. This appears:

1. Because when the Scripture speaks of the wicked being sentenced to their punishment at the time when all temporal things are come to an end, it then speaks of it as everlasting, as in the text and elsewhere. It is true that the term "forever" is not always in Scripture used to signify eternity. Sometimes it means "as long as a man lives." In this sense it is said that the Hebrew servant, who chose to abide with his master, should have his ear bored, and should serve his master forever. Sometimes it means "during the continuance of the state and church of the Jews." In this sense, several laws which were peculiar to that church, and were to continue in force no longer than that church should last, are called statutes forever (see Exodus 27:21 and 28:43). Sometimes it means "as long as the world stands." So in Ecclesiastes 1:4: "One generation passeth away, and another generation cometh; but the earth abideth for ever."

And this last is the longest temporal duration that such a term is ever used to signify. For the duration of the world is the longest of things temporal, as its beginning was the earliest. Therefore, when the Scripture speaks of things as being before the foundation of the world, it means that they existed before the beginning of time. So those things which continue after the end of the world are eternal things. When heaven and earth are shaken and removed, those things that remain will be what cannot be shaken, but will remain forever (Hebrews 12:26–27).

But the punishment of the wicked will not only remain after the end of the world, but is called "everlasting," as in the text: "These shall go away into everlasting punishment." So in 2 Thessalonians 1:9–10: "Who shall be punished with everlasting destruction from the presence of the Lord, and from the glory of His power, when He shall come to be glorified in His saints." Now, what can be meant by a thing being everlasting, after all temporal things are come to an end, but that it is absolutely without end?

2. Such expressions are used to set forth the duration of the punishment of the wicked as are never used in the Scriptures of the New Testament to signify anything but a proper eternity. It is said not only that the punishment shall be forever, but forever and ever. Revelation 14:11: "The smoke of their torment ascendeth up for ever and ever." Revelation 20:10: the devil "shall be tormented day and night, for ever and ever." Doubtless the New Testament has some expression to signify a proper eternity, of which it has so often occasion to speak. But it has no higher expression than this: if this does not signify an absolute eternity, there is none that does.

3. The Scripture uses the same way of speaking to set forth the eternity of punishment and the eternity of happiness, yea, the eternity of God Himself. Matthew 25:46: "These shall go away into everlasting punishment, but the righteous into life eternal." The words "everlasting" and "eternal" in the original are the very same. Revelation 22:5: "And they (the saints)

shall reign for ever and ever." And the Scripture has no higher expression to signify the eternity of God Himself than that of His being forever and ever, as Revelation 4:9: "to Him who sat on the throne, who liveth for ever and ever"; as also in the 10th verse, and in 5:14, 10:6, and 15:7.

Again, the Scripture expresses God's eternity by this: that it shall be forever, after the world has come to an end. Psalm 102:26–27: "They shall perish, but Thou shalt endure; yea, all of them shall wax old like a garment; as a vesture shalt Thou change them, and they shall be changed. But Thou art the same, and Thy years shall have no end."

4. The Scripture says that wicked men shall not be delivered till they have paid the uttermost farthing of their debt (Matthew 5:26) and the last mite (Luke 12:59), the utmost that is deserved; and all mercy is excluded by this expression. But we have shown that they deserve an infinite, an endless punishment.

5. The Scripture says absolutely that their punishment shall not have an end. Mark 9:44: "Where their worm dieth not, and the fire is not quenched." Now, it will not do to say that the meaning is "their worm shall live a great while," or that "it shall be a great while before their fire is quenched." If ever the time comes that their worm shall die, if ever there shall be a quenching of the fire at all, then it is not true that their worm dies not, and that the fire is not quenched. For if there is a dying of the worm and a quenching of the fire, let it be at what time it will, nearer or further off, it is equally contrary to such a negation—it dieth not, it is not quenched.

Second, there are others who allow that the expressions of the threatenings denote a proper eternity; but then, they say, it does not certainly follow that the punishment will really be eternal because God may threaten and yet not fulfill His threatenings. Though they allow that the threatenings are positive and peremptory, without any reserve, yet they say that God is not as obliged to fulfill absolute positive threatenings as He is to fulfill absolute promises, because in promises a right is conveyed that the creature to whom the promises are made will claim, but there is no danger of the creature's claiming any right by a threatening. Therefore I am now to show that what God has positively declared in this matter indeed makes it certain that it shall be as He has declared. To this end, I shall mention two things:

1. It is evidently contrary to the divine truth positively to declare anything to be real, whether past, present, or to come, which God at the same time knows is not so. Absolutely threatening that anything shall be is the same as absolutely declaring that it is to be. For any to suppose that God absolutely declares that anything will be, which He at the same time knows will not be, is blasphemy, if there is any such thing as blasphemy.

Indeed, it is very true that there is no obligation on God arising from the claim of the creature as there is in promises. They seem to reckon the wrong way who suppose the necessity of the execution of the threatening to arise from a proper obligation on God to the creature to execute consequent on His threatening. For indeed the certainty of the execution arises the other way, on the obligation there was on the omniscient God in threatening to conform His threatening to what He knew would be future in execution. Though, strictly speaking, God is not properly obliged to the creature to execute because He has threatened, yet He was obliged not absolutely to threaten if at the same time He knew that He should not or would not fulfill, because this would not have been consistent with His truth. So that from the truth of God there is an inviolable connection between positive threatenings and execution. They who suppose that God positively declared that He would do contrary to what He knew would come to pass therein suppose that He absolutely threatened contrary to what He knew to be truth. And how anyone can speak contrary to what He knows to be truth, in declaring, promising, or threatening, or any other way consistently with inviolable truth, is inconceivable.

Threatenings are significant of something; and if they are made consistently with truth they are true significations, or significations of truth, that which shall be. If absolute threatenings are significations of anything, they are significations of the futurity of the things threatened. But if the futurity of the things threatened is not true and real, then how can the threatening be a true signification? And if God in them speaks contrary to what He knows, and contrary to what He intends, how He can speak truth is inconceivable.

Absolute threatenings are a kind of predictions; and though God is not properly obliged by any claim of ours to fulfill predictions unless they are of the nature of promises, yet it certainly would be contrary to truth to predict that such a thing would come to pass which He knew at the same time would not come to pass. Threatenings are declarations of something future, and they must be declarations of future truth if they are true declarations. Its being future alters not the case any more than if it were present. It is equally contrary to truth to declare contrary to what at the same time is known to be truth, whether it is of things past, present, or to come, for all are alike to God.

Besides, we have often declarations in Scripture of the future eternal punishment of the wicked in the proper form of predictions, and not in the form of threatenings. So in the text: "These shall go away into everlasting punishment." So it is in those frequent assertions of eternal punishment in

Revelation, some of which I have already quoted. Revelation is a prophecy, and is so called in the book itself; so are those declarations of eternal punishment. The like declarations we have also in many other places of Scripture.

2. The doctrine of those who teach that it is not certain that God will fulfill those absolute threatenings is blasphemous in another way, and that is as God, according to their supposition, was obliged to make use of a fallacy to govern the world. They own that it is needful that men should apprehend themselves liable to an eternal punishment that they might thereby be restrained from sin, and that God has threatened such a punishment for the very end that they might believe themselves exposed to it. But what an unworthy opinion does this convey of God and His government, of His infinite majesty, wisdom, and all-sufficiency! Besides, they suppose that though God has made use of such a fallacy, yet it is not such a one but that they have detected Him in it. Though God intended men should believe it to be certain that sinners are liable to an eternal punishment, yet they suppose that they have been so cunning as to find out that it is not certain. And so God had not laid His design so deep but that such cunning men as they can discern the cheat and defeat the design because they have found out that there is no necessary connection between the threatening of eternal punishment and the execution of that threatening.

Considering these things, is it not greatly to be wondered at that Archbishop Tillotson, who has made so great a figure among the new-fashioned divines, should advance such an opinion as this?

Before I conclude this head, it may be proper for me to answer an objection or two, that may arise in the minds of some.

OBJECTION 1. It may be here said, "We have instances

wherein God has not fulfilled His threatenings. There is His threatening to Adam, and in him to mankind, that they should surely die if they should eat the forbidden fruit."

ANSWER. I answer, it is not true that God did not fulfill that threatening. He fulfilled it, and will fulfill it in every jot and tittle. When God said, "Thou shalt surely die," if we respect spiritual death, it was fulfilled in Adam's person in the day that he ate. For immediately his image, his holy spirit, and original righteousness, which was the highest and best life of our first parents, were lost; and they were immediately in a doleful state of spiritual death.

If we respect the moral death, that was also fulfilled. Adam brought death upon himself and all his posterity, and he virtually suffered that death on that very day on which he ate. His body was brought into a corruptible, mortal, and dying condition, and so it continued till it was dissolved. If we look at all that death which was comprehended in the threatening, it was, properly speaking, fulfilled in Christ. When God said to Adam, "If thou eatest, thou shalt die," He spoke not only to him and of him personally; but the words respected mankind, Adam and his race, and doubtless were so understood by him. His offspring were to be looked upon as sinning in him, and so should die with him. The words do as justly allow an imputation of death as of sin; they are as well consistent with dying in a surety as with sinning in one. Therefore, the threatening is fulfilled in the death of Christ, the Surety.

OBJECTION 2. Another objection may arise from God's threatening to Nineveh. He threatened that in forty days Nineveh should be destroyed, which yet He did not fulfill.

ANSWER. I answer, that threatening could justly be looked upon no in other way than as conditional. It was of the nature of a warning, and not of an absolute denunciation. Why was Jonah sent to the Ninevites but to give them warning that they might have opportunity to repent, reform, and avert the approaching destruction? God had no other design or end in sending the prophet to them but that they might be warned and tried by him, as God warned the Israelites, Judah and Jerusalem, before their destruction. Therefore the prophets, together with their prophecies of approaching destruction, joined earnest exhortations to repent and reform that it might be averted.

No more could justly be understood to be certainly threatened than that Nineveh should be destroyed in forty days, continuing as it was. For it was for their wickedness that that destruction was threatened, and so the Ninevites took it. Therefore, when the cause was removed, the effect ceased. It was contrary to God's known manner to threaten punishment and destruction for sin in this world absolutely, so that it should come upon the persons threatened unavoidably, let them repent and reform and do what they would. Jeremiah 18:7–8: "At what instant I shall speak concerning a nation, and concerning a kingdom, to pluck up, and to pull down, and to destroy it; if that nation against whom I have pronounced turn from their evil, I will repent of the evil that I thought to do unto them." So that all threatenings of this nature had a condition implied in them, according to the known and declared manner of God's dealing. And the Ninevites did not take it as an absolute sentence of denunciation; if they had, they would have despaired of any benefit by fasting and reformation.

But the threatenings of eternal wrath are positive and absolute. There is nothing in the Word of God from which we can gather any condition. The only opportunity of escaping is in this world; this is the only state of trial wherein we have any offers of mercy or place for repentance.

IV. I shall mention several good and important ends which will be obtained by the eternal punishment of the wicked.

1. Hereby God vindicates His injured majesty. Wherein sinners cast contempt upon it and trample it in the dust, God vindicates and honors it, and makes it appear, as it is indeed, infinite, by showing that it is infinitely dreadful to condemn or offend it.

2. God glorifies His justice. The glory of God is the greatest good; it is that which is the chief end of the creation; it is of greater importance than anything else. But this is one way wherein God will glorify Himself, as in the eternal destruction of ungodly men He will glorify His justice. Therein He will appear as a just governor of the world. The vindictive justice of God will appear strict, exact, awful, and terrible, and, therefore, glorious.

3. God hereby indirectly glorifies His grace on the vessels of mercy. The saints in heaven will behold the torments of the damned: "the smoke of their torment ascendeth up for ever and ever." Isaiah 66:24: "And they shall go forth and look upon the carcasses of the men that have transgressed against me: for their worm shall not die, neither shall their fire be quenched, and they shall be an abhorring unto all flesh." And in Revelation 14:10 it is said that they shall be tormented in the presence of the holy angels and in the presence of the Lamb. So they will be tormented in the presence also of the glorified saints.

Hereby the saints will be made the more sensible how great their salvation is. When they shall see how great the misery is from which God has saved them, and how great a difference He has made between their state and the state of others, who were by nature, and perhaps, for a time, by practice, no more sinful and ill-deserving than any, it will give them a greater sense of the wonderfulness of God's grace to them. Every time they look upon the damned, it will excite in them a lively and admiring sense of the grace of God in making them so to differ. This the apostle informs us is one end of the damnation of ungodly men. Romans 9:22–23: "What if God, willing to show His wrath, and to make His power known, endured with much long-suffering the vessels of wrath fitted to destruction: and that He might make known the riches of His glory on the vessels of mercy, which He had afore prepared unto glory?" The view of the misery of the damned will double the ardor of the love and gratitude of the saints in heaven.

4. The sight of hell torments will exalt the happiness of the saints forever. It will not only make them more sensible of the greatness and freeness of the grace of God in their happiness, but it will really make their happiness the greater, as it will make them more sensible of their own happiness; it will give them a more lively relish of it; it will make them prize it more. When they see others who were of the same nature, and born under the same circumstances, plunged in such misery, and them so distinguished, oh, it will make them sensible how happy they are! A sense of the opposite misery in all cases greatly increases the relish of any joy or pleasure.

The sight of the wonderful power, the great and dreadful majesty, the awful justice and holiness of God, manifested in the eternal punishment of ungodly men, will make them prize His favor and love vastly the more. And they will be so much the more happy in the enjoyment of it.

Application

1. From what has been said, we may learn the folly and madness of the greater part of mankind in that, for the sake of present, momentary gratification, they run the venture of

enduring all these eternal torments. They prefer a small pleasure or a little wealth or a little earthly honor and greatness, which can last but for a moment, to an escape from this punishment. If it is true that the torments of hell are eternal, what will it profit a man if he gains the whole world and loses his own soul? Or what shall a man give in exchange for his soul? What is there in this world which is not a trifle and lighter than vanity in comparison with these eternal things?

How mad are men who so often hear of these things and pretend to believe them; who can live but a little while, a few years, who do not even expect to live here longer than others of their species ordinarily do, and who yet are careless about what becomes of themselves in another world, where there is no change and no end! How mad are they when they hear that if they go on in sin they shall be eternally miserable, that they are not moved by it, but hear it with as much carelessness and coldness as if they were in no way concerned in the matter—when they know not but that it may be their case that they may be suffering these torments before a week is at an end!

How can men be so careless of such a matter as their own eternal and desperate destruction and torment! What a strange stupor and senselessness possesses the hearts of men! How common a thing is it to see men who are told from sabbath to sabbath of eternal misery, and who are as mortal as other men, so careless about it that they seem not to be at all restrained by it from whatever their souls lust after! It is not half so much their care to escape eternal misery as it is to get money and land, to be considerable in the world, and to gratify their senses. Their thoughts are much more exercised about these things, and much more of their care and concern is about them. Eternal misery, though they lie every day exposed to it, is a thing neglected; it is but now and then thought of, and then with a great deal of stupidity and not with concern enough to stir them up to do anything considerable in order to escape it. They are not sensible that it is worth their while to take any considerable pains in order to avoid it. And if they do take pains for a little while, they soon leave off, and something else takes up their thoughts and concern.

Thus you see it among young and old. Multitudes of youth lead a careless life, taking little care about their salvation. So you may see it among persons of middle age, and with many advanced in years, and when they certainly draw near to the grave. Yet these same persons will seem to acknowledge that the greater part of men go to hell and suffer eternal misery, and this through carelessness about it. However, they will do the same. How strange is it that men can enjoy themselves and be at rest when they are thus hanging over eternal burnings, at the same time having no lease of their lives and not knowing how soon the thread by which they hang will break, nor indeed do they pretend to know. And if it breaks they are gone; they are lost forever, and there is no remedy! Yet they trouble not themselves much about it, nor will they hearken to those who cry to them, who entreat them to take care for themselves and labor to get out of that dangerous condition. They are not willing to take so much pains; they choose not to be diverted from amusing themselves with toys and vanities. Thus, well might the wise man say in Ecclesiastes 9:3: "The heart of the sons of men is full of evil. Madness is in their heart while they live, and after that they go to the dead." How much wiser are those few who make it their main business to lay a foundation for eternity, to serve their salvation!

2. I shall improve this subject in a use of exhortation to sinners to take care to escape these eternal torments. If they are eternal, one would think that would be enough to awaken

your concern and excite your diligence. If the punishment is eternal, it is infinite, as we said before; and therefore no other evil, no death, no temporary torment that ever you heard of, or that you can imagine, is anything in comparison with it, but is as much less and less considerable not only as a grain of sand is less than the whole universe, but as it is less than the boundless space which encompasses the universe. Therefore here:

(1) Be entreated to consider attentively how great and awful a thing eternity is. Although you cannot comprehend it the more by considering, yet you may be made more sensible that it is to suffer extreme torment forever and ever; to suffer it day and night, from one year to another, from one age to another, and from one thousand ages to another, and so adding age to age and thousands to thousands, in pain, in wailing and lamenting, groaning and shrieking and gnashing your teeth, with your souls full of dreadful grief and amazement, with your bodies and every member full of racking torture without any possibility of getting ease, without any possibility of moving God to pity by your cries, without any possibility of hiding yourselves from Him, without any possibility of diverting your thoughts from your pain, without any possibility of obtaining any manner of mitigation or help or change for the better.

(2) Do but consider how dreadful despair will be in such torment. How dismal will it be when you are under these racking torments to know assuredly that you never, never shall be delivered from them; to have no hope—when you shall wish that you might be turned into nothing, but shall have no hope of it; when you shall wish that you might be turned into a toad or a serpent, but shall have no hope of it; when you would rejoice if you might but have any relief after you shall have endured these torments millions of ages, but

The Eternity of Hell Torments

shall have no hope of it. After you shall have worn out the age of the sun, moon, and stars in your dolorous groans and lamentations, without rest day and night, or one minute's ease, yet you shall have no hope of ever being delivered. After you shall have worn a thousand more such ages you shall have no hope, but shall know that you are not one whit nearer to the end of your torments; but that still there are the same groans, the same shrieks, the same doleful cries incessantly to be made by you, and that the smoke of your torment shall still ascend up forever and ever. Your souls, which shall have been agitated with the wrath of God all this while, will still exist to bear more wrath. Your bodies, which shall have been burning all this while in these glowing flames, shall not have been consumed, but will remain to roast through eternity, which will not have been at all shortened by what shall have been past.

You may, by considering, make yourselves more sensible than you ordinarily are; but it is a little you can conceive of what it is to have no hope in such torments. How sinking would it be to you to endure such pain as you have felt in this world without any hopes, and to know that you never should be delivered from it, nor have one minute's rest! You can now scarcely conceive how doleful that would be. How much more to endure the vast weight of the wrath of God without hope! The more the damned in hell think of the eternity of their torments, the more amazing will it appear to them; and alas! they will not be able to keep it out of their minds. Their tortures will not divert them from it, but will fix their attention to it. Oh, how dreadful will eternity appear to them after they shall have been thinking on it for ages together, and shall have so long an experience of their torments!

The damned in hell will have two infinites perpetually to amaze them and swallow them up: one is an infinite God, whose wrath they will bear, and in whom they will behold their perfect and irreconcilable enemy; the other is the infinite duration of their torment.

If it were possible for the damned in hell to have a comprehensive knowledge of eternity, their sorrow and grief would be infinite in degree. The comprehensive view of so much sorrow, which they must endure, would cause infinite grief for the present. Though they will not have a comprehensive knowledge of it, yet they will doubtless have a vastly more lively and strong apprehension of it than we can have in this world. Their torments will give them an impression of it. A man in his present state, without any enlargement of his capacity, would have a vastly more lively impression of eternity than he has if he were only under some pretty sharp pain in some member of his body, and were at the same time assured that he must endure that pain forever. His pain would give him a greater sense of eternity than other men have. How much more will those excruciating torments which the damned will suffer have this effect!

Besides, their capacity will probably be enlarged; their understandings will be quicker and stronger in a future state; and God can give them as great a sense and as strong an impression of eternity as He pleases to increase their grief and torment. Oh, be entreated, you who are in a Christ-less state, and are going on in a way to hell, who are daily exposed to damnation, to consider these things. If you do not, it will surely be but a little while before you will experience them; and then you will know how dreadful it is to despair in hell; and it may be before this year, or this month, or this week is at an end, before another sabbath, or ever you shall have opportunity to hear another sermon.

(3) That you may effectually escape these dreadful and eternal torments, be entreated to flee to and embrace Him who came into the world for the very end of saving sinners

from these torments, who has paid the whole debt due to the divine law and exhausted eternal in temporal sufferings. What great encouragement is it to those of you who are sensible that you are exposed to eternal punishment, that there is a Savior provided who is able, and who freely offers to save you from that punishment, and that in a way which is perfectly consistent with the glory of God, yea, which is more to the glory of God than it would be if you should suffer the eternal punishment of hell. For if you should suffer that punishment you would never pay the whole of the debt. Those who are sent to hell never will have paid the whole of the debt which they owe to God, nor indeed a part which bears any proportion to the whole. They never will have paid a part which bears so great a proportion to the whole as one mite to ten thousand talents. Justice, therefore, never can be actually satisfied in your damnation; but it is actually satisfied in Christ. Therefore He is accepted of the Father, and therefore all who believe are accepted and justified in Him.

Therefore believe in Him; come to Him, commit your souls to Him to be saved by Him. In Him you shall be safe from the eternal torments of hell. Nor is that all, but through Him you shall inherit inconceivable blessedness and glory which will be of equal duration with the torments of hell. For as at the last day the wicked shall go away into everlasting punishment, so shall the righteous, or those who trust in Christ, go into life eternal.

The End of the Wicked Contemplated by the Righteous

or

The torments of the wicked in hell no occasion of grief to the saints in heaven

"Rejoice over her, thou heaven, and ye holy apostles and prophets; for God hath avenged you on her." Revelation 18:20

In this chapter we have a very particular account of the fall of Babylon, or the antichristian church, and of the vengeance of God executed upon her. Here it is proclaimed that Babylon the great is fallen and become the habitation of devils and the hold of every foul spirit and a cage of every unclean and hateful bird; that God gave commandment to reward her as she had rewarded others, to give unto her double according to her works; in the cup she had filled, to fill to her double, and how much she had glorified herself and lived deliciously, so much torment and sorrow to give her. And it is declared that these plagues are come upon her in one day, death, mourning, and famine; and that she should be utterly burnt with fire because strong is the Lord who judges her.

These things have respect partly to the overthrow of the antichristian church in this world, and partly to the vengeance of God upon her in the world to come. There is no necessity to suppose that such extreme torments as are here mentioned will ever be executed upon papists, or upon the antichristian church, in this world. There will indeed be a dreadful and visible overthrow of that idolatrous church in this world. But we are not to understand the plagues here mentioned as exclusive of the vengeance which God will execute on the wicked upholders and promoters of antichristianism, and on the cruel antichristian persecutors, in another world.

This is evident by verse 3 of the next chapter where, with reference to the same destruction of antichrist which is spoken of in this chapter, it is said, "Her smoke rose up for ever and ever." In these words the eternal punishment of antichrist is evidently spoken of. Antichrist is here represented as being cast into hell, and there remaining forever after; he has no place anywhere else but in hell. This is evident by verse 20 of the next chapter where, concerning the destruction of antichrist, it is said, "And the beast was taken, and with him the false prophet that wrought miracles before him, with which he deceived them that had received the mark of the beast, and them that worshipped his image. These both were cast alive into a lake of fire burning with brimstone."

Although the wicked antichristians have in all ages gone to hell as they died, and not merely at the fall of antichrist, then the wrath of God against antichrist, of which damnation is the fruit, will be made eminently visible here on earth by many remarkable tokens. Then antichrist will be confined to hell and will have no more place here on earth, much after the same manner as the devil is said at the beginning of Christ's thousand-year reign on earth to be cast into the bottomless pit, as you may see in the beginning of the twentieth chapter. Not but that he had his place in the bottomless pit before; he was cast down to hell when he fell at first. 2 Peter 2:4: God "cast them down to hell and delivered them into chains of darkness." But now, when he shall be suffered to deceive the nations no more, his kingdom will be confined to hell.

In this text is contained part of what John heard uttered upon this occasion, and in these words we may observe:

1. To whom this voice is directed: to the holy prophets and apostles, and the rest of the inhabitants of the heavenly world. When God shall pour out His wrath upon the antichristian church, it will be seen and taken notice of by all the inhabitants of heaven, even by holy prophets and apostles. Neither will they see as unconcerned spectators.

2. What they are called upon by the voice to do: to rejoice over Babylon, now destroyed and lying under the wrath of God. They are not directed to rejoice over her prosperity, but in seeing her in flames and beholding the smoke of her burning ascending up forever and ever.

3. A reason given: for "God hath avenged you on her." In other words, God has executed just vengeance upon her for shedding your blood and cruelly persecuting you. For thus the matter is represented, that antichrist had been guilty of shedding the blood of the holy prophets and apostles, as in Revelation 16:6: "For they have shed the blood of saints and of prophets." And in Revelation 18:24: "In her was found the blood of prophets, and of saints, and of all them that were slain on the earth." Not that antichrist had literally shed the blood of the prophets and apostles, but he had shed the blood of those who were their followers, who were of the same spirit, and of the same church, and same mystical body. The prophets and apostles in heaven are nearly related and united to the saints on earth; they live, as it were, in true Christians in all ages. So that by slaying these, persecutors show that they would slay prophets and apostles if they could; and they indeed do it as much as in them lies.

On the same account, Christ says of the Jews in His time that "the blood of all the prophets, which was shed from the foundation of the world, may be required of this generation, from the blood of Abel, unto the blood of Zechariah, which perished between the altar and the temple; verily I say unto you, it shall be required of this generation" (Luke 11:50–51). So Christ Himself is said to have been crucified in the antichristian church: "And their dead bodies shall lie in the street of the great city, which spiritually is called Sodom and Egypt, where also our Lord was crucified" (Revelation 11:8). So all the inhabitants of heaven, all the saints from the beginning of the world, and the angels also are called upon to rejoice over Babylon because of God's vengeance upon her wherein He avenges them. They, all of them, had in effect been injured and persecuted by antichrist. Indeed, they are not called upon to rejoice in having their revenge glutted, but in seeing justice executed, and in seeing the love and tenderness of God towards them, manifested in His very severity towards their enemies.

SECTION 1

When the saints in glory shall see the wrath of God executed on ungodly men, it will be no occasion of grief to them, but of rejoicing.

It is not only the sight of God's wrath executed on those wicked men who are of the antichristian church which will be occasion of rejoicing to the saints in glory, but also the sight of the destruction of all God's enemies; whether they have been the followers of antichrist or not, that alters not the case if they have been the enemies of God and of Jesus Christ. All wicked men will at last be destroyed together as being united in the same cause and interest, as being all of Satan's army. They will all stand together at the day of judgment as being all of the same company.

And if we understand the text to have respect only to a temporal execution of God's wrath on His enemies, that will not alter the case. The thing they are called upon to rejoice at is the execution of God's wrath upon His and their enemies. And if it is matter of rejoicing to them to see justice executed in part upon them or to see the beginning of the execution of it in this world, for the same reason will they rejoice with greater joy in beholding it fully executed. For the thing here mentioned as the foundation of their joy is the execution of just vengeance. "Rejoice, for God hath avenged you on her."

PROPOSITION 1. The glorified saints will see the wrath of God executed upon ungodly men. This the Scriptures plainly teach us: the righteous and the wicked in the other world will see each other's state. Thus the rich man in hell and Lazarus and Abraham in heaven are represented as seeing each other's opposite states in the 16th chapter of Luke. The wicked in their misery will see the saints in the kingdom of heaven. Luke 13:28: "There shall be weeping and gnashing of teeth, when ye shall see Abraham, and Isaac, and Jacob, and all the prophets in the kingdom of God, and you yourselves thrust out."

So the saints in glory will see the misery of the wicked under the wrath of God. Isaiah 66:24: "And they shall go forth and look on the carcasses of the men that have transgressed against Me: for their worm shall not die, nei-

The End of the Wicked

ther shall their fire be quenched." And Revelation 14:9–10: "If any man worship the beast and his image, and receive his mark in his forehead, or in his hand, the same shall drink of the wine of the wrath of God, which is poured out without mixture into the cup of His indignation; and he shall be tormented with fire and brimstone, in the presence of the holy angels, and in the presence of the Lamb." The saints are not here mentioned, being included in Christ as His members. The church is the fullness of Christ and is called "Christ" in 1 Corinthians 12:12. So in Revelation 19:2–3, the smoke of Babylon's torment is represented as rising up forever and ever in the sight of the heavenly inhabitants.

At the day of judgment, the saints in glory at Christ's right hand will see the wicked at the left hand in their amazement and horror, will hear the judge pronounce sentence upon them, saying, "Depart, ye cursed, into everlasting fire, prepared for the devil and his angels," and will see them go away into everlasting punishment. But the Scripture seems to hold forth to us that the saints will not only see the misery of the wicked at the day of judgment, but the aforementioned texts imply that the state of the damned in hell will be in the view of the heavenly inhabitants, that the two worlds of happiness and misery will be in view of each other. Though we know not by what means, nor after what manner, it will be, yet the Scriptures certainly lead us to think that they will in some way or other have a direct and immediate apprehension of each other's state. The saints in glory will see how the damned are tormented; they will see God's threatenings fulfilled and His wrath executed upon them.

PROPOSITION 2. When they shall see it, it will be no occasion of grief to them. The miseries of the damned in hell will be inconceivably great. When they shall come to bear the wrath of the Almighty poured out upon them without mixture, and executed upon them without pity or restraint or any mitigation, it will doubtless cause anguish, horror, and amazement beyond all the sufferings and torments that ever any man endured in this world, yea, beyond all extent of our words or thoughts. For God, in executing wrath upon ungodly men, will act like an Almighty God. The Scripture calls this wrath "God's fury" and "the fierceness of His wrath." And we are told that this is to show God's wrath and to make His power known, or to make known how dreadful His wrath is and how great is His power.

The saints in glory will see this and be far more sensible of it than now we can possibly be. They will be far more sensible how dreadful the wrath of God is and will better understand how terrible the sufferings of the damned are; yet this will be no occasion of grief to them. They will not be sorry for the damned; it will cause no uneasiness or dissatisfaction to them; but, on the contrary, when they have this sight it will excite them to joyful praises. These two things are evidences of it:

1. That seeing the wrath of God executed upon the damned should cause grief in the saints in glory is inconsistent with that state of perfect happiness in which they are. There can no such thing as grief enter to be an allay to the happiness and joy of that world of blessedness. Grief is an utter stranger in that world. God has promised that He will wipe away all tears from their eyes and there shall be no more sorrow. See Revelation 21:4 and 7:17.

2. The saints in heaven possess all things as their own, and therefore all things contribute to their joy and happiness. The Scriptures teach that the saints in glory inherit

all things. This God said in John's hearing when he had the vision of the new Jerusalem in Revelation 21:7. And the Scriptures teach us to understand this absolutely of all the works of creation and providence. 1 Corinthians 3:21-22: "All things are yours, whether Paul, or Apollos, or Cephas, or the world, or life, or death, or things present, or things to come; all are yours." Here the apostle teaches that all things in the world to come, or in the future and eternal world, are the saints'—not only life but death. Men and angels and devils, heaven and hell, are theirs to contribute to their joy and happiness. Therefore the damned and their misery, their sufferings, and the wrath of God poured out upon them will be an occasion of joy to them. If there were anything whatsoever that did not contribute to their joy, but caused grief, then there would be something which would not be theirs.

That the torments of the damned are no matter of grief, but of joy, to the inhabitants of heaven is very clearly expressed in several passages of this book of Revelation, particularly by 16:5-7 and 19:1-7.

SECTION 2

Why the sufferings of the wicked will not be cause of grief to the righteous, but the contrary.

1. NEGATIVELY. It will not be because the saints in heaven are the subjects of any ill disposition, but, on the contrary, this rejoicing of theirs will be the fruit of an amiable and excellent disposition. It will be the fruit of a perfect holiness and conformity to Christ, the holy Lamb of God. The devil delights in the misery of men from cruelty, and from envy and revenge, and because he delights in

misery for its own sake from a malicious disposition.

But it will be from exceedingly different principles, and for quite other reasons, that the just damnation of the wicked will be an occasion of rejoicing to the saints in glory. It will not be because they delight in seeing the misery of others absolutely considered. The damned suffering divine vengeance will be no occasion of joy to the saints merely as it is the misery of others, or because it is pleasant to them to behold the misery of others merely for its own sake. The rejoicing of the saints on this occasion is no argument that they are not of a most amiable and excellent spirit, or that there is any defect on that account, that there is anything wanting which would render them of a more amiable disposition. It is no argument that they have not a spirit of goodness and love reigning in them in absolute perfection, or that herein they do not exceed the greatest instances of it on earth as much as the stars are higher than the earth or the sun brighter than a glowworm.

And whereas the heavenly inhabitants are in the text called upon to rejoice over Babylon because God had avenged them on her, it is not to be understood that they are to rejoice in having their revenge glutted, but to rejoice in seeing the justice of God executed and in seeing His love for them in executing it on His enemies.

2. POSITIVELY. The sufferings of the damned will be no occasion of grief to the heavenly inhabitants as they will have no love or pity for the damned as such. It will be no argument of want of a spirit of love in them that they do not love the damned, for the heavenly inhabitants will know that it is not fit that they should love them because they will know then that God has no love or pity for them, but that they are the objects of God's eternal hatred. And they will then be perfectly conformed to God in their wills

The End of the Wicked

and affections. They will love what God loves and that only. However the saints in heaven may have loved the damned while here, especially those who were near and dear to them in this world, they will have no love for them hereafter.

It will be an occasion of their rejoicing as the glory of God will appear in it. The glory of God appears in all His works, and therefore there is no work of God which the saints in glory shall behold and contemplate but what will be an occasion of rejoicing to them. God glorifies Himself in the eternal damnation of the ungodly men. God glorifies Himself in all that He does, but He glorifies Himself principally in His eternal disposal of His intelligent creatures: some are appointed to everlasting life and others left to everlasting death.

The saints in heaven will be perfect in their love for God. Their hearts will be all aflame of love for God, and therefore they will greatly value the glory of God and will exceedingly delight in seeing Him glorified. The saints highly value the glory of God here in this world, but how much more will they do so in the world to come! They will therefore greatly rejoice in all that contributes to that glory. The glory of God will, in their esteem, be of greater consequence than the welfare of thousands and millions of souls. Particularly:

(1) They will rejoice in seeing the justice of God glorified in the sufferings of the damned. The misery of the damned, dreadful as it is, is but what justice requires. They in heaven will see and know it much more clearly than any of us do here. They will see how perfectly just and righteous their punishment is, and therefore how properly inflicted by the supreme Governor of the world. They will greatly rejoice to see justice take place, to see that all the sin and wickedness

that have been committed in the world are remembered of God and have their due punishment. The sight of this strict and immutable justice of God will render Him amiable and adorable in their eyes. They will rejoice when they see Him who is their Father and eternal portion so glorious in His justice.

Then there will be no remaining difficulties about the justice of God, about the absolute decrees of God, or anything pertaining to the dispensations of God towards men. But divine justice, in the destruction of the wicked, will then appear as light without darkness and will shine as the sun without clouds; and upon this account they will sing joyful songs of praise to God, as we see the saints and angels do when God pours the vials of His wrath upon antichrist in Revelation 16:5-7. They sing joyfully to God on this account, that true and righteous are His judgments (Revelation 19:1-6). Seeing God so strictly just will make them value His love the more. Mercy and grace are more valuable on this account. The more they shall see of the justice of God, the more they will prize and rejoice in His love.

(2) They will rejoice in it as it will be a glorious manifestation of the power and majesty of God. God will show His own greatness in executing vengeance on ungodly men. This is mentioned as one end of the destruction of the ungodly: "What if God, willing to show His wrath, and make His power known, endured with much long-suffering the vessels of wrath fitted to destruction?" (Romans 9:22). God will hereby show how much He is above His enemies. There are many now in the world who proudly lift up themselves against God. There are many open opposers of the cause and interest of Christ. Psalm 73:9: "They set their mouth against the heavens, and their tongue walketh through the

The End of the Wicked

earth." Then God will show His glorious power in destroying these enemies.

The power of God is sometimes spoken of as very glorious, as appearing in the temporal destruction of His enemies. Exodus 15:6: "Thy right hand, O Lord, is become glorious in power; Thy right hand, O Lord, hath dashed in pieces the enemy." But how much more glorious will it appear in His triumphing over, and dashing in pieces all at once, all His enemies, wicked men and devils together, all His haughty foes! The power of God will gloriously appear in dashing to pieces His enemies as a potter's vessel. Moses rejoiced and sang when he saw God glorify His power in the destruction of Pharaoh and his host at the Red Sea. But how much more will the saints in glory rejoice when they shall see God gloriously triumphing over all His enemies in their eternal ruin! Then it will appear how dreadful God is, and how dreadful a thing it is to disobey and condemn Him.

It is often mentioned as a part of the majesty of the glory of God that He is a terrible God. To see the majesty and greatness and terribleness of God appearing in the destruction of His enemies will cause the saints to rejoice; and when they shall see how great and terrible a being God is, how will they prize His favor! How will they rejoice that they are the objects of His love! How will they praise Him the more joyfully that He should choose them to be His children and to live in the enjoyment of Him!

It will occasion rejoicing in them, as they will have the greater sense of their own happiness by seeing the contrary misery. It is the nature of pleasure and pain, of happiness and misery, greatly to heighten the sense of each other. Thus the seeing of the happiness of others tends to make men more sensible of their own calamities; and the seeing of the calamities of others tends to heighten the sense of our own enjoyments.

When the saints in glory, therefore, shall see the doleful state of the damned, how this will heighten their sense of the blessedness of their own state, so exceedingly different from it! When they shall see how miserable others of their fellow creatures are who were naturally in the same circumstances with themselves; when they shall see the smoke of their torment and the raging of the flames of their burning, and hear their dolorous shrieks and cries, and consider that they are, in the meantime, in the most blissful state, and shall surely be in it to all eternity, how will they rejoice!

This will give them a joyful sense of the grace and love of God toward them because hereby they will see how great a benefit they have by it. When they shall see the dreadful miseries of the damned, and consider that they deserved the same misery, and that it was sovereign grace, and nothing else, which made them so much to differ from the damned that, if it had not been for that, they would have been in the same condition; but that God from all eternity was pleased to set His love upon them, that Christ has laid down His life for them, and has made them thus gloriously happy forever—oh, how will they admire that dying love of Christ which has redeemed them from so great a misery, and purchased for them so great happiness, and has so distinguished them from others of their fellow creatures! How joyfully will they sing to God and the Lamb when they behold this!

SECTION 3

An objection answered

OBJECTION. "If we are apprehensive of the damnation of others now, it in no wise becomes us to rejoice at it, but to lament at it. If we see others in imminent danger of going to hell, it is accounted a very sorrowful thing, and it is looked upon as an argument of a senseless and wicked spirit, to look upon it otherwise."

When it is a very dead time with respect to religion, and a very degenerate and corrupt time among a people, it is accounted a thing greatly to be lamented; and it is on this account that at such times there are but few converted and saved, and many perish. Paul tells us that he had great heaviness and continual sorrow in his heart because so many of the Jews were in a perishing state. Romans 9:1–3: "I say the truth in Christ, I lie not, my conscience also bearing me witness in the Holy Ghost, that I have great heaviness and continual sorrow in my heart. For I could wish that myself were accursed from Christ, for my brethren, my kinsmen according to the flesh." And if a neighbor dies, and his death is attended with circumstances which look darkly as to the state of his soul, we account it a sorrowful thing because he has left us no more comfortable grounds to hope for his salvation. Why, is it not then an unbecoming thing in the saints in glory to rejoice when they see the damnation of the ungodly?

ANSWER 1. It is now our duty to love all men, though they are wicked; but it will not be a duty to love wicked men hereafter. Christ, by many precepts in His Word, has made it our duty to love all men. We are commanded to love wicked men, and our enemies and persecutors. But this command does not extend to the saints in glory with respect to the damned in hell. Nor is there the same reason that it should. We ought now to love all, even wicked men. We know not but that God loves them. However wicked any man is, yet we know not but that he is one whom God loved from eternity; we know not but that Christ loved him with a dying love, had his name upon His heart before the world was, and had respect to him when He endured those bitter agonies on the cross. We know not but that he is to be our companion in glory to all eternity.

But this is not the case in another world. The saints in glory will know, concerning the damned in hell, that God never loved them, but that He hates them, and that they will be forever hated of God. This hatred of God will be fully declared to them; they will see it, and will see the fruits of it in their misery. Therefore, when God has thus declared His hatred of the damned, and the saints see it, it will be in no way becoming in the saints to love them, nor to mourn over them. It becomes the saints fully and perfectly to consent to what God does without any reluctance or opposition of spirit; yea, it becomes them to rejoice in everything that God sees fit to be done.

ANSWER 2. We ought now to seek and be concerned for the salvation of wicked men, because now they are capable subjects of it. Wicked men, though they may be very wicked, yet are capable subjects of mercy. It is yet a day of grace with them, and they have the offers of salvation. Christ is as yet seeking their salvation. He is calling upon them, inviting and wooing them. He stands at the door and knocks. He is using many means with them. He is calling them, saying, "Turn ye, turn ye, why will ye die?" The day of His patience is yet continued to them; and if Christ is seeking their salvation, surely we ought to seek it.

God is wont now to make men the means of one another's salvation; yea, it is His ordinary way so to do. He makes the concern and endeavors of His people the means of bringing home many to Christ. Therefore they ought to be concerned for and endeavor it. But it will not be so in another world. There wicked men will be no longer capable subjects of mercy. The saints will know that it is the will of God that the wicked should be miserable to all eternity. It will therefore cease to be their duty any more to seek their salvation or to be concerned about their misery. On the other hand, it will be their duty to rejoice in the will and glory of God. It is not our duty to be sorry that God has executed just vengeance on the devils, concerning whom the will of God in their eternal state is already known to us.

ANSWER 3. Rejoicing at the calamities of others now rests not on the same grounds as that of the saints in glory. The evil of rejoicing at other's calamities now consists in our envy, or revenge, or some such disposition that is gratified therein, and not that God is glorified, that the majesty and justice of God gloriously shine forth.

ANSWER 4. The different circumstances of our nature now from what will be hereafter make that a virtue now which will be no virtue then. For instance, if a man is of a virtuous disposition, the circumstances of our nature now are such that it will necessarily show itself by a natural affection; to be without natural affection is a very vicious disposition, and is so mentioned in Romans 1:31. But natural affection is no virtue in the saints in glory. Their virtue will exercise itself in a higher manner.

ANSWER 5. The vengeance inflicted on many of the wicked will be a manifestation of God's love for the saints. One way whereby God shows His love for the saints is by destroying their enemies. God has said, "He that toucheth you, toucheth the apple of Mine eye" (Zechariah 2:8). And it is often mentioned in Scripture, as an instance of the great love of God to His people, that His wrath is so awakened when they are wronged and injured. Thus Christ has promised that God will avenge His own elect (Luke 18:7), and has said that if any man offend one of His little ones, "it were better for him that a millstone were hanged about his neck, and that he were drowned in the depth of the sea" (Matthew 18:6).

So the saints in glory will see the great love of God to them in the dreadful vengeance which He shall inflict on those who have injured and persecuted them; and the view of this love of God to them will be just cause of their rejoicing. Thus, in the text, heaven and the holy apostles and prophets are called to rejoice over their enemies because God has avenged them of them.

SECTION 4

The ungodly warned

I shall apply this subject only in one use, of warning to ungodly men. And in order to do this I desire such to consider:

1. How destitute of any comforting consideration your condition will be if you perish at last. You will have none to pity you. Look which way you will, before or behind, on the right hand or left; look up to heaven or look about you in hell, and you will see none to lament your case or exercise any pity towards you in your dreadful condition. You must bear these flames; you must bear that torment and amazement, day and night, forever, and never have the comfort of considering that there is so much as one who pities your case.

There never will be one tear dropped for you.

(1) You have now been taught that you will have no pity from the created inhabitants of heaven. If you shall look to them, you will see them all rejoicing at the sight of the glory of God's justice, power, and terrible majesty manifested in your torment. You will see them in a blissful and glorious state; you will see Abraham, Isaac, and Jacob, and all the prophets in the kingdom of God; you will see many come from the east, from the west, from the north and from the south, and sit down in that glorious kingdom; and you will see them all with one voice and with united joy praising God for glorifying Himself in your destruction. You will wail and gnash your teeth under your own torments and with envy of their happiness; but they will rejoice and sing (Isaiah 65:13–14): "Therefore thus saith the Lord, Behold, My servants shall eat, but ye shall be hungry; behold, My servants shall drink, but ye shall be thirsty; behold, My servants shall rejoice, but ye shall be ashamed; behold, My servants shall sing for joy of heart, but ye shall cry for sorrow of heart, and shall howl for vexation of spirit."

(2) God will exercise no pity towards you. If you might have His pity in any degree, that would be of more worth to you than thousands of worlds. That would make your case to be not without comfort and hope. But God will exercise no pity towards you. He has often said concerning wicked men that His eye shall not spare, neither will He have pity (Ezekiel 5:11; 7:4, 9; and 8:18). He will cast upon you and not spare. You will see nothing in God, and receive nothing from Him, but perfect hatred and the fierceness of His wrath; nothing but the mighty falls or outpourings of wrath upon you every moment; and no cries will avail to move God to any pity, or in the least to move

Him to lighten His hand, or assuage the fierceness and abate the power of your torments.

Jesus Christ, the Redeemer, will have no pity on you. Though He had so much love to sinners as to be willing to lay down His life for them, and offers you the benefits of His blood while you are in this world, and often calls upon you to accept them, yet then He will have no pity upon you. You will never hear any more instructions from Him. He will utterly refuse to be your Instructor; on the contrary, He will be your Judge, to pronounce sentence upon you.

(3) You will find none who will pity you in hell. The devils will not pity you, but will be your tormentors like roaring lions or hell-hounds to tear you in pieces continually. And other wicked men who shall be there will be like devils; they will have no pity on you, but will hate, curse, and torment you. And you yourselves will be like devils: you will be like devils to yourselves and will be your own tormentors.

2. *Consider what an aggravation what you have heard under this doctrine will be to your misery.* Consider how it will be at the day of judgment when you shall see Christ coming in the clouds of heaven, when you shall begin to wail and cry, as knowing that you are those who are to be condemned. And perhaps you will be ready to fly to some of your godly friends, but you will obtain no help from them. You will see them unconcerned for you, with joyful countenances ascending to meet the Lord, and not the less joyful for the horror in which they see you. And when you shall stand before the tribunal at the left hand, among devils, trembling and astonished, and shall have the dreadful sentence passed upon you, you will, at the same time, see the blessed company of saints and angels at the right hand rejoicing, and shall hear them shout forth the praises of God while

they hear your sentence pronounced. You will then see those godly people, with whom you shall have been acquainted, and who shall have been your neighbors, and with whom you now often converse, rejoicing at the pronunciation and execution of your sentence.

Perhaps there are now some godly people to whom you are near and dear, who are tenderly concerned for you, who are ready to pity you under all calamities and willing to help you; they are particularly tenderly concerned for your poor soul, and have put up many fervent prayers for you. How will you bear to hear these singing for joy of heart while you are crying for sorrow of heart and howling for vexation of spirit, and even singing the more joyfully for the glorious justice of God which they behold in your eternal condemnation?

You who have godly parents, who in this world have tenderly loved you, who were wont to look upon your welfare as their own and were wont to be grieved for you when anything calamitous befell you in this world, and especially were concerned for the good of your souls, industriously sought and earnestly prayed for their salvation: how will you bear to see them in the kingdom of God, crowned with glory? Or how will you bear to see them receiving the blessed sentence and going up with shouts and songs to enter with Christ into the kingdom prepared for them from the foundation of the world while you are among a company of devils and are turned away with the most bitter cries, to enter into burnings prepared for the devil and his angels? How will you bear to see your parents who in this life had so dear an affection for you now without any love toward you, approving the sentence of condemnation, when Christ shall with indignation bid you depart, wretched, cursed creatures, into eternal burnings? How will you bear to see and hear them praising the Judge for His justice exercised in pronouncing this sentence, and hearing it with holy joy in their countenances, and shouting forth the praises and hallelujahs of God and Christ on that account?

When they shall see what manifestations of amazement there will be in you at the hearing of this dreadful sentence, and that every syllable of it pierces you like a thunderbolt, and sinks you into the lowest depths of horror and despair; when they shall behold you with a frighted, amazed countenance, trembling and astonished, and shall hear you groan and gnash your teeth, these things will not move them at all to pity you, but you will see them with a holy joyfulness in their countenances, and with songs in their mouths. When they shall see you turned away and beginning to enter into the great furnace, and shall see how you shrink at it, and hear how you shriek and cry out, yet they will not at all be grieved for you, but at the same time you will hear from them renewed praises and hallelujahs for the true and righteous judgments of God in so dealing with you.

Then you will doubtless remember how these, your glorified parents, seemed to be concerned for your salvation while you were here in this world. You will remember how they were wont to counsel and warn you, and how little you regarded their counsels, and how they seemed to be concerned and grieved that there appeared no more effect of their endeavors for the good of your souls. You will then see them praising God for executing just vengeance on you for setting so light by their counsels and reproofs. However here they loved you and were concerned for you, now they will rise up in judgment against you and will declare how your sins are aggravated by the endeavors which they, to no purpose, used with you to bring you to forsake sin and practice virtue, and to seek and serve God; but you were obstinate under all and would not hearken unto them. They will declare how inexcusable you are upon this account. And when the Judge shall execute the more terrible wrath upon you to this account, that you have made no better improvement of your parents' instruction, they wil joyfully praise God for it. After they have seen you lie in hell for thousands of years, and your torment shall yet continue without any rest day or night, they will not begin to pity you then; they will praise God that His justice appears in the eternity of your misery.

You who have godly husbands, wives, brothers, or sisters with whom you have been wont to dwell under the same roof, and to eat at the same table, consider how it will be with you when you shall come to part with them, when they shall be taken and you left. Luke 17:34–36: "I tell you, in that night there shall be two men in one bed; the one shall be taken and the other left. Two men shall be in the field; the one shall be taken and the other left." However you may wail and lament, when you see them parted from you, they being taken and you left, you will see in them no signs of sorrow that you are not with them, that you ascend not with them to meet the Lord in the air, but are left below to be consumed with the world which is reserved unto fire against the day of the perdition of ungodly men.

Those wicked men who shall go to hell under the labors of pious and faithful ministers will see those ministers rejoicing and praising God upon the occasion of their destruction. Consider, you who have long lived under Mr. Stoddard's ministry[*] and are yet in a natural condition,

---

[*] Solomon Stoddard, Edwards's grandfather and predecessor at Northampton

how dreadful it will be to you to see him who was so tenderly concerned for the good of your souls while he was here, and so earnestly sought your salvation, to see him rising up in judgment against you, declaring your inexcusableness, declaring how often he warned you; how plainly he set your danger before you and told you of the opportunity that you had; how fully he set forth the miserable condition in which you were and the necessity there was that you should obtain an interest in Christ; how movingly and earnestly he exhorted you to get into a better state, and how regardless you were; how little you minded all that he said to you; how you went on still in your trespasses, hardened your necks and made your hearts as a rock and refused to return! How dreadful will it be to you to hear him declaring how inexcusable you are upon these accounts! How will you be cut to the heart when you shall see him approving the sentence of condemnation which the Judge shall pronounce against you, and judging and sentencing you with Christ as an assessor in judgment—for the saints shall judge the world (1 Corinthians 6:2)—and when you shall see him rejoicing in the execution of justice upon you for all your unprofitableness under his ministry.

 3. *Consider what a happy opportunity you have in your hands now.* Now your case is very different from the case of wicked men in another world of which you have now heard, and particularly in the following respects:

  (1) God makes it the duty of all the godly now to be concerned for your salvation. As to those who are damned in hell, the saints in glory are not concerned for their welfare and have no love or pity towards them; and if you perish hereafter it will be an occasion of joy to all the godly. But now God makes it the duty of all the godly to love you

with a sincere goodwill and earnest affection. God does not excuse men from loving you for your ill qualities; though you are wicked and undeserving, yet God makes it the duty of all sincerely to wish well to you, and it is a heinous sin in the sight of God for any to hate you. He requires all to be concerned for your salvation, and by all means to seek it. It is their duty now to lament your danger and to pray for mercy to you that you may be converted and brought home to Christ.

Now the godly who know you desire your salvation and are ready to seek and pray for it. If you are now in distress about the condition of your souls, you are not in such a forsaken, helpless condition as those who are damned; but you may find many to pray for you, many who are willing to assist you by their advice and counsels and all with a tender concern, and with hearty wishes that your soul may prosper. Now some of you have godly friends who are near and dear to you; you are beloved of those who have a great interest in heaven and who have power with God by their prayers. You have the blessing of living under the same roof with them. Some of you have godly parents to pray for you and to counsel and instruct you, who, you may be sure, will do it with sincere love and concern for you. And there is not only the command of God; God has not only made it the duty of others to seek your salvation, but has given encouragement to others to seek it. He gives encouragement that they may obtain help for you by their prayers, and that they may be instruments of your spiritual good. God reveals it to be His manner to make our sincere endeavors a means of each other's good. How different is the case with you from what it is with those who are already damned! And how happy an opportunity have you in your hands if you would but improve it!

(2) Now you live where there is a certain order of men appointed to make it the business of their lives to seek your salvation. Now you have ministers, not to rise up in judgment against you, but in Christ's stead to beseech you to be reconciled to God (2 Corinthians 5:20). God has not only made it the duty of all to wish well to your souls, and occasionally to endeavor to promote your spiritual interests, but He has set apart certain persons to make it their whole work in which they should spend their days and their strength.

(3) Christ Himself is now seeking your salvation. He seeks it by the aforementioned means, by appointing men to make it their business to seek it. He seeks it by them; they are His instruments, and they beseech you in Christ's stead to be reconciled to God. He seeks it in commanding your neighbors to seek it. Christ is represented in Scripture as wooing the souls of sinners. He uses means to persuade them to choose and accept their own salvation. He often invites them to come to Him that they may have life, that they may find rest to their souls, to come and take of the water of life freely. He stands at the door and knocks and ceases not, though sinners for a long time refuse Him. He bears repeated repulses from them, and yet mercifully continues knocking, saying, "Open to Me, that I may come in and sup with you, and you with Me." At the doors of many sinners He stands thus knocking for many years together. Christ is become a most importunate suitor to sinners that He may become their sovereign. He is often setting before them the need they have of Him, the miserable condition in which they are and the great provision that is made for the good of their souls; and He invites them to accept this provision, and promises it shall be theirs upon their mere acceptance.

Thus how earnestly did Christ seek the salvation of Jerusalem, and He wept over it when they refused. Luke 19:41–42: "And when He was come near, He beheld the city, and wept over it, saying, If thou hadst known, even thou, at least in this thy day, the things which belong unto thy peace! But now they are hid from thine eyes!" And Matthew 23:37: "O Jerusalem, Jerusalem, thou that killest the prophets, and stonest them which are sent unto thee, how often would I have gathered thy children together, even as a hen gathereth her chickens under her wings, and ye would not!" Thus Christ is now seeking your salvation; such an opportunity have you now in your hands. Consider, therefore, how many means Christ is using with you to bring you to salvation.

Besides those things which have been now mentioned, some of you have a degree of the inward strivings and influences of the Spirit, which makes your opportunity much greater. You have Christ's internal calls and knockings. All the persons of the Trinity are now seeking your salvation. God the Father has sent His Son, who has made way for your salvation and removed all difficulties, except those which are with your own heart. And He is waiting to be gracious to you. The door of His mercy stands open to you. He has set a fountain open for you to wash in from sin and uncleanness. Christ is calling, inviting, and wooing you; and the Holy Ghost is striving with you by His internal motions and influences.

4. *If you now repent before it is too late, the saints and angels in glory will rejoice at your repentance.* If you repent not till it is too late, they will, as you have heard, rejoice in seeing justice executed upon you. But if you now repent, they will rejoice at their welfare, that you who were lost are found, that you who were dead are alive again. They will rejoice that you

are come to so happy a state already, and that you are in due time to inherit eternal happiness (Luke 15:3–10). So that if now you will improve your opportunity, there will be a very different occasion of joy in heaven concerning you than that of which the doctrine speaks—not a rejoicing on occasion of your misery, but on occasion of your unspeakable blessedness.

5. If you repent before it is too late, you yourselves shall be of that joyful company. They will be so far from rejoicing on occasion of your ruin that you yourselves will be of that glorious company who will rejoice in all the works of God, who will have all tears wiped away from their eyes, to whom there will be no more death, nor sorrow, nor crying, and from whom sorrow and sighing shall flee away. You yourselves will be of those who will rejoice at the glorious display of God's majesty and justice in His wrath on His enemies. You will be of those who shall sing for joy of heart at the day of judgment while others mourn for sorrow of heart and howl for vexation of spirit; and you will enter into the joy of your Lord, and there shall never be any end or abatement of your joy!